old bears

old bears

The Class of 1956 reaches its fiftieth reunion,
reflecting on the Happy Days
and the unhappy days

By Dave Newhouse

Foreword by Darryl Brock

North Atlantic Books
Berkeley, California

To Patsy, my life support through stormy seas

⌒

Published by
North Atlantic Books   Cover design by Sean Connelley
P.O. Box 12327   Book design by Brad Greene
Berkeley, California 94712

Printed in the United States of America

Old Bears is sponsored by the Society for the Study of Native Arts and Sciences, a nonprofit educational corporation whose goals are to develop an educational and crosscultural perspective linking various scientific, social, and artistic fields; to nurture a holistic view of arts, sciences, humanities, and healing; and to publish and distribute literature on the relationship of mind, body, and nature.

North Atlantic Books' publications are available through most bookstores. For further information, call 800-337-2665 or visit our website at www.northatlanticbooks.com.

Substantial discounts on bulk quantities are available to corporations, professional associations, and other organizations. For details and discount information, contact our special sales department.

1-55643-711-0
978-1-55643-711-3

1 2 3 4 5 6 7 8 9 BERRYVILLE 14 13 12 11 10 09 08 07

table of contents

foreword

By Darryl Brock

Most of the guys in my men's discussion group are in our sixties now, which means we were teenagers in the 1950s. One night, we started talking about the shock of catching unexpected reflections of ourselves in mirrors or windows, and having the startled reaction, "Who's that old geezer?" Which led us to consider if that isn't who we think we are, what mental pictures of ourselves are we carrying around?

Which, in turn, launched us on an interesting experiment: We took turns bringing snapshots from our pasts and sharing our lives. We talked about various selves as shown in the photos and how we related to them now. In my case, it turned out I basically thought I was still the "me" pictured some fifteen years ago; it came the closest to my private self.

But the image I spent the most time looking at was my high school senior picture, from which a crew-cut-topped young face regarded me with confident good humor. I felt least in touch with that one. I remember trying to act back then as if I understood the ways of the world, but it's been clear for a long time that there was a hell of a lot I didn't know—couldn't possibly have known. That fresh-faced senior seemed almost a stranger, and I realized it would be no easy task to get in touch with him. Other fellows in the group had similar reactions—a shared sense of remoteness from their high school personas. So much time had passed. And things had changed so drastically.

Getting back to the 1950s is like trying to wedge through a dense scrim shaped first by the explosiveness of the 1960s, then overlaid with thick cultural deposits from the '70s, '80s and '90s, and finally capped by current grim trends of the new century. The '50s lie somewhere behind all that in what often seems, at this distance, a tranquil, cozy world.

There are Gallup polls showing that older Americans regard the 1950s as the period of their greatest contentment. Small wonder that the Fonz's TV series was titled "Happy Days."

I grew up in Oxnard, California, a place probably not very much like Menlo Park or Atherton, two towns which fed into Menlo-Atherton High School, the genesis of this book. Back then, Oxnard was a modest agricultural town surrounded by citrus groves and fields of lima beans and sugar beets. The old farm families, many of them Austrians and Germans who had arrived in the 1880s, formed the social aristocracy, later joined by enterprising downtown merchants.

It was a town with a distinct center, a spacious town square with a quaint gazebo, wide walks, and shade trees—the whole of it flanked by towering royal palms. I played trumpet in the high school band, and at Christmastime, we formed a brass ensemble and played carols from the gazebo. I can still conjure sense-memories of those chilly nights with their ringing harmonies and glowing colored lights.

Around the plaza were shops and businesses—probably we'd call them boutiques now—bearing the names of local families: Diener's Men's Clothes, Sweeney's Ice Cream Parlor, Pringle's Bootery, Dolly Lehmann's Ladies' Fashions. I went to school with kids from those families. Few out-of-town franchises had yet encroached, the first mall hadn't yet been built, and so we shopped locally, except for the rare occasions when we made the long drive to Los Angeles to visit its gigantic new May Company. During vacations, high school girls sought jobs clerking or gift-wrapping in the stores. Boys found work in the citrus packing houses or pumping gas in "service stations" that still actually provided service.

The war and postwar boom years had brought newcomers, but the area retained a solid sense of community. A daily newspaper, the Oxnard Press Courier, chronicled events and recorded our births, marriages, deaths. We still knew each other—maybe not everybody personally, but in a generalized way—and our respective social niches were reflected in residential patterns: poorer families in the southern parts of town, affluent in the northern portions. A Latino barrio lay, literally, on the wrong side of the tracks. Things weren't always friction-free, to say the least, but we were all still together.

Along with this connectedness, a 1950s small town could also promote a stifling conformity. I remember adults remarking, in nudge-snicker fashion, "He drinks" or "She's divorced." It was a snide, Peyton Place world view that would be heavily attacked in the '60s. That conventionality also lent stability in certain ways, however. Most of us took for granted that you could train for a career and enjoy a vocation the rest of your life. Same for marriage. People didn't jump around nearly so much then, and the notion of living with someone on a trial basis was unthinkable.

Our adolescent relationships reflected this, too, a lot of us "going steady," emulating marriage. Girls wore our rings as pendants on necklace chains; some knitted dice to adorn our cars' rear view mirrors. There was a sense of, if not outright ownership, certainly possession and linked destinies. And we wanted this to be obvious—manifest at first glance. So we rode around town, cruising the "main," from Foster's Freeze to the Blue Onion, back and forth, girls very close, no daylight between us. Our teen love would last forever—or so we wanted to believe.

In my part of the world, cars were important badges of identity. Want to know who I am? Check out my wheels! My car was a pampered 1950 Ford coupe, lowered ("raked") in front with a customized grill, leaded-in hood, and elaborate pinstriping. Chrome spaghetti headers spilled down from the hood and led back to twin exhausts. I'd had special tuck-and-roll Naugahyde upholstery made in Tijuana, but the crowning glory was the exterior paint, "Titian red," a deep burgundy flecked with gold. And did my alter ego ever gleam in that Southern California sunshine.

I remember listening to certain Everly Brothers songs and yearning to be somewhere else, doing something else. Maybe it was a Jack Kerouac—or pre-Dylan—thing, wanting to be out on the edge, going, going, gone. But that urge wasn't very well defined, in general, beyond wanting to be a sports hero, I have trouble reconstructing the precise nature of my dreams then. I'm sure they were grandiose and unrealistic. The stuff of youth.

And wasn't that, really, the strength, the vitality, of the '50s for us? We were all so young then.

We had no way of knowing how radically our towns would soon change, or how things would turn out for us. Our youthful ignorance was both our power and our limitation. We each had our hopes and fears and dreams—and for an interval that can seem painfully brief now, we had our high-school friends and peers.

Dave Newhouse has pulled off a wonderful feat in plunging himself into the past and putting together this remarkable book. Thanks to him, we are provided this remarkable opportunity to meet old selves once again.

introduction

Sometime in 2004, the shocking realization zapped me like a lightning bolt. My fiftieth high school reunion was coming up in two years. Fifty years! We tend to measure our lives in small increments, but my four years at Menlo-Atherton High School now calculated to a half-century ago.

Good golly, Miss Molly!

For the last thirty of those fifty years, this formless title had lingered inside my head: "Travels Through The People I've Known." The title had no shape because I couldn't define its parameters. Which people? What period of time? It all crystallized in 2004: Menlo-Atherton's Class of 1956.

I had attended previous class reunions, but this one would be dramatically different. We were now senior citizens. We had lived a full life or as close to a full life as we could have imagined on graduation day in '56, when most of us grabbed our diplomas and disappeared from one another's lives.

What had happened to these classmates? My curiosity was tweaked. With three-hundred and fifty-two graduates, there was no way of knowing how all of their lives had turned out. Some graduates hadn't been to a single reunion, which made me even more curious. It was time to hit the road.

I put out feelers among a handful of classmates with whom I had stayed in reasonably close contact. The first positive response came from Diane Sullivan Gayer Reynolds, everyone's crush at M-A. I had a thing for Diane along with a fifty other boys at M-A. My first kiss happened at Diane's house, but not from Diane. It was a grammar school party, a flashlight dance, an innocent time. Diane married her high school sweetheart and became a Navy jet pilot's widow soon afterward.

She re-married badly on the rebound, bore two children, then divorced. We set up an interview.

I knew I was on the right track when Diane spoke openly of the hard road she had chosen in life, the detours and the dead ends. She was stalked by an M-A classmate in her sixties. But even as a senior citizen, she was making waves as an activist. I figured if other classmates had half as intriguing a story as Diane's, I might have an interesting book after all.

I had read several high-school reunion books, but they had shorter time frames of ten- to twenty-five years after graduation. Hardly enough living. Fifty years represented a definitive picture of one's life. That's why I purposely chose a first-person book format, because of the many years involved. Also because most classmates hadn't ever been interviewed; they weren't public figures. And a third reason: I didn't want to make enemies.

That last point can't be stressed enough, because as the interviews progressed, some very personal quotes and experiences were stricken after the interviewees read them over. One classmate didn't experience her first orgasm until she was forty-five. Excised. A family suicide damaged a classmate's soul. Excised. A preconceived teen pregnancy remains hidden from a classmate's child to this very day. Excised. A husband's continuous womanizing. Excised. Alcohol and/or drug issues left damaging imprints on other classmates. Excised. Thus there were lots of deletions and revisions in the returned texts.

Some classmates, though, stuck courageously by their interviews. There was the pompon girl who was institutionalized. There was the athlete who became an alcoholic, was imprisoned, and then was disbarred from practicing law. There was the Episcopal bishop who separated himself from the national church with his views on gays, including the ordination of a gay bishop.

Interviews ping-ponged back and forth, from negative to positive, depressing to uplifting, often in the same session. We think we know people after spending time with them, and four years is a significant amount of time. But classmates I thought I knew offered information about themselves I was unaware of, yet they felt it cathartic to bring it up, and even to keep it.

Some interviewees became emotional as they exposed their fears and frailties. A childhood buddy I hadn't seen in years was in the early stages of Alzheimer's, which I had no clue about until I showed up at his front door. Another friend was battling cranial cancer after having dealt with alcoholism, divorce, and a drugged-up daughter.

Two women revealed they were adopted; both had located their birth parents. Our class valedictorian didn't have one serious romance at Menlo-Atherton, then wed her English professor at Stanford, who was thirteen years older. An editor of M-A's school newspaper in 1956 and her minister-in-the-field husband both worked for farm labor activist Cesar Chavez.

There also was the comely classmate who passed the bar and began practicing law at the retirement age of sixty-three. Our class speed demon turned out to be the nephew of the man who invented television. Our class nerd made puppets in high school before meeting Jim Henson and launching, together, "The Muppets" and "Sesame Street." And the Class of '56's most prominent college dropout became a multi-millionaire.

At the end of each interview, I asked classmates to look at their M-A graduation pictures and try to remember what they were thinking at the time regarding the future. Then I asked them what that same yearbook face would say about how their lives had turned out. Their answers were quite revealing.

Thirty-one interviews were done, and thirty-two individual chapters written, including my own. Three classmates pulled out; too much personal angst, they said. Two reconsidered, but one of them left again, saying "I can't deal with this right now."

Few M-A faculty members are left from 1956, but one had extremely nice things to say about our class (he actually remembered us). Then a Class of 2006 graduate discussed how Menlo-Atherton had changed over a half-century—changed dramatically, and not necessarily for the better.

Where had those fifty years gone? Gone away, gone too fast.

Ain't That A Shame.

In 1956, Menlo-Atherton High School, which borders the wealthy communities of Menlo Park and Atherton, thirty miles south of San Francisco, was perceived as a "country club." That somewhat-accurate image changed in the 1960s when students got into drugs and M-A experienced a militant period, including campus race riots. Then came homosexuality, weakened school spirit, and more aggressive student-teacher relationships, some of it sexual. New-age issues confronted M-A as it lurched into the Twenty-First Century.

Ah, Sweet Little Sixteen.

M-A had opened in the fall of 1951 on the cusp of the carefree "Happy Days" generation that permeated the decade. But the Fifties were anything but a mindless slice of American life. Those crucial ten years brought about the advent of television's popularity, plus rock 'n' roll, civil rights, the Salk polio vaccine and the space program. The 1950s changed America—culturally, technologically, politically, musically.

Elvis the Pelvis, anyone?

Other Fifties happenings: The "Peanuts" comic strip, Disneyland, Rosa Parks, "Willie, Mickey and the Duke," Bill Russell, Wilt Chamberlain and the rewriting of basketball's rule book, Roger Bannister and the four-minute mile, James Dean, "Playboy" magazine, Queen Elizabeth's coronation, "The Tonight Show," Kentucky Fried Chicken, McDonald's, Dick Clark and "American Bandstand," "I Love Lucy," the first compact car (Nash Rambler), the first credit card, the first transatlantic passenger jet, the "Barbie" doll, 3-D movies and America's greatest sex symbol, Marilyn Monroe.

The New York Giants and Brooklyn Dodgers launched Major League Baseball's westward expansion in 1958, to San Francisco and Los Angeles, respectively. The San Francisco Giants still are awaiting their first World Series championship, leaving them five behind the Los Angeles Dodgers.

And, oh, yes, Alaska and Hawaii achieved statehood in the Fifties.

That decade also benefitted from an unparalleled economic boom.

America had rebounded mightily from World War II, both as a world leader and as a generous benefactor back home. Jobs were plentiful; the federal minimum wage was one dollar in 1956. The housing industry flourished in accommodating post-war "baby boomer" families; the average cost of a house was $17,800. Home life never was better, even though the average weekly take-home pay for a worker with three dependents was $74.04. The husband managed to support the family while the wife stayed home and baked cookies for the kids behind white picket fences. America was "Ozzie and Harriet." Life was simpler and cheaper: A three-cent postage stamp; a quarter for a gallon of gas. And the Dow Jones Industrial Average marked a new high of 500.24 points in 1956.

But life wasn't altogether peaceful. School integration occurred in the Deep South as highly resistant Southern red necks turned scarlet. When the Soviet Union exploded its first atomic device, America panicked, fearful of a nuclear attack. Bomb shelters were dug in back yards all across the USA.

These shelters wouldn't be needed, except for children's war games. However, America in the 1950s found more war raging in Korea, a conflict that lasted three years. General Douglas MacArthur, commander of the United Nations forces, was "fired" by President Harry Truman for insubordination. America's greatest general, MacArthur returned home in disgrace to give his infamous "Old soldiers never die, they just fade away" military farewell speech.

By then, communism was entrenched in China and Eastern Europe, fueling additional alarm in Americans over a possible Red invasion. One misguided American, Senator Joseph McCarthy, capitalized on this growing insecurity by starting a "Red Scare" campaign, accusing government figures and Hollywood celebrities alike of being closet communists. McCarthy ruined many lives with his cruel witch hunt. Finally, mercifully, fellow senators condemned him.

But to kids approaching high-school age in the Fifties, troubling issues flew over our heads. Our biggest diversion was a whole new wave of technology that had engulfed the country. Americans were mesmerized by the television craze, sitting transfixed in front of their TV sets, staring hypnotically at the test pattern on the screen while awaiting the day's programming. Kids were glued to "Howdy Doody," "Kukla, Fran and Ollie," "Time for Beany," "Crusader Rabbit." Parents shooed the kids away at night in order to watch Milton Berle and Dagmar, Sid Caesar and Imogene Coca, Jackie Gleason, Ed Sullivan, and The Colgate Comedy Hour. Make 'em laugh they did.

In the Fifties, Americans had little to fear, not even fear itself. Teenagers at Menlo-Atherton fell right into step, although not necessarily into the two-step, for America now danced to a faster, hipper beat. The jitterbug was in. Ballad singers Patti Page, Frankie Laine, Georgia Gibbs and Joni James were on the way out, clearing room for such rhythm and blues legends as Fats Domino, Little Richard and Chuck Berry. There were dance parties to the 45 r.p.m. records of rock 'n' roll icons Buddy Holly, Jerry Lee Lewis, Bill Haley and the Comets, The Platters and, of course, Elvis Presley.

Yes, the 1950s introduced fast food, but don't blame the Happy Days kids for the fact that three out of every five Americans today are overweight, and one out of every five is obese. It's also not our fault that nineteen percent of all meals are now consumed inside the automobile.

And though we teenagers witnessed television's takeover of the land, don't blame us for the TV trash that's strewn over the various networks. We take no responsibility for Jerry Springer, Bill O'Reilly, Geraldo Rivera, all those redundant judge shows, that truly idiotic reality TV, the foul-mouthed comedy acts—where have you gone, Red Skelton?—the TV poker epidemic, Regis and Kathie Lee, Regis and Kelly, and the robotic Stone Phillips.

Yes, we watched the birth of rock 'n' roll, but don't blame us because rap music promotes the killing of policemen while also demeaning women as "bitches" and "ho's." Radio shock jock Don Imus was fired in 2007 for calling the Rutgers University women's basketball team "nappy headed ho's," even though Imus is too old to listen to rap, and too full of himself to know the difference. Imus is a Happy Days kid, but don't blame him on us. He doesn't look happy. At M-A, we'd have stepped all over his blue suede shoes.

Fifties kids, though, weren't exactly role models in terms of race matters. M-A experienced some integration back then, with black kids coming over from East Palo Alto's large African-American community. Blacks and whites mixed uneasily at M-A, but we co-existed. That wasn't the case at M-A during the consciously aware, "lean on me, you're my brother" Sixties.

In the Fifties, we thought, foolishly, that we were cool dressers. Girls wore poodle skirts and sweater-skirt outfits. Boys wore Pendleton shirts, and khaki and "wheat" pants. And Levis with the belt loops cut off and pant cuffs rolled twice as tightly as possible. Two pairs of Levis lasted an entire school year—unwashed—thus able to stand in a corner at night.

Only girls wore earrings in the Fifties. That's no longer the case. Tattooes covered sailors' biceps, strictly a man's thing. That's no longer the case. In the Fifties, we could make out a song's lyrics. That's no longer the case. We knew very little about drugs. That's no longer the case. A six-pack of Country Club malt liquor was our biggest vice, because sex wasn't that readily available. That's no longer the case.

Fifties' rebels wore their jeans low; the "draped" look. That's true today, too, although there's more butt showing and baggier bottoms. The "duck's ass" hairdo of the Fifties was a bad-ass look, but not nearly as gross as today's "Goth" look. Fifties' kids were clean cut and preppy as a rule. Twenty-First Century kids are sloppy, preferring the ghetto look.

Get A Job?

Good luck looking like that.

What's really different, and deadly, about generations fifty years apart: In the Fifties, campus differences were settled with fisticuffs. Today, they're settled with guns. Kids are killing kids, randomly, routinely. This is the scariest change in America since the 1950s, exceeding war and terrorism. And these kid killers are of varied ethnicities: White kids at Columbine High School in Colorado; Black kids in the urban ghetto; Mexican kids in rural farm country; an Asian at Virginia Tech, the worst mass murder in U.S. history.

"Happy Days" have evolved, unhappily, into "Homicide Days."

How did the Fifties shape up against other decades of the Twentieth Century? The first decade introduced the automobile, the airplane and baseball's World Series. Radio, jazz, silent pictures and World War I highlighted the Teens. The Roaring Twenties produced talkies, Charles Lindbergh, Prohibition and the National Football League. The Thirties gave us The Great Depression and Franklin Delano Roosevelt, the only U.S. president elected four times. The Forties are remembered for World War II and the integration of baseball by Jackie Robinson. The Sixties brought multi-assassinations (Jack and Bobby Kennedy, Dr. Martin Luther King, Jr.) and multi-revolution: Vietnam, protests, marches, the drug culture, flower children, communal living, the pill, Black Power. The Seventies produced a woman's right to choose, women's collegiate sports, the first President to resign from office, and disco. The computer and rap music soared in popularity in the Eighties, when the Berlin Wall came down. The Nineties were marked by the fall of communism in the Soviet Union, Desert Storm, and the dot.com boom.

So, then, how did the Fifties stack up? Clearly, it was the decade of comfort and conformity. But the Happy Days kids were changing, too, perhaps against their will, and possibly without their own awareness. Jack Kerouac wrote "On The Road" in the mid-1950s, and America would never be the same. Kerouac represented the "beat" generation, which embodied non-conformity and was a precursor to the Hippie lifestyle of the 1960s that positively railed against conformity.

The Sixties' poet, a disheveled, mumbling Bob Dylan, had taken over in popularity from the Fifties' perfect-casting boy next store, Pat Boone. The coffee house had replaced the malt shop. The times, indeed, were a-changin'.

And the year 1956 was no more significant, and likely less historic, than any other year of that what-me-worry? decade. Actress-socialite Grace Kelly married Prince Rainier III of Monaco. Marilyn Monroe wed playwright Arthur Miller; thirty years after they divorced, he called her "highly self-destructive." Don Larsen of the New York Yankees pitched the only World Series perfect game, against neighboring Brooklyn. "My Fair Lady" opened in New York City. "As The World Turns"

premiered and soap-opera TV was born. Rocky Marciano retired undefeated as heavyweight boxing champion. Althea Gibson won the French
Open; the first black to win a major tennis tournament. Dean Martin
and Jerry Lewis performed their last comedy act together. "Around The
World in 80 Days" won the Oscar for best picture.

And Menlo-Atherton High School's fifth senior class graduated on
June 15, 1956. Some of us played poker in the stands that warm, starry
night. Some of us smelled of alcohol. Most of us worried about our
futures. The Menlo-Atherton band, directed by Edward Brown, opened
with Mendelssohn's "War March of the Priests," "The Star-Spangled
Banner," and Handel's march from "Scipio." Most of us could sing the
anthem, sober, but we were oblivious to the other two selections, sober
or otherwise. Class president Bill Brodie introduced salutatorian Rhoda
Maxfield and valedictorian Josephine Booth. M-A's A Cappella Choir
sang the spiritual "Soon Ah Will Be Done" to the three-hundred and
fifty-two graduates, only three of whom were African-American.

Then the choir and the graduates joined together for the school
hymn: "Maroon and Gold of Menlo-Atherton," with the bulk of the
class clueless as to the lyrics. After a cornet duet by graduates Jim Reinhardt and Lance Fuller to "Trifolium" by Leidzen, another musical mystery to most of us, principal Nicholas M. Nugent presented our class
for graduation. Sequoia School District president Rex Turner accepted
us, for better or worse. After a recessional, "Land of Hope and Glory"
by Elgar, we hugged our parents and headed for the graduation dance,
our final event together before we stumbled as a group into a strange,
sobering world.

Fast forward to June 2006. The Class of 1956 held its fiftieth reunion
barbecue at a nearby country club. Where else? Slightly more than one-
hundred graduates, roughly one-third of the class, showed up, a
respectable turnout. Old girl friends were eager to see old boy friends.
Old boy friends were just as eager. Old friends, regardless of gender,
revisited with one another and even made the acquaintances of classmates they either hadn't the time or inclination to get to know at M-A.

We relived old memories, of Marquard's, the drive-in restaurant that was our everything in the Fifties. Cruising 'Quard's, that was the thing to do. However, 'Quard's is long gone; it's now a hole in the ground. An office complex and garage, we were told, will rise in its place in 2007.

This reunion, though, was a time to create new memories, to see what we now look like as senior citizens. Not that bad, really, especially the ladies. It was our best reunion. The main reason, everyone agreed, was that we still were alive. There was a sense of loss for those classmates who had died. On that somber note of mortality, this fiftieth reunion was no place, then, for meaningless, materialistic minutiae—bragging about second homes, time shares, yachts and social status.

For classmates now regarded themselves as that Fifties icon, Fats Domino, reacted after being rescued off the floating roof of his detached New Orleans home during Hurricane Katrina: "I'm Alive and Kicking," the title song of his most recent album, at age seventy-eight. Go get 'em, Fat man.

In 1956, we were frisky and somewhat fearless, much like bear cubs taking our first steps. By 2006, we had become "Old Bears," having slowed down considerably, but still bear-ing our teeth, even if they weren't the same teeth we had at M-A.

What really stood out, though, about this fiftieth reunion was the impressive group of graduates: Doctors, men of cloth, lawyers, professors, architects, artists, authors, captains of industry. My wife, who didn't attend M-A, marveled at the class's "intellectualism." Fifteen classmates had been accepted by Stanford; only one didn't attend for financial reasons. Fifty years later, the best and the brightest of us, the achievers and the dreamers, we mixed so easily in our white and blue collars that a fifty-fifth reunion was being discussed even before we bade our farewells.

Driving away, I thought of Diane Sullivan Gayer Reynolds, who missed the reunion because of illness. I recalled asking Diane after this book's first interview why she had agreed to tell her life story. "Because you seemed so serious about this," she replied, "that I wanted to help you."

Nearly fifty years later, that is tremendous trust. To the other "Old

Bears" who showed similar trust, I can't thank you enough. It was fun, but mostly educational, getting a second opportunity to know and understand you better. Traveling back through your lives, it was the journey of a lifetime.

—Dave Newhouse
Oakland, CA.
May 2007

Cheers!

Bill Brodie

★ 1 ★

The My Way Guy

Bill Brodie was M-A's senior class president in 1956. He was the brother of a famous quarterback, and a top athlete himself, Bill later became a successful attorney. But as the child of an drinking family, his alcoholism ruined his law career and sent him to prison. Undaunted, he did it "my way."

I don't think about why I drink as much as I have. It's just something I've enjoyed. Maybe there's some big, hidden psychological thing. But if there is, I'm not aware of it, and I'm not trying to find out about it. It's a personal choice.

Contrary to the opinion of some, I've had a happy life, though the last thirty years haven't been easy. I wouldn't suggest anybody go through it. I don't think a lot of people could go through it. There's no question that alcohol has had a detrimental affect on my life, having a law practice and then not having a law practice. I was making a helluva good living.

Would I do something different if I had a chance to do it over again? I don't know. I don't seem to be doing a helluva lot of things different, though I do manage alcohol better now. I don't get drunk. Or if I do get drunk, I don't drive. Anything over two or three drinks, I don't drive.

I usually didn't get too far out of control before. I just got drunk. The problem was I had about six drunk drivings. Now I'm working as a bartender at Harry's Hofbrau in Redwood City. It's a good job, six hours a day. The pay's good and I make enough money to take care of all my needs and to save some dough. With my drinking history, why am

I a bartender? It's a lot of fun, and you don't drink on the job. It's easy not to because it's not allowed. So people can't buy you drinks.

I don't think I'm missing out on a lot in life. I walk a lot. I play golf. I read a lot. I've read all of Robert Ludlum's books. I like Dan Brown, and I read lots of sports books. Goals? I'm thinking I might like to go to Ireland. We Brodies are Irish. Other than that, I can't think of a lot of things I'd do. Maybe marry some old broad with a lot of money. Hah, hah, hah.

I've been married twice. I'm 0-for-2 in that department, but at least I haven't married again. I have a daughter, Lisa. We're real tight. We don't dwell on things. It's just, "I love you." I've gone through a lot of stuff, but I still have a great deal of self-confidence. I'm terribly optimistic all the time that I'm going to be fine. I don't find anything terribly wrong with me. I still like who I am.

So it hasn't been all bad. I've crossed paths with some interesting people, like Bing Crosby and Al Davis. I attended the Academy Awards in a tuxedo, sat at the same dinner table with Walt Disney and Loretta Young, and I got to know the Hollywood scene.

John Brodie is my older brother, an All-American quarterback at Stanford and an All-Pro with the San Francisco 49ers during his seventeen years with that franchise. Some people think it was difficult for me living in my brother's shadow. They're wrong. John and I are very close. He's my best friend, though we don't have to say anything about it. Being John Brodie's brother had favorable consequences. He was such a good athlete that people thought, maybe, it runs in the family. So I got a look at quarterback probably before most people would have. I was lucky being his brother.

John is three years older than me. We have a sister, Katie, who is eight years younger than I am. She lives in Hayden Lake, Idaho, and is one of three elected county commissioners there. She is a big fish in a little pond, loves what she is doing, and she is damn good at it. My daughter, Lisa, lives there, too. The Brodie family has gone up to Hayden Lake every summer since I was thirteen. That's where I met Bing Crosby and his family. I became very close to Lindsay Crosby, Bing's youngest of four sons from his first marriage.

My father, Aloysius Leo Brodie, was an athlete at the University of North Dakota, where he played four years of football and four years of basketball. He got into the insurance business and met my mother, Margaret, in Seattle, where she attended the University of Washington. John was born in San Francisco. I was born in Los Angeles as my father's career moved around.

My father was into group insurance. He became involved in the Richmond ship yards, where Kaiser kept facilities for all the industrial accidents that occurred there. Henry Kaiser and Dr. Sidney Garfield, who married sisters, started what was to become the Kaiser Foundation Health Plan. Dr. Garfield is considered the founder of the medical part. My father got a hold of Eric Holtman, an actuary whom my dad knew in the insurance business. The two of them figured out a scheme to charge so much per bed per day. My dad sold the health plan, particularly with federal employees, and making two dollars per member. He had five sales people working for him and he signed up two hundred thousand members pretty quickly. This made him wealthy.

I was pretty rebellious. At thirteen, I took my dad's car and went hot-rodding with my buddies on winding Skyline Boulevard in the Oakland hills. I crashed into another car. Nobody was hurt, but I took off after the accident because I knew the police would be looking for me. So I took a piece of chrome home with me and woke up my mother, because I knew my dad had this violent Irish temper. She told me I had to tell my father. He was sleeping in another room. So I did, and he said, "Did you rob any place?" I told him I hadn't. He called the police. There was an all-points bulletin out for me. So here come the police asking for my driver's license. They were stunned to find out I was thirteen; I was already six-foot-three. I was suspended, couldn't drive until I was seventeen, and I was put on juvenile probation.

When I turned fourteen, I removed my father's car again because I wanted to go see my baseball coach, George Powles. I spent a great deal of time at his house socially. George was a helluva guy. He was responsible at McClymonds for putting more guys in the big leagues than any other high school coach in the country. Anyway, I took my dad's car the night before he had a meeting with Henry Kaiser, who was going to retire the old man because he was making too damn much money. My father woke up with a toothache that night and decided to go to the hospital. But when he got to the garage, no car.

Around 10 p.m., in comes Billy. The old man started to ask me what in the hell I was doing. Halfway through, he hit me in the face, knocking me back on the couch. When I bounced back up, he said, "Put your hands down." I did and he whacked me again. I wasn't fighting, and he was a big, tough guy. Then he told me to go to bed. In the morning, I look out the window, and he was going to meet Henry Kaiser with casts on his two broken hands.

The old man hit John, too. The most memorable time happened when John was sixteen. He wasn't home on time for dinner, and you had to be there at 7 p.m. because dinner was a fairly formal thing in our home. By the time John got home, the old man was out of his chair. John lied about where he had been—we had checked around—and the old man pops him. John said, "The only reason you hit me is you know I won't hit you back." And my father said, "Is that right? Put up your dukes." Before John could, the old man splattered his nose, breaking it. John slid down the wall. I helped him up the stairs to get some treatment. From that point on, John had difficulty breathing.

I was playing in the Police Athletic League when my old man came to see me pitch for the first time. I hit four or five batters. He was so scared that he took out an insurance policy on me. When I was fifteen, pitching for Tech's varsity, I threw a two-hitter against Alameda. But I also struck out Hall of Fame great Frank Robinson, though he probably won't remember. As a Tech sophomore, I started at end on the varsity football team. The coach knew I had a good arm, so he put in this end-around pass. I threw one of the longest passes of the year in northern California to John Hardy. In my junior year, I threw seven or eight end-around passes and completed most of them.

By that time, John was a star at Stanford. My parents were avid fans and wanted to be closer to John. So they sold the home in Oakland and we moved to Atherton, a few miles from the Stanford campus.

Oakland Tech was one-third black, with a lot of Asian and Mexican kids. And not a very affluent school. Anyone who had dough went to Piedmont High or to private schools. Menlo-Atherton wasn't anything like Tech, ethnically or financially. Very few blacks attended M-A when I transferred there. Atherton is a wealthy environment. Every guy at M-A wore Levis and Pendleton shirts. I didn't have Levis or Pendletons at the time. I'd walk down the halls and these senior girls would bump into me intentionally, to josh me around a bit. I didn't understand it at first. Girls were much more forward at M-A than at Tech.

I arrived at M-A in the middle of my junior year and went out for baseball. I met two seniors on the team, Leon Finegold and Troy Ratliff, and we worked out together. The guys I hung out with, like football stars Duncan Ferguson and Pete Welch, were older. I couldn't drive, so classmate Don DeFeo, who lived around the corner, drove me to school. Or his father, a doctor, would drive.

That spring, I won five or six games. I think I was second in the league in strikeouts. I threw a couple of one-hitters, and lost some two-hitters and three-hitters. On my pickoff moves, the ball would hit the first base-man instead of his glove. Baseball, though, was my best sport. I knew more about the game than our coach, Howie Costello, who was foot-ball-oriented. Playing for George Powles, you really learned the game.

American Legion ball wasn't as big in the Menlo Park area as it was in Oakland. I played a few games, then left for Hayden Lake in Idaho, a family retreat. When I came back to Menlo Park, I worked out for foot-ball with Wade Hampton, a shifty halfback, and Bill Hilton, a big, fast athlete who was being moved from end to fullback. The football coaches, Costello and Don Dorfmeier, knew about my end-around passes at Tech. Howie told me, "We don't have a quarterback." I told him I would give it a try. My brother worked with me in the gym on footwork and handoffs, things like that.

I didn't start the first game against Los Gatos, but I threw two touch-down passes, one to Jerry Angelo, and we won, 37-13. I started the next game. We were ahead just before halftime when one of their guys kneed me deliberately in the groin. They had to carry me off, but I played in the second half and we won, 20-0. On the bus ride home, I passed out. My balls looked like two grapefruits. The doctor was quite impressed with this injury.

And this happened when I was running for senior class president, which Hampton put me up to, even helping me with my candidate's speech. But as I walked up to the podium very bowlegged from my injury, I heard a few snickers from those who knew of my condition. I was elected, but couldn't play in our third game, which we lost to Lincoln of San Jose, 14-6. I was back the next week against San Mateo, and we won, 20-13, as I had a good day passing and running. We beat Sequoia, 31-2, then lost to Palo Alto, 13-6, when I stunk up the joint. I had success previously throwing across the middle to flanker Hal Turner, but Palo Alto scouted that play pretty well. Hilton scored our only touchdown on a sixty-yard run. Once he got by people, nobody could catch him.

My parents let me drink in the house from the time I was fifteen. After games that fall, guys on the team would have a few beers together. After the Palo Alto game, ten of us got kicked off the team. Somebody made an ass of himself, and the mother of the girl whose house we were drinking at called the dean of boys, Jimmy Coffis. He had been a football star at Stanford in the 1930s, and he kicked us off the team. A father of one suspended player was ready to punch Coffis. But I'll say this for Coffis, he held his ground, saying that we had broken training and were off the team.

Howie and Don hadn't talked to us about not drinking during the season. At least, I didn't hear the speech. My father was mad, but only because I was suspended. Jefferson beat us in our final game, 13-0. We played eight games, lost three, and in two losses, I didn't play. But it was enough for USC to offer me a football scholarship.

In high school, I dated Sue Barron, who was one class behind me. She was very pretty and we got along pretty well. She had a car and I didn't. I didn't get my license until just before I graduated from M-A. Dating took a lot of time, but on Friday nights, the boys would go out and get whoopee. You had to bring a case of Country Club malt liquor to get into this one party at Chuck Weesner's house.

Menlo-Atherton was pretty laid back. It was a fun thing being class president, although I don't think I did anything exciting. I do remember directing traffic one day in the parking lot when we decided, as a senior prank, to keep the teachers from parking there. Our principal, Nick Nugent, came up to me and said, "You have fifteen minutes to clean up this mess or you don't graduate." We got it cleaned up pretty quick.

I played basketball as a senior, but I wasn't very good and quit halfway through the season to get ready for baseball. I didn't pitch as well my last year for two reasons: I hadn't played much baseball the summer before and playing quarterback really screwed up my arm. Opponents told me I threw the ball twice as hard the year before. Before the San Jose game, I had three or four beers even though I was the starting pitcher that day. I don't know why I did that. It wasn't very smart at all. I was wild all day.

But USC still wanted me. One reason why I was sold on USC was Lindsay Crosby, who was a big USC booster. But I almost didn't go there because of something that happened at the graduation party my parents threw for me at our house. My parents drank excessively. That night at the party, my dad was in the bag and pushed my mother. I was known as "Bones" at M-A because I was so thin. But by graduation time, I was seventeen, six-foot-four and weighing one hundred and ninety pounds, from lifting weights in order to get ready for USC football. So I picked up the old man and threw him into a window.

"Get yourself out of this house," he yelled. My mother was in tears. She gave me a check for fifty bucks and told me I'd better leave. So I packed up and drove to Woodland, to the parents' home of Sue Blevins, who would marry my brother in another year. Sue's father was a doctor. He got me a job driving a tractor, which I hadn't ever done. I was sent out to this field to clean out the irrigation between the beets. But I was off-kilter with the tractor and pulling out the beets instead. This guy came screaming after me, madder than I've ever seen anybody get mad. It was also the hottest summer you could imagine. After four or five days, I'm out of there, driving to Idaho in the brand-new 1956 green-

and-white Chevrolet convertible my father bought me when I graduated. So getting kicked out of the house wasn't all bad.

I was paid for my sloppy farm work, so I had a hundred bucks when
I got to Idaho. I'm pretty fat financially. Back then, gas was twenty-five
cents a gallon. And I had an invitation to come up to Idaho as the guest
of the Crosbys. After arriving, I made inquiries at Washington State
and Washington about playing at either school. Both were interested. I
actually thought I was going to Washington, my mother's school, when
Bing picked up on this. He said, "Wait a minute. This has gone too far.
You've got to talk to your father to see what he thinks. And where do you
really want to go?" I had the utmost respect for Bing. He was so damn
nice to me. I wanted to go to USC. So I called my father. We talked it out
that I should go to USC as planned.

Bing didn't counsel me all that much, but he was very strict with his
own boys. They had to toe the line, to be in at a specific time. Those
deadlines didn't apply to me. If I wanted to stay out later, I could. You
could drive at fourteen in Idaho, so I had a license to drive there. Any
place I went with the Crosbys, I got to drive. Whenever we went to
town in Bing's ostentatious Cadillac, he told me not to stop unless there
was a stop sign. Wherever we walked, he'd say, "Bill, you walk in front
of me. Lindsay, you walk behind. And don't you dare slow down or
stop." People would literally grab Bing. He said hello to everybody, but
he never stopped walking. Once, when two drivers saw that it was him,
they crashed into each other.

Bing was a delight to be around, singing all the time, perfectly natural, very interested in sports. He had a sense of humor. At Oakland
Tech, we had a game with Oakland High. John had a game at UCLA
the next day. So after my game, I'm driving in my football uniform to San
Francisco Airport, where I changed clothes, so I could get to Los Angeles. The day after the Stanford-UCLA game, Bing said to me, "That was
kind of tough on John, wasn't it?" UCLA won, 72-0.

My first year at USC, our freshman team played Stanford's fresh-
men in the morning game at Stanford, right before the varsity game
between the two schools. We won our game. I threw three touchdown

passes and got some pretty good press. Then John won, 27-19. It was the only time John and I were on the same football field the same day. And it was a pretty good day for the Brodies.

I didn't play baseball that year at USC because they wanted me to concentrate on football. Then I red-shirted in football my sophomore year, meaning I had a year of eligibility I was saving for later on. I did travel with the team to Notre Dame and got to suit up. Then in spring practice, I got into an altercation with Al Davis, the same guy who owns the Oakland Raiders. He was my backfield coach at USC. I thought he was a terrible horse's ass. He was very impressed with Al Davis, always showing off for the alumni on the sideline. He spent more time looking at the sideline and prancing around than actually coaching.

He didn't think I knew what the hell I was doing. On one play, I turned wrong, something like that, and he threw a blocking bag at me. Then he ordered me to go over and hold the bag. I threw the bag back at him and we got into it. After they pulled me off him, I was told to go down to the showers. That was it. I told the coaches I wasn't going to play football anymore.

I went to see Rod Dedeaux, the legendary USC baseball coach. He told me to play summer league, to see how I would do. I played semi-pro ball with a team out of Oakland, with a lot of George Powles' players. My arm wasn't as good as it once was, but I could still throw. Then I played baseball my last two years at USC. I started some games, but mostly relieved. We were on probation then, so we weren't eligible to play in the postseason.

I had a good time at USC. Jon Arnett, USC's All-America halfback, was a senior when I was a freshman. He was very helpful in getting me introduced around campus. One of my cousins was Helen of Troy, a big honor at USC. My aunt, or my father's sister, married Tom Kalmus, who invented and also owned the rights to technicolor. So I had a helluva entree down there. What a house they had in Bel Air, with their own movie theater. Lindsay Crosby took me all over town, introducing me to lots of fun people.

One night, I had dinner at the Kalmuses. Walt Disney and Loretta

Young are there with a bunch of other fancy folks. My aunt pulled me aside and said, "Billy, do you like to go shopping?" I said, "Certainly." She told me to meet her at this men's store. I always dressed well, but not for this league. My aunt bought me two suits, a sport coat, a tuxedo and a bunch of shirts. She spent five hundred to a thousand bucks, which was a lot of money back them, although not to my aunt or her husband.

A year later, my uncle wasn't feeling well on the night of the Academy Awards. So my aunt asked me to escort her. We drove up in this limousine. I'm wearing the tuxedo she bought me. As I walked up this red carpet with this beautiful lady, my cousins are running behind the line yelling, "There's Bill Brodie." It was embarrassing. I enjoyed that lifestyle, though, and felt comfortable in it, but I was kind of awe-struck, too.

I dated Sue Barron throughout college, though we dated others, too. She was in fashion school in New York; we had some horrendous phone bills. We'd see each other during the summer. With college coming to an end, I had to figure out something to do. First, I had to graduate. I hadn't read a book in college until my senior year. I'd go to tutors then wind up tutoring half my Sigma Chi fraternity brothers. I was smart enough to get by, but I had to petition to take nineteen and twenty-two units my last two semesters at USC to graduate on time. I made it, but I had to go to the whip.

Bill Tarr, who played fullback at Stanford, and Ted Poulus put the bug in my ear to go to law school. I applied to Hastings in San Francisco and was accepted. Sue and I got married after my first year. We lived with my parents, and I'd take the train to San Francisco. The next year, we got an apartment in Menlo Park. Sue worked at Philco, became pregnant, and Lisa was born in April of my last year of law school. I didn't pass the bar the first time I took it in 1963. Working on the docks, loading trucks, I wasn't serious enough. I passed it the next time and was admitted to the California bar in 1964.

I lost the first five law cases I tried, then won the next twenty-five or thirty. I enjoyed trying cases. I have a little bit of ham and had fun cross-examining. Don Layne asked me to join his firm in Palo Alto. Then a third person, John Germino, joined us, and we became the law firm of Layne, Brodie and Germino, with seventeen attorneys eventually working for our firm.

I did civil and criminal law, tried a lot of cases, and was pretty damn good at both. I bought a home in Los Altos, not far from John's, for fifty-thousand dollars. Leon Finegold's dad came out and put in a pool for ten-thousand dollars one summer when Sue, Lisa and I were in Idaho. We were fat and happy, and we stayed that way for a good while.

One night, while having dinner with some friends at our house, the phone rang. It was John, who said, "I'm in Houston. Get your butt on an airplane—there's one at 9 p.m.—and get down here. It's worth twenty-thousand dollars to you." I said good night to our guests and made the plane. The Houston Oilers were ready to sign John to a longterm contract. Al Davis now was commissioner of the American Football League, and he had devised a plan to sign four top National Football League quarterbacks, including John and Roman Gabriel of the Los Angeles Rams.

John was signing yearly contracts with the 49ers, so his contract was up. His first 49ers contract was for seventeen-thousand, five-hundred. Houston owner Bud Adams was ready to give him an overall package of one-point-one million dollars. I made sure we memorialized it by writing the terms down on a cocktail napkin, which Adams then signed.

I wanted to keep the cocktail napkin as proof. But John had a sinus condition—from our father's fist—and somewhere in the night, he blew his nose in that cocktail napkin, then flushed it down the toilet. Only Bud Adams didn't know that. But the 49ers matched Houston's offer and John stayed with the 49ers. When it was all said and done, I actually got fifty-thousand dollars, which paid for the house in Los Altos.

But by that time, I was drinking a lot and had, at least, one drunk driving ticket. I was carousing, staying out late, and things started deteriorating. I put in the necessary time at my law firm, then I'd go out drinking. I was very professional, still sharp in my practice. I never had one complaint from a client. I wasn't worried about losing money because the firm was doing very well. I just enjoyed the drinking. I had fun. It was weird. I had a lot of laughs, and that conduct persisted. But somewhere in there, I had to go get another drunk driving.

Sue didn't like it, and I didn't like it, so I moved out. I can't really explain it. We didn't go to marriage counseling; we pretty much knew it was over between us. I moved in with Mike Skuse, who was working at The Winery, a restaurant in Palo Alto. I drank there practically every night after work. Sue moved up to Spokane, Washington, near a lady friend. Sue then remarried a nice guy. Not seeing Lisa all the time was rough. She was about eight when we divorced. Sue was very good about weekend visitation rights. I'd fly Lisa down at least once a month. We'd have a wonderful time, then putting her back on the plane was horrible. Both of us cried.

Lindsay Rand was a secretary at our law firm. We started dating, then got married in 1974. We divorced five years later. I hadn't cut down on my drinking and we were having problems. But my drinking wasn't the main reason our relationship went to hell. It was an incident involving her father, an unforgivable act of his, I felt. So I moved out. Then I had some setbacks, a couple more drunk drivings, and I got suspended from the bar for six months.

Then in 1987, I got another drunk driving that was undeserved. But some cocaine was found in the car in a small white bindle, a quarter of a gram, with no fingerprints of mine found anywhere. I've used cocaine, but I wasn't using it then. The car belonged to Lisa, but I'd had possession of it for a long time. I'm not sure if the cocaine was planted, but I have my ideas. But now the authorities had some big-time charges. They sentenced me to two years jail time, although I was given probation if I would spend five months in the San Mateo County Jail in La Honda, near Half Moon Bay. Then after that, I would do a live-in rehab in Scotts Valley, by Santa Cruz, for two months.

I agreed to go to La Honda. I was embarrassed, but that's all. It's just something you get through. I wasn't interested in joining Alcoholics Anonymous because I didn't want to stop drinking. The La Honda halfway house had the Twelve Steps program used by AA. The Twelve

Steps are bullshit. I had weekends where I could come home. One weekend, I had a dinner date, then dropped the woman off. She wanted me to stay and I didn't want to. I'm not sure if she called the police, but indications are she did. Anyway, I got stopped on Woodside Road for drunk driving. The judge sentenced me to the full term, four years at San Quentin.

I was at San Quentin actually six months, a really miserable experience, with some miserable characters. It's something you can't really describe. You're so confined, and everything you do is confined. You get some yard time, but mostly you're going to meals or you're locked up in your cell. I didn't have any men coming on to me sexually. I wasn't involved in any fights. I was called O.G., for old gangster.

After my time there, I went to Susanville for twelve months. Susanville is a low-risk facility. I was a librarian, then I was a clerk running inmates in and out of the facility. I still had my law practice, so I did legal work for inmates. I handled two divorces, including one for the guy running the jail. I was paid in apples, things like that. After Susanville, I was sent to a halfway house in San Mateo. I was gone for eighteen months total, but I still had eight months parole left.

Coming back from a golf tournament in Santa Cruz, I got in a fender-bender. I didn't pass go and went directly to jail in Santa Clara on yet another drunk-driving charge. Then I was moved to Santa Rita. By that time, my license to practice law had been suspended.

But that was it for me as far as jail time. I was put in an assistance program for lawyers with drinking problems. If I would go to a live-in rehab facility in Florida for two months, at a cost of thirty thousand dollars, the assistance program would put up so much of it and I would owe them the rest. I told them they were crazy; I wasn't going to be locked up again. I had had enough. I wasn't going to listen to that bullshit again.

I could practice law again if I want to go through all the hoops, but I don't know if I want to work that hard. The state bar would make me re-take an aptitude test. I took it four years ago and scored an eighty-three, a pretty good score. If I took it again and passed, and I went into this program in Florida, I could be re-admitted to the bar in a year or less. But I would have to give up my bartender's job, which I really enjoy.

I don't think drinking has shortened my life span. I've never had any major health problems. You find out who your true friends are when you've had the problems I've had. There are fair-weather friends who just avoid you. I don't push myself on anybody. If they don't want me around, I'm gone.

I still have the support of my family. My brother had a stroke a few years ago. I got there the day after he was admitted to the hospital in Palm Desert. The doctor said the prospects of his coming out of this alive were not very good. He had ninety-two percent and ninety-six percent blockages of his two carotid arteries. The doctor was not optimistic. But the next day, the doctor told me that John's going to make it. I said, "Wow! What a change." The doctor said, "It's him."

The third day at the hospital, John and I were having the damndest time communicating. He couldn't say what he wanted to say, and I couldn't figure it out. So he started laughing, and I started laughing, and we got hysterical. That's why, I'm sure, the doctor said he's going to make it.

John understands what it is he wants to say. It's all there and he can't enunciate it, so it's frustrating for him. He's limited in his speech, but he still does the speech therapy, the walk therapy, and both are getting better. His right hand is claw-like and he can't grip a golf club. That's all he wants to do, play golf. I tried to close his right hand around the club, but it's difficult to do. However, with his one good hand, he hit the ball one-hundred and seventy yards down the middle. Why am I helping him? I can't hit it one-hundred and seventy yards down the middle with two hands.

As my dad aged, the two of us got along much better. My parents moved to Hayden Lake, where they spent their final years. The old man sat under a tree at night and we'd talk about all kinds of things. He died at sixty-six in 1968. My mom, who was ten years younger, lived until she was seventy-six.

I'm still in Menlo Park, living in a condominium. Menlo is a comfortable lifestyle, terribly familiar. I know the people, though I'm not overly impressed with the prices. To buy a house, you're not going to get much for a million five-hundred. Downtown Menlo Park has been upgraded since we were in high school. Fancier stores and restaurants, and more of them.

What stood out about the Fifties for me was Frank Sinatra and Elvis Presley. My mother wasn't too crazy about Elvis. Frank sang "My Way." I can empathize; those words could be my own. My old man liked the Mills Brothers. Our teenage songs, "Walk Over The Bridge" and "Sh-Boom," didn't knock his socks off. We all change with time. You kinda remember the music you grow up with, but I find the rap that kids are listening to today appalling.

What do I see looking at my M-A graduation picture? Probably that I wanted to talk to the girl pictured on the left of me, Barbara Boucke, or the girl pictured on the right, Joanne Broeren. They look pretty good. But the kid that I was, the future looked kinda rosy to him, awful bright.

If he looked at me now, he'd probably be a little disappointed that he didn't achieve as much as he could have or should have. But, then again, maybe he'd just as soon go have a pop with me and see what's going on. That would be fine by me. I've got nothing to hide. As I said, I've had a happy life.

Smartest one in the room

Josephine Booth

★ 2 ★

The Intellectual

Josephine Booth Grieder was M-A's valedictorian in 1956: No. 1 out of 352 graduates. She married her Stanford English teacher, who was thirteen years older. She earned a doctorate, taught French at Rutgers, went through alcoholism and a divorce, and now divides her time between Paris and New York.

My high-school class' fiftieth reunion—the first reunion I had attended since leaving Menlo-Atherton—was a far more dramatic moment than one might expect. That's because before the reunion, I was cleaning out my office at Rutgers University, the same office I had lived in for thirty-seven years. I was retiring from teaching. So I was concluding one life and coming back to revisit another.

Barbara Rhoades, or "Bittle," was the only person in our M-A class I had kept in contact with over the years. So fifty years later, there was this band of people....well, the initial shock gave way to something that was very impressive. So many interesting people, and I was immensely touched by how many people wanted to talk to me. It makes me misty-eyed now to think about it, and I was misty-eyed even at the reunion. I guess they liked me more than I thought when I was at M-A, although I really didn't care back then whether they liked me or not. For I was a terrible snob about all those people whose social class I didn't fit into.

Menlo-Atherton was a very strange amalgam of very wealthy kids, pretty wealthy kids, lots of middle-class kids, not so wealthy kids, kinda poor kids, and poor kids. Bittle and I became friends in the fourth grade. When she moved across El Camino Real to Creek Drive, she moved into an entirely different social circle. I met that circle at M-A, but I never entered it.

The person I was in high school was ambitious and impatient. I figured out the only way to improve myself socially was through intellectual pursuits—journalism and drama, primarily. I was features editor on the school newspaper. I acted in school plays. I was Commissioner of Publications.

I didn't feel above people; I felt beside them. I was a snob, though, in not paying attention to them. My interests were separate from theirs. I had no desire to share in the dances or all the marks of social success, like cashmere sweaters, which my parents couldn't really afford, or my own good-looking car. Sports didn't interest me. Being a cheerleader didn't mean anything to me. That kind of popularity, dating jocks and all of that, didn't interest me. I felt on the fringe, but I had my own little group.

I don't want to give the impression that high school was boring for me, because it wasn't. I did go to games, because they were fun. M-A was a time of opportunity, things to learn and do. I was chosen for Girls State, a wonderful honor. I applied for and was accepted to a six-week high school theater workshop at Northwestern University in Evanston, Illinois, between my junior and senior years. I couldn't act, except superficially. What made me valuable in acting was I could memorize quickly and I remembered my lines. I wasn't one of the glamorous stars; I used to play fathers and dogs. These were character roles, and there was a reason for that. I was fat. I didn't lose weight until my senior year. But the experience at Northwestern opened my eyes to the fact that I didn't have acting talent and I better try something else.

Being class valedictorian was a mark of distinction. I really wanted that because it validated what I had been doing. I think I had a 3.92 grade-point average. There was a girl in our class, Carolyn Isabella, who had something like a 3.95 GPA. By a faculty decision, I was named valedictorian because Carolyn hadn't been at M-A the full four years. My IQ is 152, though I know classmate Emily Bartholomew was innately more intelligent than I am.

I'm the liberal in my family, even though I handed out Eisenhower-Nixon bumper stickers in a Menlo Park shopping mall in 1956. But I evolved. I consider capitalism as much of an ideology as an economic theory. This twinning of the religious and the economic always has been a part of the American character. And it's the worst part, because having a firm belief in one of the two makes people totally intolerant of anyone who does not share their views. I do believe there is such a thing as benevolent capitalism. Warren Buffet's forty-four-billion-dollar gift to the Gates Foundation is a stunning example. But practiced on a large or small scale, it doesn't really matter, because capitalism is a dehumanizing process that reduces other people to a collection of wants and needs.

Is our political system the best we can have? In theory, it is. But how did it come to pass that politicians have become so venal? They no longer serve office as a civic duty. Politics has become a profession with its own corrupt morality. Winston Churchill said, "Democracy is not a good system, but there aren't any better." Democracy has its flaws and its holes, but the Constitution has produced fundamentally decent Americans.

My family was partially educated. My mother had a B.A. and B.F.A. from the University of Denver. My father couldn't afford to go to college and became a salesman. My brother was a pilot for FedEx. I do have an interesting family background. My paternal great-grandfather was the first undertaker in Los Angeles County. My father's uncle was a Keystone Kop in those Mack Sennett silent-screen comedies. And my father's side of the family is related to General William Booth, founder of the Salvation Army.

My father was a first-class salesman, but what he was best at was traveling. He loved to travel. His great pleasure on the weekends was to get in the car and drive up to the Mother Lode or to San Mateo Memorial Park in the mountains close by. We took a family trip around the country, which opened my eyes to other possibilities, to a world I wanted to access.

Our family was not comfortable financially, largely because my father took care of the budget. He told me, "You can have anything you want as long as we can afford it." Consequently, what he gave me was immense, like the opportunity to go to Stanford, although its tuition was much lower back then, and I was on a scholarship. I do think it's remarkable that fourteen kids from our M-A graduating class attended Stanford. It says a whole lot about the quality of the people in our class, and their level of intelligence.

Our Stanford freshman class was about a thousand students, two thirds men and one third women. The women generally were known as the "Stanford turkeys." Presumably, women who got into Stanford were smart, but ugly. Of course, that wasn't true. Some of the most ravishing women I've known in my life were in that freshman class. I had two roommates that year, one of them a blonde model type with a ponytail. I walked into the room and she said, "You have the awfulest hair I've ever seen." My hair at M-A was like a Prince Valiant cut with bangs. My roommates sat me down and cut it all off. I've worn my hair like this, a pixie, ever since. It fits my face.

What I felt intellectually when I got to Stanford—and this is going to sound terrible—was how happy I was not to be the smartest person in the room. I was certainly one of the more ignorant Stanford students. And all because Menlo-Atherton didn't do a very rigorous job of teaching literary and historical classics. In freshman English at Stanford, my teacher, Ted Grieder, gave me the first F of my life on a paper. I got a C for the first quarter, another first, then a B the second quarter, and an A the third quarter. Ted was an excellent teacher. I was tremendously impressed with him because he represented education and how much there was to learn.

Ted was older than I was by thirteen years. We had coffee together late in my freshman year, but he had the hots for another Stanford student, a Mack Truck heiress. I worked as a campus guide at Hoover Tower. One day, Ted stopped by. He had just passed his dissertation defense and gotten a job teaching English at the University of Nevada in Reno. It somehow came up that I was going to Iowa that summer to visit my roommate, and I would be driving back to California with her cousin. The two of us stopped off in Reno and had dinner with Ted. Then Ted and I had a drink. We were engaged by Christmas.

Ted and I wed in August, 1958. I transferred to Nevada. The first thing Ted said to me after we got to Reno was that I would take education classes and stenography. I said, "What!" And he said, "Well, you're either going to be a secretary or a teacher after college." I broke into tears. But I took those classes, and as it turned out, I fell in love with teaching.

I've often tried to figure out if I was in love with Ted. I certainly was in love with everything he represented. He was an older man. He may have been in the Army during World War II; he made up a lot of stories later on. His education and degrees were impressive. In terms of experience, he liked wine and food. He represented all the things in a man I'd never seen before. He was slightly shorter than I was, so that gave me pause. And he was a thoroughly disagreeable, unpleasant guy, though I didn't know it right then.

The marriage lasted seventeen years. For the first ten, it was certainly compatible. I always thought a student-teacher marriage was like something out of a fairy tale. Then Ted had a nervous breakdown one day while in class. It was a blessing, really, because he wasn't very good at writing and he would have never gotten tenure at any university. So he decided to go to library school at UC-Berkeley while I taught school in San Pablo. In 1963, he was hired as chief acquisitions librarian at UC-Davis, where I finished a master's degree in French. After three years, he got an offer from New York University to be its acquisitions librarian. We both knew that this was the big time. We found an apartment and I went on to get my Ph.D in Comparative Literature at NYU. Then I was hired right away to teach French at Rutgers.

Ted had a drinking problem. I wasn't so temperate either. We moved from one brownstone in SoHo to another one in Hoboken, New Jersey. Ted was perfectly happy. He could watch all the television he wanted, because he had one floor of the house and I had another floor. We had kind of a bottom floor where we ate together. We had total separation, eventually even at night.

I drank so heavily that I would black out and wake up the next morning to interminable reproaches. Finally in the summer of 1975, I quit drinking and set out to analyze my behavior. Why was I drinking this much? Clearly because I was trying to get Ted's attention, and clearly I was not succeeding in a positive way. Why did I want his attention? Because I wanted something to depend on, it appeared. But wasn't I independent? No, I wasn't, apparently.

Suddenly, I realized a startling and profound truth: I now knew as much about everything as Ted did. All those things he had represented before marriage had become my property. Then the final question: Why was I wasting my life with this thoroughly disagreeable, unpleasant person who expected me to work full time and clean house, cook, take out the garbage, work in the garden, and pay all the bills? I moved back to New York and filed for divorce. A friend said, "What took you so long?" In 1976, I divorced and got tenure.

I have had and continue to have a wonderful life. People often think a career in academics must be monotonous and dull. On the contrary. Teaching provides immediate communication and—on the good days— the satisfaction of seeing students learn. Scholarship—you don't get promoted if you don't publish—supplies the intellectual challenge and pressure that stimulate the mind. Administration—not all faculty choose to participate, but I did—offers opportunities to improve and structure the future. I was department chair at Rutgers from 1983 to 1987 and again from 1999 to 2005, when I ended my teaching career. During the last nine years, I was Director of the Graduate Program in Liberal Studies. And three different times, I directed the Junior Year Abroad in France Program. Imagine having to live in France.

Rutgers has been incredibly good to me, and it has been good to me in retirement. I'm writing a book about lions in Paris architecture. I bought a small place in Paris in 1994. I don't rent it out. Paris is heaven on Earth, the perfection of the moment, where everything is complete within itself. The French represent to me knowledge and standards that I must live with, eagerly. New York and Paris are alike; both are intense and great walking cities. I shop identically, I take public transportation, I go to the theater and museums. I live in Paris twice a year and in New York twice a year. I hope I am not sounding smug, but I am certainly satisfied with life.

Looking at our high school yearbook, what was I thinking back then? About the excitement of going to Stanford. What would the girl in that picture say about how her life has turned out? To perfection.

Holy! Holy! Holy!

David Schofield

★ 3 ★

The Voice of God

The Rt. Rev. John-David Schofield is Bishop of San Joaquin, one of six Episcopal dioceses in California. Along with delivering God's message, he has received messages from God and experienced one vision of Jesus Christ. His conservative views have created heated controversy within the national church.

Growing up in a home with parents who sought God, I was no stranger to the idea that God would provide guidance and direction to those who asked. My father was British and a member of the Church of England before coming to America, hence an Anglican. My mother came from a very puritanical New England family that traced its roots back to the religion of the Pilgrim Fathers, American Revolution and General Israel Putnam, who was George Washington's man in the Northern Colonies.

If the name Putnam sounds familiar, the night before the Battle of Bunker Hill (actually Breed's Hill), he told his men, "Don't shoot 'til you see the whites of their eyes." So I have this famous ancestor. Curiously, my parents' personalities in no way reflected their backgrounds. Dad was generous and outgoing. Mom reflected her Beacon Hill upbringing and was reserved and shy. Yet they shared their love of God, the daily reading of scripture, prayer, and waiting on Him in what they called their "quiet time."

By 1948, my father, after four heart attacks and acting on his doctor's advice, decided the climate of Massachusetts was too harsh. He would seek milder climates. To do this, the family packed up and took off on the adventure of a lifetime—a tour of the South Pacific. Then it was agreed upon in the family that the San Francisco Peninsula offered everything anyone could want, including a wonderful climate. So after vacationing in Fiji, New Zealand and Hawaii, off to Palo Alto and Menlo Park we headed.

Willow Elementary School and Ravenswood Junior High School led me to Menlo-Atherton—a school one of my father's companies supplied materials for during its construction. It was in high school that I saw my first opera, "La Bohème." I've loved the opera ever since, and I go as often as I can. At M-A, I pursued my child's interest in theater, appearing in various plays. I also became interested in writing. One of the most practical things I learned in high school was how to type. Writing and typing became tremendously useful to me later in life, composing editorials for The San Joaquin Star, the official newspaper of the Episcopal Diocese of San Joaquin.

High school was a wonderful time for me. I made very good friends with Jackie DeWitt, Mickey Pierce, Dick Parks and Gordy Plaisted. I had a facility to relate to people. I find it tedious to be by myself. I loved the music of the times. Teresa Brewer was my sweetheart, singing "I Don't Want a Ricochet Romance." Two movie stars, Audrey Hepburn and June Allyson, stole my heart.

By my junior year, I already was thinking of the priesthood. Sitting in Holy Trinity Church in Menlo Park, I listened to one of the worst sermons I had ever heard. I thought, "I can do better than that." I had studied Spanish and Latin in high school, and Russian on my own. I thought I could serve the church well in many different cultures. Eventually, I also studied Greek, Hebrew and a little bit of French. When I told my Spanish teacher, Rosa Choplin, that I wanted to be a priest, she replied, "What a waste. You would be wonderful in the diplomatic corps with your facility of languages. You could have influence all over the world."

In the fall of 1956, I found my way back to New England, entering Dartmouth College. There I made my first retreat at Holy Cross Monastery on the Hudson River. As an undergraduate, a book written by C. Kilmer Myers entitled "Light the Dark Streets" kindled a desire within me to follow in this priest's footsteps and minister to street gangs in slum areas. It didn't take long to discover that no one was taking me seriously. Then instead of serving in the slums while I went through the General Theological Seminary in New York City, I was sent to St. James on Madison Avenue, where children were dropped off to Sunday School by chauffeurs.

The dream of being a slum priest, though, would not die. My ordination in 1963 at Grace Cathedral in San Francisco could have opened Hunter's Point—the city's naval yards—for such a ministry. But because of a facility with language that was encouraged by my studying on Stanford University's foreign exchange program at La Universidad Autonoma de Guadalajara. I had requested to be sent to San Francisco's Mission District, where I would be able to use my Spanish. But no such luck. I was sent to San Francisco's Pacific Heights, where I was also called to serve as chaplain at the Presidio's Letterman Army Hospital. However, by 1965, I was free to follow my dream. After a short stint at St. George's in Paris, at long last I received a call to serve in London's East End at Our Most Holy Redeemer with St. Philip of Clerkenwell.

It didn't take long before my dream turned into a nightmare. Living across the street from a pub, which was next door to Woolworth's, and a factory that was operating twelve hours a day, not to mention street stalls selling everything from jellied eels and kitchen ware to shoes, well, this wasn't the romantic life I had imagined. Depression reared its ugly head. While classmates from high school and college wrote me glowing letters of success, marriage and family life, my two rooms at the top of a church tower seemed more barren than they probably were. I welcomed the respite that a week at Stacklands Retreat House in Seven Oaks, Kent, England, offered. I had no idea how that one bleak November week would change my life forever.

The retreat at Stacklands did not begin well. The elderly priest who was serving as conductor couldn't have been worse. Starting on the opening night, I thought to myself that if I weren't in a depression when I arrived, this retreat would drive me into one. By the fourth day, even the retreat conductor suspected things weren't going well. He called a group of us young priests into the chapel and said, "I'm going to set my notes aside." I thought it couldn't get worse, and it might get better. For his notes hadn't done anything for him up to this point.

Without introduction, our conductor described how Jesus invited Peter to step out of the boat and join him by walking on water. Pausing and looking at us, he said, "What I'm about to say, I believe, is meant for one of you in this chapel." He paused, then continued: "When God asks the impossible of you, and you say 'Yes,' He'll make it possible."

On the way to the retreat, I already had decided what I was going to do. Living a celibate life was not for me. Therefore, I was determined to leave the slums, go back to the United States and, most importantly, get married. It was not a blessing, then, to hear an inner voice speaking to me. It had a quality of sadness about it. Over and over again, the words "Your vows" were repeated. It was almost as if Jesus Christ were standing next to me and weeping over me. I knew in my heart I was disappointing Him.

No matter how I tried to focus on something else, I couldn't get those words out of my mind. After the half hour, we were required to kneel on the slate floor of the chapel. I made my way out to the formal gardens, where I hoped the voice would be silenced. It wasn't. "On to my bed" was my next thought. By taking a nap, I could blot the whole thing out. Impossible. So sitting on my bed, I decided to go into a cold-blooded rebellion. I would return to the chapel, where I was determined to say one word: "No."

After I prayed, I waited for something to happen. Nothing did. Emboldened, I proceeded to tell God how we ran things in the Church of England. I explained that I knew many holy and effective priests who were happily married. In the midst of these explanations, the voice broke through to me a second time. This time it was in the form of a question: "But what would it be like if you just said 'Yes' to me without any strings attached?" My first thought was that by agreeing to such a thing, I wouldn't have a leg to stand on. Why, I could be returned to the East End of London and left there until my dying day.

Without warning, I became aware of a sense of excitement welling up inside of me. This may seem like nothing unless, of course, you have been through sixteen months of depression as I had. In a depression, there are no feelings. Now it seemed as if a little green shoot, something like the first crocus of spring, was rising up inside me. I found myself longing to say "yes" to God. What an exciting life to wake up each morning not knowing whether by the end of day the Lord might have transported you to South Africa, Australia, Canada or Alaska.

Just as I was about to reverse what I had said, the voice came a third time. This time, it was the Lord revealing the "fine print" of the contract. "It's not your body nor even your drives that I want," He said. "I want your heart and mind, and I want them one-hundred per cent pure." What a demand! No normal human being could do what He was asking. Then almost immediately the words of the elderly priest that were spoken only an hour earlier in the chapel came to mind: "When God asks the impossible of you and you say 'Yes,' He'll make it possible."

With all my heart, I wanted the pure heart and mind He was asking of me. So I said, "God, if you will make this happen, then that is what I want." As I prayed these words, I was looking up at the altar. To my utter amazement, I watched transfixed as Jesus came out of the tabernacle where the consecrated bread and wine of Communion were reserved. He was dressed as the King of kings. On his head was a crown of gold, but it was living gold. The crown kept its shape, but the gold moved. A long red cape from His shoulders extended back to the altar. Slowly, He came down the aisle toward me. He never touched me, nor did He speak. But as He drew closer, wave after wave of love washed over me. Instead of surrounding me, these waves were like x-rays. They penetrated my whole being.

Before this, I thought I knew what love was. I didn't. And even though I couldn't have told you what was happening to me, whatever this ecstasy was, I didn't want it to end. I wasn't aware of the moment. I lost sight of Him. It is likely that I was totally preoccupied with the enormous love he continued to pour into me. In the days that followed, I tried to make sense out of what had happened. Because I had never known anyone who had had such an experience, I concluded that God had asked something of me, and I was willing to say "Yes." He had blessed me. That unforgettable day was Nov. 17, 1966.

In the months that followed, changes came over me that I hadn't ever associated with the vision of the Lord. Not only did the Bible come alive for me in a way it never had before, it took on a new authority. I discovered in the pages of Scripture things I was beginning to experience. My prayer life deepened. I was astounded when people who were critically ill or terminal were healed when I prayed. I was in the midst of a love affair with God.

After a year of these remarkable changes, my boss called me into his study. He was concerned. "You are forever singing and laughing and whistling," he said, "yet nothing in your life has changed." Fearing I was on the edge of some kind of nervous breakdown, he insisted I receive counseling. It was only after this, through three close friends, that I learned I had received what is called the Baptism of the Holy Spirit.

By 1968, the priest who had written the book that began this spiritual odyssey for me was now the Bishop of California. In London for the 1968 Lambeth Conference for Bishops from around the world, Bishop C. Kilmer Myers said to me, "I want you to come home to California. You are only on loan to the Church of England." By October, 1969, he appointed me to be the vicar and retreatmaster of the tiny Church and Retreat House of St. Columba in Inverness. Lovely as the location was on Tomales Bay on the Point Reyes National Seashore of West Marin, that first year was the loneliest I had ever experienced. My friends who had opened so many doors for me in the Spirit were all in England, and my new assignment felt like I was doing time.

True, I had said "Yes" to God, but doubts about returning to the United States crowded my mind. Then little by little, I fell in love with my parishioners. And the small church family began to grow almost immediately. I conducted retreats. I found preaching and teaching rewarding, especially as I became aware of how many people seemed to be drawn to St. Columba from all over the Bay Area and as far away as Sacramento. I watched with amazement as lives were being changed. Healings were taking place. People were being set free from life-long addictions. I couldn't have been happier.

Out of the blue, I received a telephone call from a young priest in the Diocese of San Joaquin, which represents the central third of California. I had known this young priest for some time, but I wasn't prepared for the suggestion he was about to make. He wanted to place my name in nomination for the bishop of the diocese. All I could do was laugh. "Wait a minute," he said. "When I've come to you for counsel, you have told me not to be cavalier, but to pray. Now I am asking you to follow your own advice."

I agreed, not knowing whether or not I was being serious. The young priest asked how long I was going to spend in prayer, because the deadline for applications was approaching rapidly. "Give me three days," I responded. On the third day, he telephoned to ask if I had heard anything from the Lord. I said I had, and felt God had simply said to me, "Let your name stand."

When the news of the nominations became public, I assured the people of St. Columba's that there was no way on God's green earth I could be elected. I told them my name was a last-minute addition. The search committee had planned on presenting only four names; I was the fifth, and only by the slim margin of one vote. On the day after the election, when I heard no news, I told my congregation that, just as I had suspected, someone else must have been elected.

That evening, I learned differently. The phone rang and a caller purporting to be Bishop Victor Rivera said I had been elected that day. "You do accept, don't you?" he asked. I stammered out something of a positive response, to which he said, "Good, I'll call you tomorrow morning." And with that, he hung up. I was almost certain this was a joke being played by a friend of mine, disguising his voice and adding the Puerto Rican accent of Bishop Rivera.

Reality hit me the next morning at six o'clock with the phone ringing by my bedside. It was a writer for the New York Times requesting an interview. "You're the most conservative candidate to be elected as bishop in the Episcopal Church in years," he announced. It was true. I told the interviewer I still was in bed because it was early on the West Coast. I thought I could gather my wits if he would call back in a few hours. But before I could get my bearings, controversy began to swirl about me.

The Fresno Bee published a headline announcing "Next Episcopal Bishop A Practicing Roman Catholic." Charges leveled by those who opposed me from within the Diocese of San Joaquin ranged from "The election was bogus" to "He's breaking the Church's law by refusing to ordain women" to "He's against homosexuals." By the time the General Convention was called to order in Detroit, Michigan in the summer of 1988, I was to be put on trial. I stood before fourteen judges for two days as each charge was addressed. The unanimous decision of the judges was acquittal. My name was permitted to go before the House of Deputies and the House of Bishops. Both Houses confirmed the election.

What I will never forget is standing before a congregation of four thousand on Sunday, Oct. 9, 1988. An old adage says: "A man's perspective on life changes when he reaches fifty." I can confirm that, because three days prior to my consecration as the fourth Bishop of San Joaquin, I celebrated my fiftieth birthday. At least, I think I celebrated. I have no memory of the day at all. Relatives from England and friends from all over the United States began to arrive in Fresno for the "Big Day." More than six hundred people accepted my invitation to an open house. While still in our pajamas, a cousin of mine looked out the front window and exclaimed, "You'll never believe this. They're lined up out onto the sidewalk and down the street." Everyone in the household was kept busy making sandwiches, cutting cake and brewing gallons of coffee until late at night.

The actual service the previous day had been glorious. One detail that escaped the notice of most came at the moment Edmond Lee Browning, the Presiding Bishop, changed my name as he laid his hands on me. It was then that he joined my monastic name, John, to my baptismal name, David. From then on, I became John-David. In one sense, it was a little thing. But names have tremendous power. Changing a name makes an impact. And I would need to make a wide impact as the Diocese of San Joaquin is larger in land mass than the state of Iowa, stretching from the southern tip of Sacramento to the northern tip of Los Angeles.

As a young priest, I remember worrying about the passage of Scripture that warns: "Beware when all men speak well of you." In the nineteen years since my consecration. I've discovered I don't have that worry any more. Like other public figures, I've learned to live with statements that I supposedly made, but haven't made. And also with the motives that have been attributed to me, but in actual fact, have never occurred to me. A priest friend who finds himself in similar circumstances said to me, "I have to read the newspaper now to know what I am thinking."

As an Anglo-Catholic, I have never swerved from supporting the traditional position that ninety per cent of liturgical Christians (including Roman Catholicism and the many different Churches of Eastern Orthodoxy) do not ordain women to the priesthood or the episcopate. The women's caucus of my own church has been quick to charge me with being a "woman hater." Nothing could be further from the truth. I have gladly ordained a number of women deacons for the Diocese of San Joaquin, and I find their ministries effective, sensitive and powerful.

Today a huge controversy rages over what liberals would like the public to believe about an issue that may well cause a massive schism in the Church. Those of us who do not agree with them are called "homophobes" or haters of homosexual persons. The serious question that faces the Church, however, is not primarily one of human sexuality. On the contrary, that which could split the Church—I am talking not only about The Episcopal Church of the United States, but the seventy million persons who make up the Anglican Communion throughout the world—concerns the authority of Scripture.

What liberals could not have foreseen when they ignored the pleas of many parts of the Anglican Community and the Archbishop of Canterbury himself as they confirmed and consecrated a man as Bishop of New Hampshire, who had divorced his wife, abandoned his family, and had been living with another man for eleven years, was that this was not a "justice issue," but a series of actions that ran contrary to the clear reading of the Bible. The consequences of such unilateral actions and arrogant disregard of the rest of the Anglican Community, not to mention the majority of Christians throughout the world, may prove, in the end, disastrous. Already thousands of believers have left the Episcopal Church, and others are making plans to do so.

Am I, as I have been accused, against gays? I believe that love bids us to reach out with healing. In fact, I have supported a powerful ministry on the campus of the Cathedral of St. James in Fresno, where four full-time counselors work some six days a week with individuals and small groups who are struggling with sexual addiction. The joy is to meet with those who have proven the myth wrong that there is no release from homosexuality. Scores of men who had been living in secret desperation have come into full, wholesome and healthy heterosexual lives.

A Presbyterian minister by the name of Roger Minassian came to me asking for guidance and support as he launched what he believed was God's word to him to minister to street gangs in Fresno. Now fourteen years later, more than sixteen-hundred young men have left the gangs of the city, committed their lives to Christ, and found responsible jobs, making it possible for them to marry, have families, and even buy homes. So it is that "Hope Now For Youth" was born, and whose impact reaches far beyond San Joaquin to cities plagued with gang warfare all over California. I never could have guessed forty years ago when I dreamed of being a slum priest how God would fulfill that ministry in such a different and far-reaching way that I could have never hoped for.

The wonder of knowing and serving God is that life becomes an unending adventure. The future—by our limited vision—always remains uncertain. This last year, alone, four California bishops brought charges against me in the hopes of having me deposed and removed as Bishop of San Joaquin. Their attempt to do this behind closed doors and without hope of a trial was seen for what it was. The charges were dismissed.

Many times I feel as if my diocese is an island surrounded by a sea of liberalism that, unless one is in lock step with what is politically correct, seeks to suppress us. Perhaps that is why one of my heroes is Lewis "Chesty" Puller, the most decorated man in the history of the United States Marine Corps. His portrait is framed and hanging in my breakfast nook where I can see him every day. During the Korean conflict, Chesty, who had pushed his men far north of the 38th parallel, announced: "The enemy are to the north of us. They are to the south of us as well as to the east and west of us. Men, we are absolutely surrounded. There is no way they can escape."

There are enormous forces at work within the Church today. Unfortunately, when one traces down the origin of the conflicts that are now raging, too often we find that they have less to do with God, and the work of reaching out and transforming the lives of men and women, and the Good News of what the Lord has accomplished for us in His Son rather than through money, power and property. I sense God weeping over His church. Instead of being the Body of Christ moving in the power of His Holy Spirit, it has chosen, instead, to become a human institution, well-endowed, bristling with the parapets of intrigue and legalism.

Does that make me want to give up? Never. My loyalty helps me focus—not on the creaking machinery of man-made laws, political agendas and aspirations that (no matter how charitable they sound) fall short of God's word—but the One whose voice I've heard, whose love is expressed through countless lives, and whose promise to us will endure and pass through the veil of death itself.

Now I gaze upon my Menlo-Atherton graduation picture. When that was taken, I was thinking the church can hardly wait to get me because I will be such a gift. That was arrogant, pride-filled thinking. With some of the experiences I've had in life—the school of hard knocks—I've learned it is other people who are gifts to you, and once in a while you are a blessing to others, and be thankful for every blessing you've been able to give.

If that same spiritual young man was looking at me now, he would say, "You could be in better shape. You're a fat old man." But on the whole he would say, "That's exactly what I'd thought you'd turn out to be, not necessarily a bishop, but someone who is in a position of leadership, and someone who has something to offer to others."

I am woman, watch me soar

Gerrie Keely

* 4 *

AARP Attorney
of the Year

Gerrie Keely Miller was a bright student who lost out on a college scholarship only because she was female. She then left college for financial reasons, got married, became a mother, and assisted her husband in business. Then when others her same age were retiring, she decided to become a lawyer.

The Fifties were different times for women. When I was a Menlo-Atherton High School senior, I learned I was a top candidate for the Peninsula Volunteers' annual fifteen-hundred-dollar academic college scholarship. But at my interview, they informed me that, at first, they had granted me the scholarship, but then decided to give it to a male student.

"We hope you understand," I was told, "that the reason we're doing this is because you're a girl, and you'll probably just get married and have children. So we decided to give it to a boy who has more career potential."

This was 1956, I was seventeen, and I said very sincerely, "Fine. That's wonderful. Great." Looking back on that situation, I realize this was gender discrimination, which wouldn't be tolerated in today's world.

But those times, as I said, were different. Young women I knew did not have aspirations to become professional people. We were, indeed, looking forward to getting married and having children. That's what was expected of us. We could become teachers, secretary-typists, nurses, store employees, flight attendants. Those were our career choices, basically.

I chose to be a flight attendant. Many women thought that was a glamorous life. We wore smartly tailored uniforms, spectator pumps and stylish military-type hats. We were "inspected" before each flight by a stern senior flight attendant. Stocking seams had to be straight. We wore bright-red lipstick, had beautifully polished nails, and practiced bright perky smiles.

We also put our lives on the line. One of my Reno flights had a slippery emergency landing on a foamed runway. The plane lost its landing gear. We slid and swerved all over the runway. We almost hit the terminal before finally coming to a stop. I have a box of "orchid" letters from relieved passengers who thought I was so brave and in control in the midst of a near tragedy. I kept that perky smile throughout that whole ordeal.

I was then nineteen. As a flight attendant, you couldn't be married, and you were automatically furloughed at the age of thirty-two. Today, both men and women attendants fly happily into their leathery seventies. A flying career was a way to serve people and to see the country inexpensively.

Speaking of serving people, I was the football queen my freshman year at Whitman College in Walla, Walla, Washington. My prize was I got to serve dinner to the football team for three weeks, two nights a week. It was the 1950s and I was happy to do it. Most women I knew didn't expect anything else.

Then in the late 1960s, Betty Friedan published best-selling books about the liberation of women. We were told that we should aspire to something greater than raising children. We should be out getting an education. We should be on an equal par with men in the employment arena. I never thought about that. At that time, I was happy being a good mother to my two children and a good wife to my hard-working husband.

Then I saw Gloria Steinem speak at Stanford. I was shocked that women's lib was so "in your face." She was so resentful about what she conceived as the ill-treatment of women in our society. I hadn't ever felt discriminated against as a woman—even with that scholarship incident in high school. I have always been dependent on my husband and have deferred to him over the years. But our marriage always has been a successful partnership.

I didn't wake up one day and say, "I think I'll become a lawyer." It was a gradual process. I attended Whitman as an English major, but for only two years. Although I had an academic scholarship, my father had three kids in college at the same time on his newspaperman's salary. He couldn't afford to help me finish my degree. So I became a flight attendant with the intention of finishing college after I saved some money.

When Wally and I married in 1961, I went back to school part-time and finally graduated from San Jose State at the age of thirty. In 1972, Wally and I started our family business, Miller Distributing Company. We distributed industrial adhesives, abrasives and metal-refinishing products. We became distributors for the Dupont Company and sold automotive coatings from Holland, eventually running five wholesale/retail locations in the Bay Area.

One of our employees was going to night law school. I thought that was something I might like to do. I don't know if my becoming a lawyer is genetic, but my great-great-great grandfather, Judge Robertson, was on the Virginia Supreme Court. He was responsible for getting the first African-Americans on juries. I have copies of letters Thomas Jefferson wrote to Judge Robertson.

In the mid-Seventies, while working full-time and raising two children, I went to Lincoln University Law School in San Jose four nights a week. Lincoln is accredited by the State Bar of California and was the only school in the Bay Area at the time that offered a night curriculum for working adults. I'd work in the office until it was time to pick up the kids from school, then take them home, go back to the office, come home, fix dinner, go to law classes, and then study early in the morning and on weekends.

We began with one-hundred students in our first-year class at law school. Four years later, only twenty-one were left, four of them women. This occurred a few years after Elizabeth Dole was ostracized by Harvard Law School classmates for accepting an admission that could have gone to a man.

When I graduated from law school, our family business had expanded to fifty-five employees. Wally said he needed me to work with him instead of my working for somebody else. So I stayed until we sold the business to a national company in 1996.

Then I worked toward a two-year certificate in paralegal studies at Santa Clara University in order to refamiliarize myself with the law. Bar review classes held at Stanford and Santa Clara prepared me for the bar exam. The year I passed the bar exam, the pass rate was only thirty-three percent. It was considered the toughest bar exam in the country. I was admitted to the California bar in November 2002 at the age of sixty-three.

Nancy Heinrich Hack has been my friend since the second grade at Willow School in Menlo Park. After I passed the bar and said I was going to open an office, Nancy said to me, "Are you crazy? Don't you know how old you are?" Other people said to me, "Why are you putting yourself through this? Why don't you just take it easy and travel?"

It takes a long time to build a law practice. I've handled a variety of matters so far. I worked on the defense team for a white-collar software fraud case perpetrated against Microsoft. I've assisted on sexual harassment and gender discrimination cases. I've handled some real estate transactions, trust administration and bankruptcy cases. But my focus seems to be headed toward family law. I do divorces and a lot of pro bono work. It's very stressful, but very rewarding. I'm a compassionate person and you have to set boundaries in this profession. One seasoned attorney with an Irish brogue gave me this advice: "Get out of family law as soon as ye can. It'll kill ye, darlin'."

The very first family law case I took, the lady forgot to tell me that her husband was a crack dealer and had been making death threats against her. My husband and I worried for a time about our own personal safety. It was a relief when the couple reconciled.

It's a myth that attorneys, even seasoned attorneys, know everything about the law. That is why there is so much mandatory continuing education for attorneys. Law school teaches you how to find the answers, but you can't know everything in this vast and growing profession. I'm still trying to find the level at which I will excel. I do default hearings at the Family Court, where I divorce people on Friday mornings. I call my black business suit "my divorce clothes." It's usually a happy day for the woman and man who are finally getting their papers signed by the judge.

I still have a lot to learn, but I am a life-long learner.

I usually read five books at a time. It helps that I was once a speed-reading teacher. It's my goal to self-educate. Wally teases me that I'll apply next to medical school. I hope to practice law for the next ten years, but I won't slow down after that. I'd like to take math classes to make up for my poor math education as a child. Math was the worst of my courses in school.

And being the child of an alcoholic, I had a history of not finishing things. I'd get to a point and then stop and go on to something else. Other traits of this child-of-an-alcoholic syndrome are always feeling responsible for other people, constant apologizing, and having difficulty in accepting praise. When parents are drinking, you are on your own, and you have to develop your own sense of self-worth. I am getting better at having more pride in my accomplishments. But it is a life-long struggle. My parents died while I was pursuing my law license. I like to think they know, somehow, that I finally completed a longterm goal.

My parents were a handsome couple. They met in high school in Yuba City during the Depression. My father, Bob Keely, was a hard-drinking Irish newspaperman. My mother, Marguerite Jones, was a talented musician who dreamed of attending the College of the Pacific in Stockton. Few people went to college during the Depression. So my parents married right after graduation and came to San Francisco.

My father eventually worked in retail advertising for the San Francisco Chronicle. He wrote "The Owl" column about San Francisco night clubs and restaurants. He also was an actor and president of the Palo Alto Players and Menlo Park Theater Guild. He was a Big Band singer; he sang with the Special Services band in the Navy during World War II. He appeared in a number of musicals, had a Screen Actors Guild card, and was an extra in many movies. He had a speaking part as a prison guard in the Woody Allen movie, "Take The Money And Run."

My memory of my father is that he was always gone. He was a good father to my three brothers and me, but he was hardly ever home. He was quite a ladies man, too. We don't know if my mother knew about his dalliances, but they stayed married for sixty-five years.

I wish I had been more patient with my mother after my father died. I was never unkind, but I could have been a little more sympathetic. My memories of my mother are that she was always sick. She was a life-long diabetic who never worked outside the home until my husband hired her a few days a week to answer the phone. She stayed for eighteen years. We used to call my husband, Wally, a saint for having to work with his wife and mother-in-law in the same business.

Wally's sense of humor has seen us through the ups and downs of our forty-four years of marriage. I met Wally when I was seventeen. He grew up in Minnesota, the youngest of nine children. He came to California because he had a sister in Palo Alto. She was a school librarian who helped him with his education. He attended Menlo Junior College and was editor of the school newspaper. He got his degree from Stanford, which he attended on a baseball scholarship. He was a pitcher. I thought he was the funniest guy and fixed him up with some of my high-school girl friends. In fact, we used to double-date.

After my first year at Whitman, Wally and I began dating and became great friends. He was well-read and we used to discuss literature and philosophy. After that magical summer, he went into the military. So we really didn't see each other for the next three years. Working for United Air Lines, I was based in Seattle before spending a year in Boston. I shudder when I think of myself in Boston, taking the subway home all by myself at four in the morning. I didn't know it until after I had moved back to San Francisco, but this was during the time of the Boston Strangler.

Flying out of San Francisco, I learned that Wally was living in Washington, D.C. Since United serviced Baltimore, I arranged my flight attendant's schedule in order to meet Wally in D.C. We had dinner and talked for hours and hours. That very night, we became engaged. Two months later, we were married in Alexandria, Virginia. I was twenty-two, Wally twenty-six. Nancy Heinrich Hack came from California to be maid of honor. It was a very small wedding, only nine people in attendance. We didn't have the twenty dollars to pay Reverend Johnson for conducting the ceremony. Years later, we sent him a sizable donation and a note of apology. We lived in Georgetown for two years. Wally worked for General Electric and I worked in the United States Patent Office. We moved back to the Bay Area in the early 1960s.

We have a daughter and a son, Kelly and Jeff, single professionals who live in San Francisco. They are good people and we are all great friends. One of my greatest regrets is that I will never know what's going to happen to our children when they grow old. It is my hope that I predecease them, but I won't know how their lives turn out. I'm one who likes to see the whole picture.

This needless worry must come from being brought up in such a chaotic family. I was the one who always had to be in charge. I had to be an adult before I had a chance to be a child. This is where a lot of my self-doubt comes in. That's a lot of pressure, and you're blocked in some way from getting to the end of a project. It's the old "fear of failure, fear of success" adage. I have more work to do on me. I'm trying to learn not to stress over my law cases. I've found that walking, reading, meditating and exercising all help with the stress.

Besides having to work on stress reduction, I also suffer at times from claustrophobia. I think this condition comes from being a child during World War II. We had to do mock air raid drills. I remember the air raid warden coming to the door and making us pull down our black shades and turn off all the lights so the coast would not be visible to enemy submarines. I used to hide in the closet because I thought they were coming to get us.

One of my attorney friends said to me, "You should be proud, proud of who you are, and what you have accomplished in your life." I know that lawyers often have a bad reputation. There are lots of lawyer jokes, and people think most lawyers are dishonest. I've found the attorneys I work with and work for are honorable and respectful to their clients and fellow attorneys. I've found that lawyers, male and female, are willing to help new attorneys. Every attorney I've met has a strong work ethic, much like the work ethic I both experienced and observed as a youth growing up in the 1950s.

Looking at my high-school graduation photograph, that doesn't even look like me. My best friend, Beverly Wells, and I decided not to smile. Bev was self-conscious about what she thought were her prominent teeth. I was thinking I would look sultry if I didn't smile. That's an unflattering picture of us both. I was devastated when I heard Bev died in a plane crash. And she wasn't yet forty.

But that girl with the pursed lips, me, would look at herself now and say, "What happened to your brown hair? It's blonde." That M-A Student Court judge, me, might think she did OK in life, even though it took her six decades to get back in a courtroom atmosphere.

But she doesn't think of age. She really doesn't. By the time she's eighty-five, she should be a pretty darn good lawyer.

★5★

The Puppet Man

Jerry Juhl didn't run with the "in" crowd at Menlo-Atherton. He was immersed in the insular world of puppets and in his editorship of the school newspaper, the "Bear Tracks." He later combined puppetry and journalism to win scriptwriting awards for "The Muppets." He was Jim Henson's first hire.

I wasn't happy in the halls of academia. I didn't ever feel particularly a part of it. I looked at other students with a kind of awe. I transferred to M-A my sophomore year after moving from Minnesota, where I attended this big institutional high school that was slightly down in the heels. It had up-and-down staircases and punk kids hanging out on the corner. M-A was like walking into a country club. A big, open campus, kind of glamorous, a lot of wealthy kids. Somebody in our class was given a brand-new Ford convertible for his sixteenth birthday. That just bowled me over.

When I turned sixteen and got my driver's license, there was a spare car in the family. I thought now I can drive to school. My father couldn't understand that. He said, "Take your bicycle to school." Of course I could have taken my bicycle to school. But the whole image of Menlo-Atherton was to drive your car into the school parking lot, even if the car was a twelve-year-old Plymouth. I had a hard time making my father understand that.

Puppetry pretty much consumed my life. All through my childhood and high school, I was working on puppet projects. I did birthday parties and school shows. And I made big bucks, like fifteen bucks per show.

Cookie Monster's friend
Jerry Juhl

I had a small group of friends. Some friends thought I was odd, always working on puppets.

I was a good student with a B to B+ grade point average. I wasn't an athlete; I was born without the sports gene. I took journalism, though I don't know why. I just took it as an elective, and the teacher, Doug Murray, immediately captured me. I joined the staff of the school paper. My senior year, I was the editor at a time when we changed it from a newspaper into a news magazine, on glossy paper with a photo cover.

Before editing the paper, I wrote a column with another M-A student; a high-school ripoff of Herb Caen, a very popular San Francisco columnist. His column was called "Baghdad By The Bay." Ours was called "Beardom By The Bay." That's when I first realized I liked writing. It was me circling around, trying to find a voice: A comedic voice. Doug Murray was incredibly encouraging. I owe him a lot.

I also was involved in "First Nighters," the school's drama productions. I was in some plays, mostly backstage work. I did very little getting on stage. That's why I was into puppetry, because it's a perfect refuge for people who like theater, but who want to put something between themselves and the audience. Actors walk on stage naked, if you know what I'm saying. Some people can handle that. Other people become puppeteers.

I was born in St. Paul, Minnesota. My sister, Rennie, and brother, Philip, were teenagers at that time. My father, a sweet man, had come from Denmark when he was eighteen. He was from peasant stock. His field was landscape design. My mother used to say he liked trees more than he liked people. He wasn't a particularly verbal fellow.

My mother was from Minnesota. At nineteen, she was a teacher in a one-room schoolhouse. My mother thought the only road to happiness in this world was to teach. She wanted all of her children to teach. From the beginning, I was totally uncomfortable with that idea. She was always after us to get a teaching credential. Just in case, she'd say. But if I got it, I would never do anything but teach. No, I told myself, I'm going to make puppetry work.

I became fascinated with puppetry when I was nine. I remember going to Chicago with my family and seeing a display of marionettes in a big department store. I was completely transfixed. For my birthday, I got a couple of marionettes. I was involved with puppetry from that point on. When I was eleven, I went to a national convention of The Puppeteers of America, which happened to be in St. Paul. I immediately announced I wanted to make the theater my career.

"Kukla, Fran and Ollie" was a major influence on me, just as it was to Jim Henson, who originated "The Muppets." Burr Tillstrom created "Kukla, Fran and Ollie," the beginning of puppetry on television. Tillstrom was a master at creating this family of characters that you came back to day after day. That was amazingly fascinating.

I also was obsessed with the work of Walt Kelly, who did the cartoon strip "Pogo," an interesting balance between innocence and edginess. Pogo Possum and Albert the Alligator were children in essence, but they were dealing with very edgy things. They satirized Senator Joe McCarthy at the height of the Communist witch hunt. They talked about nuclear proliferation.

When I was twelve, I built puppets of Pogo and Albert. When Kelly spoke in Palo Alto, I brought my puppets along to meet him. He then sent me an original cartoon, which I still have framed on my office wall. That was a big thing to me. No one affected my comedy sense more than Walt Kelly. I used Kelly's influence the whole time I was with "The Muppets."

I built puppets all during high school. I wasn't a good craftsman. Not at all. They were puppets on strings with wooden bodies. The heads were made out of papier mache. My mother costumed them for me. There's something about the craft of puppetry that's very introspective. Puppeteers aren't putting themselves on the line directly. They're removed from the audience. That can be good. It's harder that way to develop a monster ego.

While attending San Jose State, I did a children's show on Channel 11, or KNTV, in San Jose. It was called "Sylvia and Pup." It looked an awful lot like "Kukla, Fran and Ollie." I was Pup. There were three of us:

Sylvia Ciron and Mel Swope, our director, and me. We did five shows a week.

Mel was my college roommate. He went on to produce a number of things in Hollywood, including the television show "Fame." On "Sylvia and Pup," we worked for almost no money. And it was a lot of work. It took me five years to get my bachelor of arts degree. But we had all the free bread we wanted, because the television station was owned by the Sunlite bakers.

In college, I met my wife, Susan, who was the total opposite of me when it came to education. She loved school so much, I think she could have stayed forever. We took a couple of classes together, crammed for finals together. Her father, Robert Doerr, had been mayor of San Jose and served for a long time on its city council.

I was all set to graduate from college—and begin a long career of unemployment. The truth is, denial kicks in easily with people like me. I wanted to make puppetry a career after seeing how puppetry worked on television. But, practically speaking, this is like wishing you were going to win the lottery. It's a really high-risk enterprise.

Then I won the lottery. I met Jim Henson.

My last three summers of school, including the summer I graduated from college, I worked for the Oakland Recreation Department, which had an active program called "The Vagabond Puppets." A wonderful woman, Lettie Connell, ran this company out of a trailer that looked like a circus wagon, but which opened up into a puppet stage. We traveled around to recreation centers in Oakland doing two, three shows a day.

My third year on the job, Lettie left and I took over the program. One person who worked for me, Frank Oznowicz, later changed his name to Frank Oz and became a puppeteer for "The Muppets," performing such characters as Miss Piggy, Fozzie Bear, Cookie Monster and a small army of other Muppet figures. He later left puppetry to direct movies.

During that same summer, The Puppeteers of America held their annual festival at Asilomar, a retreat near Carmel. We were invited to do one of our Vagabond Puppet shows. Jim Henson was there with his wife, Jane, and their daughter, Lisa. Jim and Jane had been successful puppeteers back east. Jim was an alumnus of the University of Maryland, where there now is a statue of Jim and Kermit the Frog. Jim came to Asilomar looking for someone to hire, because Jane was pregnant with her second child and could no longer work full time.

Jim grew up in Mississippi, then moved to Washington, D.C., where his father worked in the Agriculture Department. Jim became obsessed with television as a child. He got into puppetry after hearing that a local TV station was looking for a puppeteer. He went to the library and read a couple of books on puppetry. He then went to the television station and auditioned. He got the job. He was all of sixteen.

By the time I met him, he had remade the face of puppetry. He had a style unlike anything that anyone had done before. Jim used what are known as hand-and-rod puppets, which had a movable mouth and little sticks to work the hands. But he was doing these strange abstract characters who weren't meant to be human or animals. Instead, they were just....creatures that he gave extraordinary life to.

Jim was twenty-four and I was twenty-two. I came back to Oakland after Asilomar. Jim and I were invited to the same barbecue. He took me out to his station wagon to show me his characters. It was like seeing aliens from outer space. Then he offered me a job. No way was I going to turn it down.

At the time, Jim had a five-minute show on the NBC station in Washington, D.C., called "Sam and Friends," which was programmed between the eleven o'clock news and the "Tonight Show." Everyone in D.C. is a news junkie, so everyone knew Jim's show. Kermit the Frog was on it, but he really wasn't a frog in those days. He was a frog-like creature—didn't look at all like he does now.

Jim's company was "The Muppets" even then. Jim came up with the name, taking the "m" from marionettes and replacing the "p" on puppets. That's the story he used to tell. I think he just liked the sound of it.

I went back to Washington thinking I would do this for a year.

Thirty-six years later, I was still with the company. Jim and I did everything, at first, including working fifteen-hour days. After a while, Frank
Oz came on as the lead puppeteer with Jim, and I happily turned to
the writing. I had bad stage fright. We'd do the Ed Sullivan Show, or
Johnny Carson, and while the other guys would be laughing, I'd be
nauseous.

Shortly after I came east to do "Sam and Friends," it was cancelled.
But, by then, Jim was getting more guest shots on national television.
On the strength of that, and with New York the center of the universe,
we picked up stakes in 1963 and moved there.

Financially, we were squeaking by. Susan and I were married in 1965.
We lived in a one-room apartment in Manhattan. I don't think I felt successful at all, just kind of happy to be working at something so interesting. It went on that way for several years. We scrounged around from
job to job, doing a lot of commercial and industrial shows to pay the
rent. We did some small stuff at the New York World's Fair, and we did
company films for IBM.

The best times for us back then were always sitting and kicking ideas
around. Jim and I played off each other's ideas. It was not a combative
situation at all. Jim did not have fights with people. He was the most
amicable man—but he also knew exactly what he wanted.

In 1967, I decided to leave the company. Because Susan and I lived
in Manhattan, we spent every penny we were making. One year later,
we saved enough money to drive our little Triumph TR4 to California.
It was a completely insane thing to do because I had no prospects at all
in California. Just before leaving New York, I was asked to write for this
new kids' show on NET—National Education Television. This was
before the days of PBS—the Public Broadcasting System. Jim and a
writer I knew, Jon Stone, were working on a format for a kids' show
that was to be done for the Children's Television Workshop, a non-
profit founded by Joan Ganz-Cooney.

Nevertheless, Susan and I wanted to move to California, figuring
most of those educational shows only lasted thirteen weeks. So I turned
down "Sesame Street." Dumb, I know. We moved to a little coastal vil-

lage called Cambria, just north of San Luis Obispo. After relocating, I got a call from Jon. He was having a terrible time finding writers for his new show.

So Jon made a deal with me. For the next four years, I contributed Muppet material to "Sesame Street." Did it all by mail and phone—we didn't have fax machines back then. Twice a year, I'd fly back to New York. It was me leading a charmed life in spite of my dumbness. Cable television hadn't come to Cambria, so I wrote for shows I couldn't see without driving twenty miles to see them. Educational TV didn't pay much in those days, but we were squeaking by. And my mother figured I was teaching.

People in the United States tend to think puppetry is for children. Jim always aimed for the adults. But with "Sesame Street," he had suddenly become one of the kings of kids' TV. He loved "Sesame Street." He protected and nurtured it to the end. I don't know what he'd think now of Big Bird doing a Ford commercial. Still, Jim wanted prime time. He got it in 1976 with "The Muppet Show."

Jim had pitched that concept for three years. For a while, he joined forces with George Schlatter, the executive producer of the "Laugh In" television comedy show. But all three networks—NBC, CBS, ABC—turned Jim's show down. About that time, Sir Lew Grade, an entrepreneur from England, told Jim he would produce the show and put it in worldwide syndication. Syndicated television was just getting off the ground, and after "The Muppet Show" became a hit, Sir Lew was promoted to Lord Lew.

But we all uprooted and moved to London, where we spent the next five years, though not twelve months out of the year. The first year, we did twenty-four shows—an entire season—and although the show was sold in the U.S. and England, it wasn't on the air anywhere. Here we were in England doing a puppet show and nobody knew who we were. We were just some completely whacky Americans being hauled to the studio every day in a rusted-out minibus.

We returned to the states for a few months, and that's exactly when the show premiered in England. There were only two TV stations in

England at the time, so if a show was a hit, it was a big hit. And we were a hit. When we went back for the second season, a fleet of limousines awaited us. Shortly after, the show premiered in the States. Within about a year, we were a hit here. By the time it was over, "The Muppet Show" was seen in one hundred and two countries by a weekly audience of two hundred and fifty million.

The whole thing was a shock to me. Did it change me? Sure. I no longer was this geeky kid from Menlo Park. We had become a hugely high-profile operation known all around the world. In 1981, after five seasons, the producers decided to end the show for business reasons. I agreed with the decision because I always think it's really sad when a television series continues on past its creative prime. And with "The Muppet Show" going into syndication, there wasn't a financial advantage in doing more of them.

So we started planning another children's show. Only this time it was a children's show with segments that could be tailored to fit the different cultures where it would be sold. That was the genesis of "Fraggle Rock," a show that ran on HBO in the early days of that network and was shown in a number of countries. I was the show's head writer and one of its producers.

The popularity of "The Muppet Show" led to Muppet movies. We shot the first movie during the summer, between seasons, when we were supposed to be off work. We shot the second movie, "The Great Muppet Caper," at the end of the last season of "The Muppet Show."

After the Fraggles, we got into a project called "The Jim Henson Hour." We shot thirteen episodes, but the network aired only nine. I was the head writer and creative producer. As Jim got older, there were more and more projects he wanted to do and less time to do them. Instead of slowing down in his fifties, he sped up. Then he did a dangerous thing. He took an hour of prime time network television and split it into two pieces.

The first half was a variety show similar to "The Muppet Show." The second half was a story that had a different feel every week. Sometimes, Jim did an hour-long story and dropped the vaudeville bit. Unfortunately, that's not the way series television works. People tune in to a series because they know what to expect.

Well, the audience didn't know what it was getting on "The Jim Henson Hour." So they didn't tune it in. NBC then moved the show around so much, there was no way it would find an audience. Jim took this hard, but still with his usual calm. I think he figured his job was to push the envelope.

Thus in the 1980s, he did two fantasy movies that were pretty dark—at least compared to the Muppet stuff. There was "The Dark Crystal" and "Labyrinth," both of which got mixed reviews and did not do great business in their first release. But they live on with a very devoted cult following.

People close to Jim Henson evangelize about him. Jim appreciated people and good work, and he did great work himself. Many people in this business get called a genius, but I really feel Jim was one of the geniuses of our generation. He pushed a lot of boundaries in a lot of different areas—film, television, puppetry.

I managed to win three Emmys for writing—two for "Sesame Street" and one for "The Muppet Show." I also have a gold record hanging in my office for "The Muppets," plus a few Writers Guild awards.

People asked me at parties what I did. I'd tell them I was the head writer on "The Muppets." These people looked at me, accusingly, and said, "Oh, you're the one who writes those jokes." Listen, the jokes were the least part of it. It was all about the characters created by this wonderful collaboration of performers, designers, builders and writers. A lot of great script ideas came from team members who weren't writers.

Jim died in 1990 of a viral strain of pneumonia that was making the rounds at that time. A very deadly strain. Jim didn't believe in spending a lot of time in doctor's offices. He felt so bad this time, though, he went to a doctor who gave him a prescription for some heavy-duty antibiotics that probably would have knocked this thing out.

Jim put the prescription in his pocket and said, "Well, if I feel bad in the morning, I'll have this thing filled." The next morning he was in intensive care. It went through him like a locomotive.

I was in northern California at the time. Frank Oz called me from New York. He was really upset that Jim was in the hospital. My first reaction and Susan's was that he'll outlive all of us. We all felt that he was just unstoppable. Then we spent twenty-four hours phoning one another until we got word that he had died. He was fifty-three.

Before dying, he and Jane had separated. But his kids took over The Jim Henson Company and run it to this day.

I've my own health issues, a kidney removed in July 2003. I'm very good at repressing this kind of stuff, but it was serious. There was a small tumor on the lining of the kidney. The best remedy: Remove the entire kidney. Since then, I've experienced some minor physical complications and follow-up treatments. Fortunately, I didn't have to cope with chemotherapy or radiation. And it seems to have gone well. I go back every three months for checkups.

I left the Henson company in 1997, but didn't want that to mean retirement. I still want to explore some stuff, do some writing on my own. I've been playing around with some fiction. In my early days, I did a children's book or two, published by a small press. People have talked to me about writing a memoir. It would be a huge undertaking, involving years of looking backwards, and I've always had problems looking back instead of ahead.

I'm totally ambivalent about television these days. I look at reality television and what the networks are doing, and I say, "Who would watch this? This is insane!" At the same time, if you're willing and able to burrow into what the cable networks are showing, this is the golden age of television in many ways.

Throughout my life, I've always tried to keep a sense of perspective. Once success hit, I was surrounded by people—not just our Muppets team but the celebrity scene in general, and the great pitfall that poses. Runaway egos. That's why it was really good that Susan and I lived in these small towns, where nobody knew what we did.

Now you're asking me to look at my high-school graduation picture. Oh, God. I looked like that for years. It wasn't that many years after my graduating from Menlo-Atherton that Jim Henson was running a puppetry festival in the Adirondacks. I was there helping out with things, and it happened that there were a few, well, rather lame performances.

I sneaked out of this one show, went into the hotel bar and ordered a martini. I was sitting at the bar, looking pretty much like my M-A graduation picture, when someone walked in and said, "What are you doing? You look like a Baptist seminary student. How can you be sitting there swilling martinis?"

So I ordered a second one.

* 6 *

Superwoman

Linda Price Williams' world changed from carefree cheers as a pom-pon girl in the 1950s to unexpected fears—mental illness in 1970 and breast cancer in 2002. Her determination, spirituality, and a devoted family helped guide her through these two crises with an emboldened perspective on life.

Looking back over the fifty years since we all graduated from Menlo-Atherton High School, I am in awe. We have seen some amazing changes in the world. Some good, some bad. I've also seen some amazing changes in me.

Positive changes.

I became interested in mental health care following a family crisis in 1970. Forever a high-energy, enthusiastic, do-it-all kind of person, I ran smack into an enormous mountain that year. It was uncharted, terrifying territory. Society wasn't ready for the challenges I was presented. It was up to my husband, John, and me to navigate the wild seas that encircled us.

We had the perfect life, a 1950s dream come true. A nice home in Mountain View, California. Three fabulous kids, ages ten, eight and six. And John's academic career teaching physical education and coaching aquatics in the Palo Alto Unified School District and for his Palo Alto Swim Club age group team gave us a moderate income, enough to pay the family bills.

My energy was running high in June, 1970. Everything was on fast forward. The kids were in competitive swimming, taking tennis les-

Way to go, girl

Linda Price

sons, and I also had an afternoon tennis class. John had a 7 a.m. swim workout at Foothill College, then another one in Palo Alto from 5 to 7 p.m. There also was laundry, meals, shopping, chores, check writing, gardening, etc. We were a family of five, and our parents lived nearby and wanted to see us. On top of this, we'd had the kitchen remodeled in May, and I was trying to paper the kitchen walls. My pace accelerated and I started losing sleep. Simultaneously, I had an incredible sense of well-being.

Because I wasn't sleeping well and was so keyed up, John thought I should get the same prescription my father had used for years. My Kaiser HMO (Health Maintenance Organization) doctor was on vacation, so another doctor filled the prescription and said, coldly, "If these pills don't work, you need a psychiatrist." Who, me? I took the pills for a few nights. They were of no help. Had I listened to that doctor and called the Kaiser Psychiatry Department right away, that summer possibly would have been much different.

Our family stayed on the fast track through July and early August. John was worried. He called Kaiser Psychiatry twice and was told, "We think we know what is wrong with your wife, but you won't get her to come in." Ominous.

One year later, the Palo Alto Times ran a story about the pending closure of the mental health portion of Agnews State Hospital, including administrator Dr. Maurice Rapport's dismay that it was closing. I sat down at the typewriter and banged out a response, using the pen name of Linda Bronson. I was then a "graduate" of Agnews, which had been a war zone for me. After Times editor Ward Winslow verified my identity, he ran the entire long story. I'm now giving Menlo-Atherton classmate Dave Newhouse approval to use the article for this book. It is part of a book-length manuscript, "Once Upon a Merry-Go-Round," that has not yet been published.

But, first, a preface to that article. On Aug. 20, 1970, John's brother in Half Moon Bay, Dale Williams, answered John's SOS call and drove to our house. It was mid-afternoon. I was singing in the shower. John announced that we were going for a ride and I was to get into the car.

I sat between John and Dale, wishing I'd had the time to get my face cream and eyeglasses, because I'm near-sighted.

I asked, "Where are we going?" No answer. John was told to bring me down to Santa Clara Valley Medical Center for evaluation. By the time we got there, I was terrified. The doctor who greeted us ordered an injection of some kind for me. Since there was no bed for me, an ambulance was called. And John and Dale were sent home.

Which now brings us to the Palo Alto Times' "Agnews Story," with a few insertions. All rights are reserved by the author, Linda Williams. This is what I wrote thirty-five years ago:

"On a hot evening, Aug. 20, 1970, I was hastily wheeled into an isolation room at Agnews and left alone behind a locked door with no more than a mattress on the floor, a heavy blanket, a pail, and a roll of toilet paper. There was no access to telephone, family, lawyer or doctor, contrary to the provisions of the Lanterman-Petris-Short Act. I was totally cut off from society in a room designed to prevent destruction of self or others, although I hadn't shown such tendencies prior to or during admission. I was hysterical with fright, however, and there was no place else to put me. No one had or took the time to explain what was happening, or even to tell me where I was.

"Side effects of the drug that was given to me forcibly set in quickly. With growing nasal congestion and a horribly parched throat, I honestly wondered if I were in the beginning stages of death at the hands of my "captors." There was a little window in the door at eye level and I could only see a hallway. Where did it go to? I screamed and hollered for hours. I got more injections, and it took several attendants to hold me down. Sometime before dawn, I curled up in a ball under the awful blanket and repeated the 23rd Psalm, "Yea though I walk through the valley of the shadow of death, I will fear no evil, for Thou are with me...." several times until I finally fell asleep. Was I back in some Eighteenth Century barbaric place?

"I could see the sun had come up through the tiny high window when a nurse unlocked the door and put down a plate of scrambled eggs, a banana, toast, and a glass of milk. I thought, 'Maybe I'm not going to die after all.' I'd had nothing to eat since breakfast the day before. Too busy. The food tasted so good, even off the floor. Another nurse arrived with the door key and asked if I would like to take a bath. As we walked along toward the bathing room, I noticed a laundry cart with ASH stencilled on it. I asked, 'Is it Ash Wednesday?' She said, 'Oh, honey, don't you know where you are? This is Agnews State Hospital.' My reaction was panic, but I kept in step with her on the way to a big, claw-footed bath tub. Water was poured on me by two nurses with pitchers, and I felt soooooo good.

"Then I was allowed on the ward with about forty other women. A few of them played cards. We could lie down in the crowded day room, which was pretty junky. Our beds were off limits all day. Everyone sat around with very little to do. One eighteen-year-old girl I befriended told me she had knocked out all the windows in her parents' home two days prior. Several of the women said, 'I heard your screams last night.' I was sorry to have disturbed their sleep. After a 'seventy-two-hour hold' on the admitting ward, I was transferred to another unit that housed about the same number of women. I was 'committed' for fourteen more days. Although not homicidal or suicidal, I was 'gravely disabled,' they had decided. So that legally qualified me for more time at Agnews.

"For seven more days, I was given medications without knowing what they were or what they were supposed to do. And I could not refuse them. I listened to my fellow patients' stories of alcoholism, attempted suicide, drug abuse, and I kept asking the nurses, 'Why am I here? Why can't I go home?'

"During the seventh night, I woke up scratching furiously, covered with a measles-like rash. I went to the nurses' station and said, 'Please help me,' holding up my nightgown. The nurse on duty gasped when she saw it all. She unlocked a nearby cupboard for Calamine Lotion and gently dabbed it on me with cotton. I looked in the open cupboard and asked her, 'Is that my jar of Avon Rich Moisture Cream?' Yes. They had taken it out of my locker so I couldn't break it and hurt myself with the glass shards. A wonderful sweater vest I was knitting that summer had also vanished from my locker and was never returned. The place was a den of thieves.

"The psychiatrist on the ward would arrive and walk very fast to his office, locking his door. I wrote him notes and slid them under the door. He was definitely not in my camp. As a busy mother with three school-age children and a part-time business, I found the long, seemingly wasted days nearly impossible to take. As I struggled to keep my equilibrium and stave off mounting panic at the idea of staying there, three things helped me to hang in there and not give up hope.

"First, along with my husband, my mother came to see me every day. Together with my Dad, they were as worried as I was, and equally frustrated in their attempts to get a diagnosis and prognosis from the elusive doctor. Secondly, I volunteered to join the kitchen staff in the cafeteria, serving meals in the chow line and doing dishes, thus using a good deal of time every day. Thirdly, a pay phone in the hall served as a link to humanity and the outside world. With a dime I borrowed from a nurse, I ran up forty-five dollars of collect calls to my family. That pay phone was a regular lifeline.

"On the eighth day, a Friday, I initiated writ of habeas corpus proceedings with a young man from the district attorney's office, who arrived on the ward looking for me. Dr. Perry, the weekend doctor, arrived the next morning and called me into his office. I had met him the weekend before and we seemed to click. 'I can help expedite your release,' he said, 'so you won't have to go before a judge.' When I asked him if he believed in God—a question I asked almost everyone that summer—he smiled and replied thoughtfully, 'Well, yes, but I don't believe He has any specific plans for me.' Monday morning, I signed the papers to change my status from 'involuntary' to 'voluntary' and walked out of Agnews with John, even though I was leaving against medical advice. 'You aren't ready,' the nurses said. 'You'll be back.' Dr. Perry told me I needed to connect with Kaiser and I had promised to do so.

"Over the next couple of weeks, it was so lovely to be off the drugs I'd received at Agnews that I postponed calling Kaiser. So I was not on any medication to help me slow down. And I was still hyper, losing sleep, feeling euphoric, on my 'writing mission,' and refusing to believe anything was wrong. If anyone suggested I still was in need of help, I could be stubborn and cantankerous. A couple of times, I ran out of the house to a local park for refuge and some peace, my heart pounding in my chest. There was no way John could reason with me. If he tried, and we argued, I fled.

"Football practice had started for John and his players, summer was evaporating, and we'd missed our annual late August vacation. So over Labor Day, we drove up to Arnold to see John's folks, and went on a camp-out at Lake Alpine. John awakened at 4 a.m. that first night as I was dragging my sleeping bag out of the tent. He asked where I was going. 'I'm going to get Steve out of the station wagon and take him fishing by the edge of the lake.' John said, 'You have to wait 'til the fish can see what you're doing if you want to catch any.' But I got Steve down there, and our hands were shaking so hard from the cold, we could hardly get the worms on the hook. By sunrise, I was talking to everyone on the shoreline. Meanwhile, John was packing our gear at the campsite. 'We're going home,' he said. He knew I still needed help. He knew it the night before when I got up at 3:30 a.m. at his parents' home to make spaghetti for dinner in camp.

"On Sept. 13, my birthday, our fifth-grade daughter, Laurie, was run over by a car on our block while roller skating with friends. I returned from shopping just after it happened. A wheel had passed over her foot and it obviously was broken. It wasn't the young driver's fault. Neighbors then watched our two other children while we took Laurie to Kaiser. She got a cast that covered not only her foot, but most of her leg. I was Miss Curiosity, wanting to see her x-rays, talking to her doctor, the staff, and other patients. I wrote 'Sold to Linda' under a painting that was part of an art exhibit in one of the halls. We picked it up later from the Los Altos artist.

"Two days later, on Sept. 15, I was whisked once again by ambulance to Santa Clara Valley Medical Center after trying to jump into the living room sofa bed we kept open for Laurie's friends who visited. I started to sign in voluntarily at the medical center because my condition was acute, according to them, and the only other place was....Agnews! I excused myself to the ladies room, tore up all my admitting papers and sent them through the plumbing. When I came out, I said to John, 'Quick, we have to get out of here. We are both in danger.' Ye gods. They locked me up in a room smaller than the one I had been locked in that first night at Agnews. This latest room had a regular bed and a window overlooking a courtyard, where a volleyball game was in progress. The window was secure, so there was no escaping. Of course, I was terrified and yelling.

"John was standing there at the main nurses' station trying to finish my admitting. Poor John. In the kitchen of our home, I had kicked him hard when it became apparent I was again headed somewhere for treatment. Then, in my crazed fear, I'd sworn I would divorce him the minute I got out. I took off my wedding rings, sent them under the locked door, and hollered, 'John Williams, look down.' He finally did, picked them up, and gave them back to me the next day. I had joined the patients on the ward. We could not use Kaiser in-patient care because those facilities were in Richmond and Concord. John had ruled them out because of the distance.

"There was more medication, and no way to refuse. On the third day, a new pill was there, and they refused to tell me what it was or what it was supposed to do. I outfoxed them by hiding it under my tongue and then spitting it out in the nearby toilet. Too many pills. 'People die from too many drugs at once,' I kept thinking. The staff's failure to explain what they were supposed to do was even more mysterious and threatening.

"Two days later, my name was called and three of us were trotted across the hospital to the blood lab to give samples. I asked the kindly escorting nurse, 'Why draw our blood?' She said, 'Well, you three women are on something where the therapeutic level is very close to the toxic level, and we have to be sure you are within a safe range.' Well, why didn't they tell me that in the first place? Another thing I did not know was that Dr. Paula Fish in Kaiser Psychiatry at Santa Clara had called my Valley Medical Center doctor and strongly suggested he start me on this new drug.

"When we got back to the ward, I went straight to the nurses' station and confessed what I had been doing, adding, 'There won't be any of that new medicine in my blood.' From then on, all my medication was served in tiny cups in liquid form, and had the most vile taste. I was through pulling tricks, but they didn't trust me.

"I was driven by a strong belief that God had specifically chosen me to write the world's greatest best-seller. I planned to use some of the proceeds to promote world peace, once and for all. To begin with, I was going to rent several 747s, equip them with bomb bays, and fly them over Vietnam with a special cargo: Billions of flower petals that would gracefully flutter down and remind all below that there still is beauty in the world. The shock might end the war. Maybe they would all refuse to go on fighting. I shared my plan with only one person, a boy of eighteen on the ward at Valley Medical. He smiled broadly and asked, 'When are you running for President?'

"For six days in all, I played volleyball, worked on projects in the occupational therapy room, took notes, met with other patients in groups, visited outside with my family, did my share of ward chores, received medication, enjoyed the private shower, and called home. I had not made any meaningful connection with my doctor there. On the fifth day, I asked a woman in a little office, 'What's your job here?' She said, 'I do the billing.' I asked, 'What does it cost to stay here?' She replied, 'Seventy-five dollars a day.' I had no previous idea of the cost, but it now came to four-hundred and fifty dollars in my case and counting. Plus there was the bill coming from the state for my time at Agnews and the two ambulance rides.

"I borrowed another dime from a nurse and, luckily, Dr. Paula Fish was at her Kaiser office. 'I want to be your outpatient,' I told her. 'Please! I'll do whatever you say.' She was very reluctant since I was in another doctor's care, but Kaiser was our insurance plan. She promised to do 'what I can.' I called John and told him to please come and pick me up in the morning. Once again, the staff said, 'You're not ready. You'll be back.'

But it was a movie I didn't want to see a third time. I left against medical advice again.

"Dr. Fish was finishing up her residency at Agnews. We had to go by there to pick up my prescriptions. First, I had to bury my feelings of terror at being anywhere near that place. From there we went to the Kaiser pharmacy in Sunnyvale, and then home with the drugs. The staff's prediction, happily, did not come true. Dr. Fish was right in her hunch about what was wrong with me. Two vitally important changes led me back to wellness. First, I became a willing taker of pills (four kinds, several times daily): Stelazine, Mellaril, Lithium Carbonate, and Cogentin to help relieve side effects. Secondly, in October, Dr. Fish truthfully answered a long list of questions I'd typed, leading me to my own discovery of the truth. She carefully explained the term 'hypomanic' and said my behavior fit that profile.

"How to define hypomanic? On a scale of one to ten, I might have been a six or seven. (Noted psychiatrist Dr. Ronald Fieve wrote in his 1975 book 'Moodswing', which I read years later: 'Wild horses could not drag in these charismatic, super organizers and go-getters when they were on top of the world and accomplishing so much....In the Sixties, we diagnosed them as hypomanics.') The next level is serious paranoia, wild spending sprees, psychosis, and much potential danger. The patient is truly disabled. Dr. Fish also kindly let me bring a tape recorder to our meetings, since it was beginning to dawn on me that there was quite a story here. And its telling might help others avoid a similar wild ride.

"Armed now with a concrete definition to research, I went to the library and read everything they had on manic episodes. It was all there. I read plenty of case histories, including a thorough one in Fortune Magazine. According to one article, a 'biochemical imbalance in the brain had led to an overproduction of norepinephrine, or adrenalin.' Hence all the energy I'd experienced in spite of little sleep. My mind literally had shut off my body's needs for sleep and rest. I lost ten pounds in the ensuing weeks. Another fascinating study with graduate students in psychology had shown that in clinical conditions of sleep deprivation, every one of them began to hallucinate. Without the full REM (Rapid Eye Movement) phase of sleep that we all must have, you are dreaming while you are walking around awake. Stir in a little paranoia about good and evil and 'they are out to get you.' Thus it's no wonder I got a date with the men in white coats.

"The nightmare ended with the drug Lithium Carbonate restoring the delicate balance of chemistry in my brain. Within ten days, I was demonstrating its worth. It can take up to two weeks to take effect. I got every blood test that was required. I was a most cooperative outpatient. In hopes that my story would help others avoid a similar experience, I began serious writing in January 1971. While working on the manuscript, I returned to Agnews to interview Dr. Perry, and to Valley Medical Center to see the head nurse. From them I learned that I had been diagnosed in both facilities as schizophrenic. But Dr. Perry and the nurse each told me, 'I knew you were not schizophrenic.' Dr. Perry told me they were giving me twelve-hundred milligrams of Thorazine while I was at Agnews. No wonder my head felt as if it were in cement. A nurse at Agnews had written 'obnoxious in a.m.' in my chart. Another nurse at Valley Medical wrote 'no insight.'

"Dr. Russel V.A. Lee, founder of the Palo Alto Medical Clinic, was a fraternity brother of my father at Stanford, and our family doctor for years. He agreed to read my manuscript and even wrote its foreword. When I picked up the manuscript from him, his comment was 'I wish you had called me. All this should have never happened to you.' We had never thought to call Russ.

"It is dehumanizing and demoralizing to be herded around with a large group of people suffering from a broad spectrum of mental and emotional disorders. The nurses can't give you specific answers, and they are too busy to do much more than give out medications. The care seems to be merely custodial, and the impersonal approach is frightening to experience. In fairness to Agnews, I wish to report that an administrator there told me that people sometimes ask to be admitted there for treatment. These people already are on the road to recovery, and may benefit from such limited care. To know one is sick and in need of help is a very big No. 1 hurdle. The docile, conforming patients fare well and are granted privileges by the group. Patients who resent being treated like convicts, and having their freedom determined by others, have a hard time.

"If Agnews has to operate on such a small budget granted by the state, then it is right to close the facility. It needs complete refurbishing and a much lower ratio of patients to staff. All of this takes money that 'isn't there.' We can and must do better for our citizens. What we do for someone against his or her will should at least be humane. It is not too much to ask."

That was my first life crisis. Now for the rest of my life.

My parents met at Stanford. They married after graduating in 1928. My father, Bill, majored in pre-law, and my mother, Lida, in Romance Languages. They were both good athletes. Dad was a tennis player, while Mom was a platform diver at Searsville Lake, when they had a diving tower by the dam. She planned to go to the Olympic Trials in New York City, traveling with a girl friend and two guys in a Model-T Ford. In those days, to qualify for the U.S. team, you only had to do a standing swan dive and a running swan. My German grandfather put a stop to Mom's travel plans, so she never made it to the Trials. As a teenager, her family rented a place at Aptos during the summer. Mom and my grandfather would swim from Aptos to the Santa Cruz pier.

In the 1960s, my parents won the club championships at the Stanford Golf Club, Mom twice. Their names are still on the wall in the clubhouse. Dad was in an insurance partnership with Kent Thoits in Palo Alto. Thoits and Price was a tough partnership; Dad got two major ulcers requiring surgery. He had Kent buy Dad out, then he went to work for Great American Insurance in San Francisco. We also rented at Aptos during the summer months. Dad arrived on Friday night. On Saturday, he'd float around in an inner tube for hours, get a royal sunburn, and say he hated the coast. Usually they shipped me off to Girl Scout camp the day school was out. Three two-week sessions back-to-back at Woodhaven in La Honda. I loved it.

Mom was a good typist, a wannabe writer. She did free lance work for

Stanford professors and local writers. When she got office jobs, she said, "I'm yours, but not on Tuesdays. That's my golf day." Even Lockheed agreed to that. She was so loved by many, and had the most wonderful giving spirit and charming personality. Dad had a lot of fun with his golf, dominoes, and his drinking buddies. But he wasn't very communicative around the house. One of his oftspoken pronouncements was "Children should be seen and not heard." Too bad they never had a son. I have one older sister, Patsy, Palo Alto High School Class of 1950.

I did well in school. I attended Las Lomitas Elementary, then enrolled at Menlo-Atherton. As far as boy friends at M-A, Bryon Farnsworth heads the list. He was class president our sophomore year, and we went steady most of that year. Our senior year, Bryon started the rumor that he and I had been intimate when we went steady. Not true. I was a good Presbyterian girl, saving myself for when it was more serious and lasting. Several people asked me about it. I was furious. At lunch, several girls and I drove over to Howatt's, an M-A hangout on Middlefield Road, and bought a gorgeous lemon meringue pie. When we got back to the school parking lot, I got out with the pie in my hand. The universe was smiling for there was Bryon heading my way across the parking lot with his arms open for a hug. I don't know if he saw the pie or not, but I got a direct hit. It was fabulous. It was worth it. What a time!

The summer after graduation was spent in the advertising department of the Palo Alto Times. It was an exciting job and they were sorry to see me head off to San Francisco State. But I wanted very much to go to college. A kind woman five blocks from the campus gave me her spare room for forty dollars a month for room and breakfast. I also had a roommate, a girl from Fair Oaks. My parents gave me fifty dollars a month, and I had to earn the rest. part-time jobs included selling football tickets and working in the book store at the start of my sophomore year, plus vacation jobs in Menlo Park.

In the fall of my freshman year, I met Mr. Wonderful in the San Francisco State law library. He was engaged to be married between semesters. I found that out on our second date. His eyes should have been in his law books. He decided to cancel the wedding in Mendocino. Easter week,

I went up to meet his family despite my mother's threat to cut off all my support if I did so. By June, I was wearing his fraternity pin.

That summer, the City of Palo Alto hired me to run the Crescent Park Elementary School playground with Olympic javelin thrower Leo Long, who was wonderful with the kids and great to work with. One night, I took the kids over to the community center for a sleepover. The next morning, we had a dawn swim scheduled at Rinconada Pool, where coach Johnny Williams was the pool manager. He had dated my sister when they were at Palo Alto High, and I had taken Red Cross life-saving classes from him my junior year at M-A.

Well, none of his life guards would go to work that early, so there he was. I hadn't been on a diving board in weeks, but had done some competing, so I was suited up and having some fun. John invited me to be on the Palo Alto Swim Club diving team that summer. He coached me into a one and a half off the three-meter board. I didn't have the sense of direction to do any twisting dives.

One day in late July, John invited me to go up to San Francisco for dinner and a play. I wrote a letter to the guy in Mendocino and said, "There is this longtime friend of the family....and I want to go." He didn't write back and I didn't see him all summer. I also told him his fraternity pin had fallen off my shirt on the Crescent Park lawn, and even though all of the kids helped me scour the grass for hours, we never found it.

I was thinking John and I were just friends. But he had fallen for me. Of course he knew of my relationship at San Francisco State. Still, he gave me a Bulova watch for my birthday in September with "no strings." I didn't want to accept it, because I couldn't promise him anything other than friendship. But he insisted and I wore it for years. Returning to college, I was in the registration line when along came Mr. Wonderful. The sidewalk shook like a San Francisco-style earthquake, and my knees shook with it.

Infatuation can override all common sense, but what happens when there are two loves in your life? Emotional chaos. Cherished friend vs. Romeo. Romeo did propose, but he wanted to run off to Reno. No thanks, I wanted a wedding. Since he had been married before (!), and had a wedding on the calendar when he met me, he didn't want to take that route. I lived that year with Jeanne Peasley, Menlo-Atherton Class of 1955, in a Stonestown apartment with two other girls. Mr. Wonderful was on the G.I. bill. He had an apartment by Golden Gate Park.

During fall semester finals, a bad bronchial infection hit me. Three weeks into the spring semester, I was still sick and coughing hard. Mr. Wonderful finally stated he didn't know how he felt about me. That did it. The next day, I checked out of school, quit my bookstore job, and went home to Menlo Park. Bus, trolley, and train. It was a ghastly day. As an aside, I had become friends with Mr. Wonderful's ex-fiancee; we both worked in the San Francisco State book store. When I felt better, I invited her down to spend the weekend in Ladera, where we'd moved in 1954. It turned out that when Mr. Wonderful wasn't with me, he was with her. We cooked his goose.

When I was finally well again, I showed up one day at the Palo Alto High pool. I climbed up to sit on the end of the three-meter board. John and the kids came out for swim practice. I still remember the look on John's face when he saw me. He had no idea about the chaos in my life because we hadn't seen each other for months. I had pretty much called off the friendship, telling him to find someone eligible. "Well, if you ever need a friend," he said, "you know where to find me." The magic words.

Mom and I then went to my cousin Monina's wedding in Mexico City in March. We were gone six weeks. I registered at the University of Mexico and got a pass to its fabulous pool and spent many days there diving. I sent John a telegram from Acapulco asking him to meet me at San Francisco International Airport. As soon as I saw him, my heart and mind screamed in tandem: "You are the one!" How lucky can a girl be?

We were engaged in June and married between semesters in 1959. The previous fall, I transferred to San Jose State to be closer to him. During that semester, I lived with M-A classmate Yvonne Layne and two other girls. John was in graduate school at San Jose State, working toward his general secondary credential. In the fall of 1959, both of us transferred to San Francisco State, so I could complete my fourth course in Social Studies, International Relations. My professor, Dr. Urban Whitaker, had taught at the University of Peking for ten years. He predicted "We are going to be at war soon in Vietnam."

It was a fabulous semester. After John and I wed, we lived in a little house in East Palo Alto. We got up three times a week at 5 a.m. to commute to San Francisco so I could make my 8 a.m. class. I'd throw up around San Bruno every trip....we were expecting Laurie in March 1960. With six more units, I finally reached upper class status.

John got his general secondary with a history minor. He was hired by Palo Alto Unified to start at Wilbur Junior High in the fall of 1962. We had bought a little house in Mountain View, when money was very tight. We moved the Palo Alto Swim Club operation to the Palo Alto Elks Club outdoor pool. Steve arrived in 1962, Pamela in 1964.

Around 1967, when Grampy Price died in Palo Alto, Mom and I found a little diary that Granny Estelle had kept over the fifty-six years of her marriage. In it, I read, "1937. Billy and Lida divorced." I ran to the phone and called Mom. "Oh, Honey," she said, "that was only the first time I divorced your father. It was final twice!"

During a checkup in January 1971, a goiter was discovered in my neck. It was caused by the Lithium. I was told that if I continued the drug, I would eventually need surgery. The decision was made, medically, for me to stop the Lithium. Everything then stayed "normal." The Women's Re-Entry Program at Foothill Community College was just what I needed. John felt badly about his crazy schedule over the years; he still wondered about any connection between his long hours and my manic episode. We farmed our kids to three Palo Alto Swim Club families and took our first trip to Hawaii, flying out on Christmas Day, 1971. Paradise!

The Re-Entry Program chairperson then called me into her office and asked when I was going to get my college degree. San Jose State had vacancies in the physical education major, and I was accepted there again. I had no plans to be a P.E. teacher, though. I discovered an innovative program on campus called New College. It was designed for students who could work independently on field work projects they created in the community, and they worked under contract with the New College professors. I thrived. My 1975 degree was "Liberal Arts, Special Major, New College." It was exciting to achieve honors. After the next six years teaching in Older Adult Education, I worked for two Silicon Valley companies in the early 1980s.

My parents were married fifty-six years in spite of their two divorces. In July 1984, Mom was diagnosed with metastic cancer—adenocarcinoma in the left lung. I was between careers. I was able to spend a lot of time with her during those tough six months. An ad in the Palo Alto Times then led me to a job with Miracle Ear in Santa Clara. I went into training and worked there a short time before working for two other hearing aid offices. I studied hard and passed the California Hearing Aid Dispensers examination. John and I then bought a wonderful practice in Sunnyvale in 1985.

At that point, I told John, "It's my turn. Do you want to die on the pool deck or retire from one of your two jobs? I need you more at home." He quit the swim club and then took flying lessons at Palo Alto Airport. He also became the bookkeeper at our hearing aid business, which I eventually sold in September, 1991, pending John's early retirement scheduled for 1993.

All three of our kids made it through college, working when they could. After visiting Pam and her family in Lincoln, when Sun City Lincoln Hills opened up sales in February 1999, we bought our current home site there and moved in that November. Two years later, we found two cabins in Blue Lake Springs in Arnold for our two Bay Area kids and their families. Now we all get together when we can in Calaveras County, where John's folks had their place from 1965 to 1997.

I played tennis twice a week in our new home in Lincoln, and was so busy that I missed my mammogram in 2001. I absolutely blanked on it. I had a mammogram in May 2002 and was told I needed a biopsy. I immediately called a woman to get a breast cancer support group going in Lincoln Hills. This led to "Bosom Buddies." Eighteen women attended our first meeting. Four years later, we grew to sixty. It turned out my tumor was two centimeters, Stage II, and buried in my right breast so deeply, no one could ever feel it. I asked for Dr. Ernie Bodai to be my surgeon. He already had operated on two-thousand women and had created the idea of the Breast Cancer Postage Stamp, which he lobbied successfully through Congress. We set the surgery date: July 23, 2002.

I chose a lumpectomy rather than a mastectomy, because the chances of survival were equal, providing the patient agrees to radiation. There aren't words to describe how I felt about having cancer. You don't know if you're going to make it or not. It's a real terror, like the worst movie you could be watching. And it's real, it hits home, you don't want it to be you, and there's no way to get away from it.

Now it's 2006, four years after the surgery, the chemotherapy and the radiation. I learned to quilt during this challenge. I recently had a successful mammogram. I asked my oncologist what my long-term future is, but wasn't given any for-sure answers. He said, "Let's get through the first five years, then we'll talk about ten." One woman in our Bosom Buddies group had a mastectomy in 1983, and she's still sailing along.

For me, a religious or spiritual life is so important as things come along. Life is not so simplistic. Religion/spirituality is for good times and bad times. All is in Divine Order and I give thanks. No matter which way this path is leading me, things are going to turn out all right. John and I have so many things going on in our life. We've traveled and still do. We spend time with our three children and six grandchildren. We're so grateful that we've had these years in retirement; we have an even stronger sense of teamwork. And we so enjoy our new community and the friends we've made.

Fifty years after high school, I look at my graduation picture and I think that life, all in all, has turned out great. Life happens. It's spectacular. My attitude is throw me into a swimming pool. I can swim.

I think the Linda of 1956 would say of the current Linda, "Way to go, girl. Well done. I am proud of you."

The Chinese Son

Wayne Chan's family tree sprouted keen intellect, solid work ethic and resiliency—strong qualities the Chans needed after immersing themselves in an American society unkind to Chinese immigrants. Wayne felt stunted socially as a teen, but he persevered to add yet another prominent branch to the tree.

My father, Shau Wing Chan, was born in Canton, China. By the time he was twelve, both his parents had died. There were five children in his family, including four boys, all of whom would come to America. There was a scholarly tradition in the family, which valued education and achievement.

My father was considered an up-and-coming scholar. He was a linguist who spoke fluent French, accent-free English, and Mandarin and Cantonese. He also had a reading knowledge of Latin. He graduated from Lingnan University in 1927 and had a choice of pursuing his graduate studies at Stanford or at the Sorbonne in Paris. Because he already had an older brother at Stanford, my dad chose Stanford. He came to the United States on a student visa in 1930 and earned his Master's degree in English in 1932 and then his doctorate in 1937.

Each of the Chan brothers earned money in America that was sent back to China to expedite bringing the next brother over. The eldest had come here in the 1920s and attended the University of Chicago, receiving a Ph.D in Comparative Literature. He became a professor at the University of Hawaii and then at Pomona College. The second oldest brother, who preceded my father at Stanford, taught Political Sci-

Everybody's best friend
Wayne Chan

ence at Loyola Marymount. The youngest brother became a dentist and practiced more than thirty-five years in Los Angeles.

Their success was predicated upon scholarly pursuits and hard work. This was a time when opportunities for Chinese in America arose primarily in the more mundane businesses and trades. Regardless of which avenue was taken, a Chinese not only had to achieve, but overachieve. My father put himself through Stanford by teaching at a Chinese language school and by editing a newspaper in San Francisco's Chinatown.

My mother's maiden name also was Chan: Anna Mae Chan. She was a native San Franciscan. As a youth, she sang at the Orpheum Theater and danced with the Flora Dora Girls. She met my father in a church where he was the organist/pianist and she often was the soloist. They married in 1935. After my father earned his Ph.D, he planned to return to China to teach English and, in the process, contribute to the modernization of his native country. He was appointed to the faculty of one of the national universities near Shanghai, just when the Japanese were bombing China. My parents lived in my father's native land in the summer and for part of the fall of 1937, then deemed life there too dangerous. They returned to the United States, listed as refugees.

Unemployed in early 1938, my father visited the Stanford campus and saw his old professor and English department chairman, William Dinsmore Briggs, who respected my father for his toughness. Briggs took dad over to the university president, Ray Lyman Wilbur. Doctor Wilbur was a visionary for diversity. After one meeting and one handshake, he appointed dad to the faculty in the fall of 1938. It was an opportunity and a favor for which dad was eternally grateful. That explains why my middle name is Lyman.

My father was an instructor of English and Chinese. He was the second Asian to serve on the school's faculty; the first was Professor Ishihashi (1912-41). My father remained at Stanford until 1972, then retired as a full professor. He served seven years as chairman of the Department of Asian Languages and established one of the first language laboratories on campus. He authored a textbook for teaching Chinese and also a Chinese-English dictionary. Both publications went through multiple edition revisions.

We moved to the San Francisco peninsula in the fall of 1939, living in rentals in East Palo Alto, South Palo Alto, and finally Menlo Park. When a house in Menlo Park went up for sale, my father tried to purchase it. The neighborhood learned of his intent and a petition was circulated, essentially making us not welcome. Undaunted, my father found a house on Live Oak Avenue in Menlo. That neighborhood was inhabited largely by Italian-Americans, and we never experienced any problems. In fact, we were friends with our neighbors. Still, Asians in Menlo Park were few in number and, fundamentally, were considered second-class citizens.

My problem as a boy: I didn't realize I was different, other than when people asked me if I was Japanese. As I grew up, this led to an identity crisis. I went to school and learned the same lessons as other kids, I sounded the same when I spoke English. I played the same games during recess. But I was visibly different. This identity issue and my basic shyness led to a kid who tried to be a good citizen and an overachiever. When I eventually realized there were girls in the world, there wasn't much to look forward to in terms of my social development. So I didn't attend any dances at Menlo-Atherton High School. And I didn't ask out any girls, for fear of rejection.

Nevertheless, I enjoyed high school. I didn't have a car. I walked to school or rode my bike. I was involved with the Stamp Club, Board of Welfare....mostly nerdy stuff. I had a circle of friends—the more studious, quiet, less-social, less-athletic members of our class. Believe me, I noticed the attractive girls as much as the next male, but I never approached any girl. My only interaction was in the classroom. I was in my own little cocoon. Looking back, I really regret my reticence.

Upon graduation from M-A, I was admitted to Stanford. From my first mid-term there as a freshman, I knew it would be an uphill fight scholastically. Some classmates were truly brilliant. I was told I was in the top ten of my class at M-A, but I was strictly an average student at Stanford.

The social scene at Stanford for a Chinese American in the 1950s and 1960s was even more acute than at M-A. Stanford was hardly diverse. For Asians there, the social attitudes of the time engendered a feeling of "stepping over the line" if we attempted to date non-Asians. In a class of nearly fourteen-hundred people, I doubt there were more than fifteen Asians, and most of them were males. It was difficult to grow socially in such an atmosphere.

I never had any doubts, though, about my choice of careers. While in grade school, I was inspired to pursue medicine by our family physician, Dr. Denistoun Wood of Palo Alto. His son, Bill Wood, became a good friend of mine from the fourth grade through high school. Dr. Wood was a knowledgeable, compassionate gentleman. Our whole family had only the greatest respect and admiration for this wonderful man. I majored in Biology at Stanford. Upon graduation, I was denied admission to medical school two successive years. So I enrolled as a graduate student at San Jose State in the Department of Psychology. I finished all my course work, but not my dissertation in the Master's program when, in 1963, I finally gained admission into medical school at George Washington University in the District of Columbia, a euphoric feeling after seven trying years. My life was going to change forever.

I had four wonderful years at George Washington, with classmates from all over the United States. Compared to my travails at Stanford, medical school was relatively easy and I performed well enough to stay comfortably in the middle of my class. Those years back East gave me the opportunity to finally leave home and to experience lifestyles different from California. I lived in a rooming house owned by the Daughters of the American Confederacy. All the occupants were medical students at George Washington. The Daughters felt medical students were too busy studying to damage their house. There were about a dozen of us. We went places together and partied together. To this day, we're still good friends, communicating frequently by e-mail.

As for my family, things changed for the better as time moved on. My father was a member of the Kiwanis Club in Palo Alto, meeting many people in the business world. He was referred to by his new comrades as an "adopted Irishman." From the late 1950s through the 1970s, he was a member of the Menlo Park Library Commission, serving as its chairman. There is a room named for him at the library. I have one sibling, younger brother Loren, who graduated from Menlo-Atherton in 1961. He then earned two degrees at Stanford and a doctorate in history from UCLA. After serving on San Jose State's faculty, he got into the technical writing field in the computer industry.

In late 1965, an acquaintance asked me for a favor. I was invited to Mr. John Lee's house on Thanksgiving Day, and there I met a young lady from New York who might want to see the sights around suburban Washington over the long weekend. The favor? I would be her tour guide. Only this request came at the last minute. I already had accepted an earlier invitation elsewhere. But I promised to be a "stand-in" on the condition that I would arrive well after dinner. I kept my promise by walking into a house of perfect strangers. I had no idea what an earth-shaking moment this was going to be.

That's how I met Elizabeth Lee, who was a school teacher at P.S. 130 in New York City after graduating from Hunter College. She was nick-named Pinky by her grandmother because of her very pink skin as a baby, and not because of old-time comedian Pinky Lee. Hardly anyone called her Elizabeth.

I showed Pinky the sights around Washington, including the Mount Vernon estate. We had a good time. She was very attractive and a socially proper girl. After my semester finals in January, 1966, I visited Pinky and her family in New York City. I continued doing this once or twice a month for six months. Pinky and I found that we had similar and compatible backgrounds, and we enjoyed many of the same things. She was the first girl I kissed. Six months after we met, we were engaged. We married the week before I graduated from medical school in 1976. We have been happily married ever since.

After medical school, we moved back to California, where I served as a rotating intern at the Santa Clara Valley Medical Center. In 1968, I was commissioned a captain in the United States Air Force medical corps, and served my two military years at the White Sands Missile Range in

New Mexico. I saw patients daily as a general medical officer. I also was chief of preventative medicine for the post. After years of pre-med, med school, and my medical internship, military life seemed like an all-expenses-paid vacation.

Seeing patients at our dispensary, I noticed there was a significant number of dermatologic problems. And I didn't have a clue about proper diagnosis or proper treatment. I traveled to William Beaumont Hospital at Fort Bliss, Texas, to see patients with the head dermatologist there. Having this minimal clinical experience and by reading textbooks, I gained a reputation as the "rash doctor." I found dermatology a challenge intellectually, and the patients generally were more pleasant, for they weren't usually very ill.

After the military, I applied for a residency in dermatology at Stanford, and was delighted to be accepted as a resident in August 1970. After three years of residency, I opened a private practice in east San Jose, an area that was medically underserved and had no dermatologists. I'm proud to be still practicing dermatology. My biggest reward: Seeing an old patient and being told that I had a positive impact on his or her life.

The world has changed since I was a teenager at Menlo-Atherton. Ethnicity and religion do not present nearly the same social barriers they did back then. Society is much more open. Pinky and I have lived on the same street in Los Altos for more than twenty-nine years. Our daughter, Lisa, has a doctorate in Immunology from UCLA. She is married and works as a post-doctoral fellow at UCLA Medical School and Hospital. Our son, Christopher, graduated from Chico State and works as an information technology recruiter.

From the time our two children were old enough to date, we taught them that ethnic origin is not an important factor socially. However, choosing decent people is paramount. Christopher hasn't ever dated an Asian. Lisa is married to a non-Asian Anglo. This is no longer the 1950s.

In retrospect, what my upbringing taught me was that I had to be tough. Basically, one needs to be honest and to have principles. I learned to reach within myself to find the strength required to push on. My dad taught me that anything worthwhile would never be handed to me, and to never give up. I thought if I was ever going to be worthy of my father, I would have to do well at school, too. I'm from the same tree as my father's son. The Chinese son.

For hobbies, I'm interested in cooking and the art of matching food and wine. I enjoy classical music and jazz. I collect toy cars and antique wrist watches. I own a 1937 Buick, just like my parents' family car.

I'm also involved with Menlo-Atherton. My high school reunions have been metamorphic. I've participated in the planning and execution of a couple of them. It has truly been fun to see and work with people I might not have known very well years ago. I've found there is nothing like the great interaction before a reunion and the feeling of satisfaction afterward in knowing that people had a good time. Reunion committee members have told me that I am now our class historian and the backbone of these reunions,

Looking at my high-school graduation picture, that young man with the crew cut, bow tie and glasses was thinking, "I better go to Stanford and get good grades." That's all that was really there then for him. He was driven in a quiet sort of way.

He would be very happy with what he has done in his life, making himself into the best person he could be. He wouldn't feel short-changed in any way. There are ups and downs in everything, but he has had a relative life of privilege.

He has been blessed.

The Completed Woman

Marilyn Hareid McDowell Powell was a student-body officer and honors student at M-A. But instead of entering college, she became a wife and mother at eighteen. From this difficult transition into adulthood, she grew in many ways—artist, activist, political-supporter, journalist, businesswoman.

When I was a junior at Menlo-Atherton, this guy came from Iowa named Gil. Gil McDowell. He seemed mature and interesting, and he was different from the guys in Menlo Park. He wasn't sophisticated. He came to school sometimes in his overalls. But he was good-looking, and I really loved this guy. I was making a decision to spend my life with him.

We were married in February of our senior year. Getting married in high school was frowned upon in the 1950s. Probably would be frowned upon today, too, but it carried more of a wallop in those days. I gave a luncheon at this big Victorian place in Menlo Park to tell my girl friends that I was married. They came unglued at hearing the news. They ran upstairs to the bathroom, crying and breaking their high-heeled shoes. After all, the whole bunch of us girls, we were just kids.

Gil and I had gotten married at the Church of the Wayfarer in Carmel. We went by ourselves. I'm not sure how my parents, who were educated people, felt about us getting married. We didn't talk much about things in our family. But my mom was terrific in setting up the wedding. There was no hint of scorn or judgment. She really took care of me. My dad didn't talk about it.

It was a very lonely time. Gil and I had each other. But everybody

Motherhood, not college

Marilyn Hareid

else was doing something else. The two of us lived separately the rest of our senior year. It was a hard time. I was torn.

It goes without saying that Gil was the man in my life. But at the same time, I had planned to attend Whitman College in Walla Walla, Washington. My parents had gone there. With my good grades, I could have gotten a scholarship. But I never applied. I wasn't going to college like the rest of my friends. I was about to become a mother.

I was pregnant when Gil and I graduated with our class in June 1956. I wasn't showing at that time and we marched with the rest of the graduates. My girl friends at M-A stuck by me. When school started the next fall, they made me feel included. Joanne Felkner was going to Mills College in Oakland. She had me help her move in. I felt really different. I had taken a different path and I didn't like it. I wanted to be part of that other world, too.

Gil and I settled into our new life. Our son, Terry, was born that fall. We first lived in an apartment in Menlo Park. College was out of Gil's frame of reference. He was a sensitive person, so he might have felt badly about my not going to college. I'm not sure. He never said anything about it. He got a job at a gas station, then at Bethlehem Steel as a crane operator.

When Terry was two or three, I went to work at Lockheed. Through M-A classmate Teddy Grindle's father, I got a very good job in material analysis and eventually had a group of men working for me. Gil hated the fact that I was going to work with all these guys. He was insanely jealous. One day, he threw me in the shower with my clothes on because he didn't want me to go.

I had seen this same jealousy of his in high school. We didn't go to a lot of parties because he didn't want to go. I got a new dress for the Senior Ball, and we didn't go to that either. It all had to do with his feeling alienated from what he saw as my successful crowd. He pulled me out of this group, and we had to make the best of it. But, ultimately, we didn't.

Looking at our respective cultures and what we wanted out of life, we were just very different. And we were so young. Who could make a marriage work in that instance anyway? Though we lived in various places in Menlo Park and Palo Alto, we were on different paths. Our goals, aspirations and the way we approached things were different. Gil probably knew we weren't well-suited to each other. Even though there was chemistry, there wasn't enough to cement a longterm relationship. So I left the marriage. I wanted something more for myself and for Terry.

Gil never paid any alimony or child support. I kept thinking he would....I guess I'm just optimistic. We weren't into litigation much in those days. I just figured I would do it on my own. Gil remarried and had two more children. He hasn't shown any interest in Terry. It hasn't bothered me. Or Terry. But now that he's getting older, Terry may be more inquisitive, wanting to know about his heritage. On St. Patrick's Day, he had this green shirt on. I asked him about it and he said, "I've got Irish relatives." I thought he meant this relative of my mother's. He said, "No, I'm talking about my birth dad." But I'm not sure if Gil is Scottish or Irish.

After the divorce, I lived in some odd situations just to get away. Answering an ad, I moved in with this woman and her child in Mountain View. It wasn't a good situation and my dad got me out of it. So I lived on my own for a while. Then I met Dick Powell.

Dick was a business major at San Jose State before being hired in administration at Lockheed. Both of us worked in the think tank in Palo Alto as opposed to Silicon Valley, and our jobs were related. Dick had a strong work ethic about never dating anyone at work, so we danced around for a while. But I had all the answers about where the parts were going to be delivered and when the missiles would fly. After a while, he asked me out. We were engaged thirteen days later, and we married two months after that on April 29, 1961.

Terry was four at the time. Dick adopted him right away. Dick was good for Terry, giving him a father figure. They had a good relationship because Terry played baseball, and Dick played baseball with him. They loved doing that. Fathers and sons always have their issues, like mothers and their sons or daughters, but Terry always has thought of Dick as his dad.

Now it's 2005. Dick and I have been married forty-four years, so it's funny to talk about my first marriage. But from that union I became a mother, and I feel a good mother. You always think of things you could have done better. You always feel bad that you didn't do a certain thing, that your kid turned out in one aspect to be this way, and you could have changed that. But you do the best you can. That's the big lesson in life to learn. Terry always said, "You did such a good job, mom."

Terry is my only child. Dick and I thought about having children, but I didn't get pregnant. We didn't try very hard. It wasn't a big issue. We didn't try invitro-fertilization; it wasn't really a known option back then. We have had a very active life as it is. We owned a very successful bicycle shop that we sold after twenty-eight years. We're still in the bike touring business, putting on tours in Europe around the time of the Tour de France. We're actually in Europe five months of the year, and we own a house in southern France in the Dordogne, near Bordeaux.

And I love art. I do plein air paintings: outdoors, mostly on location, landscapes. I belong to the Society of Western Artists. I have three pieces in a miniature show in Lincoln town, not far from where Dick and I live. I'll be part of another show in Lincoln Hills in a few months, and I'll have an open studio this fall. I've gone to painting workshops all over the United States—in Maine twice, in Scottsdale, Arizona, and in Carmel and Monterey, California, plus other workshops in Cornwall, England, in LaRochelle and in the Dordogne. I've joined lots of art clubs and sold lots of paintings. I like the satisfaction I get when one of my paintings is good. They don't all turn out. You might get one out of ten that's really good, show-worthy.

At one point, Dick and I worked to get political candidates elected. The group we became a part of decided the best way to do that was to get in the middle of things. So we started a global news service. I had tea with the candidates' wives. Soon, someone said to me, "This must be right up your alley." People saw me as pushy, but I'm a very shy person, really. I just fall into things. But that news service was stressful.

For twenty years, Dick and I also were involved with a Palo Alto group, the Creative Initiative Foundation. It was, in essence, spiritual. Its courses were built on the teachings of Jesus; not Jesus as a saint or

Christ, but as a prophet, someone who had a lot to say about how to live your life. We also worked on pesticides, nuclear power, and Beyond War. With the Cold War so prevalent at the time, and with the distinct possibility of a nuclear confrontation, we felt we had to educate people that it's important to move "beyond war" in our personal lives and as nations. To do so, we spoke all over the state. Dick and I left the group because we were needed at the bike store. But we were always grateful for the people we met and worked with.

It was a different time when I was growing up. It was simpler, gentler. We didn't have the sexual revolution. We didn't have access to everything that we have now. Drugs were never a big part of my life. They're now available on every street corner. Parents stayed together back then. That's what one did; divorce wasn't an option. Their kids paid the price, but what's better, having two parents stay together who don't love each other and who have a lousy relationship, or having kids deal with the effects of a divorce? That's what we've got now.

I don't believe my parents had a happy relationship. That was pretty common in those times. Life just wore them down, but they stayed together. The fact that parents don't stay together today isn't necessarily a good thing. That's because people take marriage vows too lightly. Any little thing that goes haywire, they're out of there.

My parents, Don and Peggy Hareid—that's Hareid as in car ride—were married during my dad's senior year at Whitman. Because Whitman was a liberal arts college, they moved to New York where dad got an engineering degree at Columbia. He then worked for Bell Laboratories, where he helped develop radar. All four of their kids were born in New York City. I'm the oldest, with two younger sisters and a baby brother.

My parents disliked the East Coast. So they moved back west, first to Washington and then to California. We lived in San Leandro for a while before moving to Menlo Park. Our first house in Menlo was at the corner of Olive Street and Santa Cruz Avenue. Then we moved to College Avenue.

My mother had an artistic side. She was a painter with a tremendous sense of wonder about the world around her, which she passed on to us. However, she thought I was a snot. I wanted to shop at Joseph Magnin's; she preferred J.C. Penney's. She wanted me to take Spanish; I took three years of French. My mother was hard on me verbally.

My dad was a perfectionist. Getting a B in high school was not acceptable. I had mostly A's and only one C that I can remember. There was a lot of parental pressure on me to perform, because I was the oldest. Even after I went back to school as an adult, I still showed my dad my grades, still trying to make points with him. He was so picky that growing up with him was difficult. But he always pushed you to do your best.

Looking back on grammar school, I was president of my eighth grade class. But there always was this sense of "What am I doing here?" I told my teacher, Ruth Rogers, "I just don't think I can do this, being president." She asked me why. "Because I don't think anyone wants me to be." She talked me out of it, and I finished the school year as president. Teen-age angst!

I had this feeling, deep down, of being inadequate. I carried it with me all through high school. I was voted Publicity Commissioner at M-A, though I don't know why I ever ran for that office. I was doing a lot of art work for one of the teachers, Stanley Dorfer, and maybe he suggested it. All we did in terms of publicity was make banners and fill showcases.

The first few years at M-A, I really liked it. I did well in my classes. I had a lot of friends. Was I popular? No one ever feels popular, I don't think. I remember someone saying to me, "You came from the right side of the tracks, so you were popular." I thought, "What is this right side of the tracks?" My family didn't have money. That was a problem in Menlo Park, where there was lots of money. Don't you remember? Whatever the image was, and whatever the reality was, I pushed myself. That wasn't always congenial to me.

But we always put a different face on things. For instance, a really significant thing happened when I was in the eighth grade. My father had his first mental breakdown, something that was always a part of his life, and our lives. I remember my mother coming to school, getting me out of my eighth-grade class, and taking me to Belmont where my father was hospitalized. That was a significant thing for an eighth-grade girl.

It stayed with me for a long time, and probably is with me today, because there always was this implication that I did it. Why? My mother was upset and didn't know how to handle it. And maybe I took it on. In her eyes, I was sort of a handful in a lot of ways.

My dad was in and out of hospitals. It was like walking on eggs, that it might happen again. Then there was the hiding of it, because mental illness made you suspect. A real nut case. Today we know that people have all kinds of mental breakdowns, yet there still is a stigma attached to it. I think my friends knew about my dad, but we didn't talk about that kind of thing in those days.

My father had a history of depression. He was in and out of his job. The company let him keep it, but it affected his progression. This was very hard on my mother. She always tried to do the right thing, even though it was too much for her. But she didn't have her spouse there to raise four children.

Life isn't always kind. I'm partially blind in my left eye. Doctors think it happened when I had German measles in grammar school. I can drive a car, but my depth perception is affected. I've had to learn how to judge distances. I do well at everything except for things that come at me really fast, like a softball. I can't bowl or play golf. I'm sure it affects how I paint; nobody else I know paints the same way I do because I see things differently. I use a more semi-impressionistic stroke—a little dot here, a little dot there, a little accent here or there. Then I had some floaters appear across my good eye five years ago at a Cow Palace garden show. It was a scary thing, a slight tear across the retina. It wasn't detached, but I could have another tear across the retina at any time. There is that risk if the gel behind the retina becomes hard, brittle, and then breaks away. It's a normal part of aging, but I hope it doesn't happen when we're in France.

Then Dick suffered angina on a bike ride. He was fifty-two and had severely clogged arteries. He had an angioplasty, but three months later he started having pains again. This time it was a minor heart attack, which happened when he had a second angioplasty. And he had a third angioplasty the day after that. Remarkably, he hasn't had another problem since. But from that difficult experience, we became vegans. And we started meditating about an hour every day. We also bike and we lift weights at the gym. Like they say, motion is lotion.

Dick and I were married in Carson City, Nevada. For a long time, I had feelings about never being able to have a big wedding. The year after we wed, Dick was called up from Navy reserves during the Berlin crisis. He was sent to Hawaii for seven months. Terry spent the first grade there. I loved the islands. While Dick was on ship, I was on the beach or driving my MG sports car. After we came back home, I went back to Lockheed. But Dick wanted me to be a normal housewife and mother, so I left.

However, being a full-time mom terrified me, so I programmed myself right into school at San Jose State. My chance, at last, to go to college. I was an art major concentrating on interior design. Bud Varty had been an M-A classmate. My sister, Cathy, dated Bud's brother, Gerry. They got me a job working with Barbara Varty, the mother, at Allied Arts in Menlo Park.

I didn't want to work full-time; I wanted to be there when Terry came home from school. Barbara became like a second mom to me and worked my hours around so that I could do both. By then I had satisfied myself that I could do college work. I had very good grades and there was no need for me to graduate. So I left college my junior year and became Barbara's assistant. We did decorator shows together. She gave me jobs on my own. When I quit to join the Creative Initiative Foundation, she was very disappointed. I think she wanted me to take over from her one day. Later on, I had my own design business.

Dick started smoking when he was fourteen. To stop, he used the reward system; he got himself a new bike. We decided to get out of Lockheed because the bike thing made a lot of sense. We bought the Bicycle Outfitter in Los Altos. We already had been on two bike tours, so we also focused on touring. When the fuel crisis hit in 1976, our business really took off. We got a bigger store, so big, in fact, that it took up the whole block.

From my teenage marriage and early motherhood, I now felt good about my personal growth. But I was more concerned with trying not to get the planet blown up. War as a means of resolving conflict is really obsolete. That's true today, I don't care what anyone says. Look what a mess we made of it in Iraq.

I think one should always be in a state of growth. And in the 1970s, there was all kinds of self-help. Dick and I have worked hard to make ourselves better. You're always trying to work out relationships, but there are bumps along the way. In the late 1980s, Dick and I separated for a period of time. Basically, after twenty-six years of marriage, he decided he wanted a different life. Maybe it was a mid-life crisis for him, but it was a shock to me. I was fifty. I thought my life was over. Dick started dating others. I didn't date because I was down on men.

We were separated nine months. The divorce papers were written up, but we never filed them. Then, somehow, we got back together. We just decided the marriage was worth saving. But we agreed to see a marriage counselor. That was a very hard time, more painful than the separation. Usually things that attract you to people are the same things that drive you nuts later. With a psychologist, you have to go through everything all over again. Somebody once said, "Whatever doesn't kill you makes you strong." There's always a good side that comes out of a separation. A lot of good things came out of ours.

We've moved around quite a bit. We had seven escrows in just two years. We've lived in Los Altos Hills, Lake Tahoe, San Francisco, Cupertino, Carmel, Los Gatos, the Santa Cruz Mountains, and now Lincoln. I wouldn't say we're wealthy. What's wealthy? We're doing all right.

And we're still working. The touring business pays the bills. It's a big job putting together a tour. You have to do the housing, the bike routes, organizing the people, getting the bikes in shape. You want it to be a good experience for those who sign up.

On one bike tour, we rode from Dordogne to Provence. I was the only one in the group who spoke French. Dick and I really liked the Dordogne, fifty miles east of Bordeaux. The Dordogne is green and doesn't have the hot Mediterranean weather. We rented a house there and left our bikes behind when we came home. Then the owner died and his wife wanted to sell the house to us. We loved the area. It's very rural farm country, great for biking, and less stressful. So we bought that house, located in the tiny village of Montagrier. There are lots of Brits there, and it's easy to make friends with them because of the common language. But we also have French friends.

I think of my life this way: Everybody does the best they can with what they've been given. I sort of lost track of my M-A girl friends because of our different lifestyles. So it has been delightful in recent years to rekindle some of those relationships, with Sue Samuels and Lynne Mokler. I'm sorry I'm going to miss our fiftieth class reunion. Dick and I will be in Europe. It would be nice to see everyone.

Gil came to one of our reunions. I'm not sure if I got him there or not. I might have prevailed on someone to get him there. I just wanted to see him. Dick and I met Gil and his wife. Gil looked all right, older. He was good friends with another classmate, Jim Filardo, and they came together. I was surprised that I didn't experience more emotion in seeing Gil. In my mind, that said to me that something was settled.

Recently, I spoke with Gil's mother. She lives in Mountain View. I called her. I've called her several times over the years to see if she was alive and OK. She and I were very close, and she had a hard time with the breakup of our marriage. Someone made her see that it was for the best. She still considers Terry her grandson even though he hasn't seen her.

You know, it's so funny to talk about this, because it's like talking about another person from a whole lifetime ago. But I can see where, in one way, that it really served me. I became a mother of a wonderful son.

My senior year at Menlo-Atherton? I was a lot healthier, for sure. That girl had the ability to laugh it all off. Somewhere underneath, something else was going on. She thought, "OK, now I'm going to graduate. I'm going to have a baby. I'm going to be in charge of a family. Is my life really over?"

Looking at herself now, she'd think it was a different life from what she projected. She would feel OK about how her life turned out, how certain strengths grew out of adversity. And there was a certain amount of getting to know herself, so that she could try to fit into this crazy world we live in.

It has all worked out.

Family of invention

Bryon Farnsworth

⋆ 9 ⋆

A Man on the Edge

Bryon Farnsworth, whose uncle invented television, moved fast at M-A, whether it was football, cars, motorcycles or girls. His thrill-seeking need for speed evolved into a career. He has cheated death, enjoyed full-throttle fun, married three times. Though retired, he hasn't fully decelerated.

At an early age, I became addicted to the thrill you get from pushing yourself to where your adrenalin starts flowing. It's almost like drugs or alcoholism, a self-induced high. To get it, you have to walk that edge, go down that narrow line. It's like riding your motorcycle on a two-by-four. I would get to that edge and try to see how long I could stay there.

That's what racing is all about, staying in control on that edge. Some people don't want to get that close. Others feel comfortable. Things kind of slow down in your mind and you're able to control that adrenalin rush.

Through racing, I became an adrenalin junkie. I played football, which gives you a different kind of adrenalin rush. In football, you can break your leg. In a motorcycle or car, you can kill yourself. Fear didn't bother me, but afterward I'd think, "Oh, my God." Because that second goes by where you're going through the air (laughter) or you're going to hit something and you think, "Oh, this is going to hurt." (More laughter). And I've crashed plenty, and broken about everything there is to break on my body.

There's a certain physical limit you can take a motorcycle to because of traction and horsepower. If you know how to get it to that edge, that edge of fear, then you feel a sense of euphoria. You can't perform when you're scared, but you can perform when you get to that point where I'm not scared yet, but if I go a little faster, I'm going to be scared. I'd get into a zone where my body just reacted without my doing or saying anything. It's like the body was controlled by a computer.

I never feared death. Once on a speedway in San Jose, I was trying for the lead and went into a wall. I fell off and broke my shoulder. The guy coming up behind me hit my motorcycle, which drove him into the wall. His face shield came down and cut his throat. I was in the same ambulance with him going to the hospital. I asked how he was doing, and they said, "He's gone." I didn't know him well, but he had a wife and a kid.

Here was evidence that what you're doing on this side of the edge or on the other side of the edge is very close. But the next time I raced, I put that guy's death out of my mind. I feel there's a Rolodex in the sky, someone else determining who hits the fence and who doesn't hit the fence, and do you break your collar bone or cut your throat and die? When it's your time, it's your time. I became a fatalist at that point. Since then, I've had so many chances to die. I rolled off a mountain on a motorcycle and went down a two-hundred-foot cliff. I got up and walked back up the mountain. I've hit cows in Mexico, went off the road in cars....I've had plenty of chances.

I had a 1934 two-door black Ford sedan at M-A, the perfect getaway car you see in those old Hollywood gangster movies. Wade Hampton and I were going to a dance with our dates and a drunk lady in a big Chrysler hit us and totaled my car. We walked away. So did the drunk lady. I remember driving over Sandhill Road's rolling hills in the dead of night with the lights off and two other guys in the car. Nothing happened. My name wasn't in the Rolodex.

But if you can't get your body to that edge in racing, you're going to be back in the pack. First-place guys can run down that narrow two-by-four without falling off. There was a picture of me in M-A's school newspaper, the "Bear Tracks." I'm sitting on my motorcycle. The headline is "Here's the Wild One," referring to the Marlon Brando motorcycle movie. I was a sophomore then, but old enough to drive. The story was written by this older girl, a junior. I dated her when I was a freshman. She then moved to Illinois. She was a nice girl, but they were all nice girls at Menlo-Atherton, from Linda Price to Beverly Wells. All the girls I dated were great.

Dating and girls came easy for me. The way my mother and father treated each other—there never were any fights at home—is how I treated girls. And they treated me nicely, too. I had my first sexual experience when I was twelve or thirteen. She was an older girl, maybe fourteen, a baby-sitter or the friend of a baby-sitter. I can't remember which, but she took advantage of me. It gave me an interest; I didn't know girls could do this. Before that, I was becoming aware of sex, but you don't know what to do. How does this play out, becoming involved with a girl in this respect? Do I play doctor with them? After that first experience, it was like, "That's how it works."

Without naming names, all through high school, there were two levels: The girls that did and the girls that didn't. And some of the girls that didn't were the upper crust. Although they wanted to, they didn't. So you'd have two girl friends at the same time that you would see differently. There was this Catholic school in Palo Alto where the girls would climb out the window, then shimmy down a tree. That was like fishing.

I was pretty active. Bill Hilton and I took a summer trip after our sophomore years, traveling from Lake Tahoe to Utah to work on my uncle's ranch. We learned a lot, if you know what I mean. It was part of growing up. We didn't have fear of AIDS. The honor system back then was a sense of obligation if the woman became pregnant. It was like God put this child on Earth partly because of me, so I have a responsibility to do the best I can for this child. And I did. They don't always have that honor system today.

My parents were Mormons. I went to church with them as a boy, but when I got to high school, I did not follow the religion. It was not a problem with them. They were the kind of parents who said, "You are who you are." They allowed me to be who I was, and that's why I was the kind of rebel at M-A who rode motorcycles and raced cars. Because my folks gave me a free reign, I wasn't as restricted as other kids in our era.

As long as I wasn't physically hurting myself, and my parents were obviously worried about that, they felt that my expressing myself was probably a better learning experience than trying to hold me back and having me do it anyway.

We had it pretty good in Menlo Park. We lived in a pretty nice area, kind of in a bubble of the world so to speak. There were no bad days; it was happy days. There was nothing wrong. No war. No problems. We had pretty much everything we wanted. Our friends were great. It was movie stuff.

And I came from a great family. My uncle, Philo T. Farnsworth, is the father of television. He invented the cathode ray tube, the scanning mechanism that transmits the electronic signal onto the television screen. And once that signal hits, it becomes light, which is the basis of the black-and-white TV picture. That old glass screen with the "gun" behind it was his concept. He dreamed up the basic principal of transmitting an image electronically as a boy of thirteen in Rigby, Idaho, while plowing a beet field. He noticed that an electrical current was like the furrows in the field. That was 1920.

Uncle Philo was an avid reader of science books and had a strong interest in electricity. He wound an armature to make an electric motor for his mother's sewing machine and washing machine. In 1922 at Rigby High School, he discussed his image projection by an electrical source concept with his science teacher and then produced a schematic of the idea. That same schematic was later used as conclusive proof by Uncle Philo in his 1934 television invention patent case against RCA, which contended it had invented television.

It was 1927 when Uncle Philo was twenty-one that his first real working television was shown to investors at the Green Street laboratory in San Francisco. Crocker Bank of San Francisco invested twenty-five thousand dollars that launched the Farnsworth Television Corporation that same year. Uncle Philo was like a mad scientist. His mind was on another planet. He has credit for more than one-hundred-and-fifty United States patents on electronics. He told me he could power a ship the size of an ocean liner with a power source the size of a refrigerator.

He never made much money, though, off television or his other concepts. He hustled around the country selling his ideas so he could continue his research. Besides television, his patents included Electron Microscope, Infrared image, Gastroscope, and the Ion Transfer Pump that led to the development of the Cyclotron at Livermore, California. He gave his patents to corporations such as ITT for funds and the necessary means of support. Because he was ethical, he didn't care about money. People pooh-poohed his idea about television. They told him, "You're crazy. It will never work." The first working television image I ever saw was 1942 in Uncle Philo's lab in Brownfield, Maine.

Though a Mormon, Uncle Philo smoked a lot, which contributed to the lung cancer that took his life in Holliday, Utah, in 1971. He was sixty-four. His widow, Elma "Pem" Gardner Farnsworth, authored a book, "Distant Vision," about Uncle Philo. She died at age ninety-eight in 2006.

My parents, Lincoln Farnsworth and Iris Fowler, were from Utah, but met in San Francisco. My father was a builder, but after my parents married, they moved to Philadelphia where dad got a job in Uncle Philo's lab. I was born in Philadelphia, but we lived all over: San Francisco again, then Fryeburg, Maine, Utah, and finally to Menlo Park. I'm the oldest of three children; Kathy is a year younger than me and Daryl five years younger.

My sophomore year at M-A, I was a starting halfback on the freshman-sophomore football team and class president. Being president was a popularity issue, not a political issue. Gee, everybody liked me so they made me president. Before my junior year, I tore up my knee in varsity football practice. That devastated me, but when I couldn't play football anymore, I lost interest. I started working at Bill Mumford's Body Shop. Nick Juvet and I bought five-dollar and ten-dollar cars from wrecking yards, fixed them up, and got them running. Then we'd head to the creek and get those cars going as fast as we could on the creek bottom, which was dry a lot of the time. Or we'd race from Marquard's out Alpine Road to Rossotti's Beer Garden, then loop back to Marquard's. I found I loved the sense of high speed.

I had jobs all through high school, so I bought my own cars mostly.

Sometimes, my dad helped out with the purchase. I really liked working on cars, making them go faster. From that experience, I thought about becoming a mechanical engineer. My favorite car in high school was a 1937 Chevy coupe, a classy looking car that I built myself and painted Pompano peach at Mumford's body shop.

After graduation, I went to College of San Mateo, a local junior college. It was three months of partying. Then with two other M-A guys, Bob Adams and Dick Baker, we decided to become Marines. I thought joining the Marines would be fun, carrying around a gun and shooting at things. I knew the moment I got to Camp Pendleton that I had made a big mistake. I wasn't the same person anymore. I belonged to that sergeant. The Marines changed my entire life, the way I thought and acted. I just watched the movie "Jarhead," and it was deja vu. You're junk, you're nothing.

But being a Marine wasn't all bad. They made you do things without thinking, to keep you alive and the person next to you alive. The Marines taught me respect for other people, to think of what's good for me in ways of reasoning. The Marine Corps does build men, but it also builds values.

I was twenty-one when I got out. I went to work at Fred Hudkins' Plymouth in the parts department, making fifty dollars a week. I met a girl, Judy, whose father owned a TV store in Mountain View. Judy was sixteen. Her mother said, "You're not going out with that ex-Marine older guy." Judy sneaked out to meet me, then one thing led to another, and our first child, Linda, was born immediately after we were married.

We probably wouldn't have gotten married otherwise, but we toughed it out. I knew Linda was my child, and I thought the only right thing to do was marry Judy and raise Linda. Then we had Lisa soon afterward. During the ten years Judy and I were married, I worked in motorcycle stores and Davie's Chevrolet dealership. I even became a Redwood City fireman for six years. I enjoyed it, but it was boring because there wasn't enough action for me.

I was racing motorcycles and traveling around the country. As a fireman, you arranged your hours so you could get off seven days in a row.

At Daytona, I met Hap Alzima, a BSA motorcycle distributor from Oakland. He needed a traveling service representative. I agreed to take the job. The fire department was happy to see me leave. I would have a broken leg or arm from racing and could only work the desk, which made me grumpy and growly.

The BSA company moved to Southern California, making Judy miserable. She missed her family in Northern California. Then the company's Northern California sales manager's job opened up. I took it and now she was happy. But BSA's sales dropped in the late 1960s. The British-based company didn't really care; their attitude was Americans would buy anything. Then a guy I knew, Joe Parkhurst, who had started "Cycle World" magazine, offered me double my BSA salary to come work for him in Long Beach. I took it. Judy wasn't happy about it, but she moved once again.

There was a love between us, but Judy didn't feel like she had her own life. I told her to get a job. Well, I was off racing in Europe, gone thirty to forty days. I came home one morning and there was a guy sitting at the table, drinking a cup of coffee, wearing my robe. Judy said, "That's it for me, I'm going back up north, and I've met somebody who will go with me." I wasn't angry. We had grown apart, staying together for the kids' sake. Judy had been unfaithful, but so had I, though not to the point where I found somebody I wanted to spend my life with. I wanted to stay married to Judy, but I can't blame her for leaving. She had followed me wherever I had to go. Then she found someone who would help her start the flower store she wanted. And she's still married to that man. But my next marriage wouldn't go so well.

Kawasaki hired me to develop motorcycles for the American market. Here was a multi-million-dollar Japanese company asking for my input. I worked on a bike, the Kawasaki 900Z, that became the hot rod of the industry when it came out in 1973. I lived in Japan during this time, but when the bike was ready, we took it to Daytona and set the world twenty-four-hour endurance record, breaking it by more than thirty miles per hour. We ended up setting seventy-three world records. We kicked ass.

And we were heroes. Kawasaki rose to No. 2 in the business. I stayed with them until 1979, trying to keep them improving, but probably irritating somebody high up in the company. I was still racing, winning a truck race in Mexico in a Toyota, and winning my solo motorcycle class, thirty-eight years and older, in the Baja 1000 Race. My last Baja win was 1992, teaming up with some guys to take the fifty-and-older motorcycle class.

Judy and I divorced in 1972. A year later, I married Lana, a sweet girl from Aberdeen, South Dakota. It might have been one of those hot tub romances. I realized I had made a big mistake, and she said, "Yeah, you're right." She went back to South Dakota. We were only together a couple of years. I was divorced again and single for another twenty years. I was into the same analogy of a lot of single guys: Why buy the car when I can just rent them?

Susie was the biggest change of my life. She was a school principal when I met her, with two children of her own. Susie had been divorced several years. I was working for Isuzu and living in a condo. I helped Susie with a car problem. Her two kids came over and helped me work on my bike. There was a movie Susie and I wanted to see. We started a relationship, then she moved in with me. Because she was a principal, I didn't think that would look good, her living in sin. So I suggested we get married. Susie didn't care if we got married or not, just so we were happy together and we respected each other. I loved her and her son and daughter. That's what mattered most.

Unfortunately, my parents never got to spend their golden years together. My mother decided after thirty-five years, she didn't want to be married to my father anymore. She reunited with someone we knew in Maine years before, a man whose wife had died. My mom wanted to spend the rest of her life with this man. These kinds of things happen to people. Both my parents re-married wonderful people, and had wonderful second marriages. My mom's the only one still alive, but she has Alzheimer's and doesn't even recognize me.

My career took me to Prescott, Arizona, for three years, and to San Diego, where I worked for the U.S. division of KTM Motorcycles from

Austria. Then Isuzu employed me for ten years to manage their fleet of press vehicles. We got all kinds of ink, Isuzu was happy, and I was making good money. Volvo's p.r. firm hired me to facilitate press relations in America. With this guy from Sweden, we drove the Alcan Highway from Anchorage, Alaska, all the way to the Arctic Circle and Prudhoe Bay and back again. This was a dream job, the frosting on my career.

I won some racing medals for Volvo in the Alcan Rally and at Infineon Raceway in Sonoma, California. I won ten gold medals in China driving Volvo's electric car, with each win worth a thousand dollars. I retired after China. I was sixty-five and I wanted more time to ride my bike. But if they ask for my assistance now, I'll do it because I can always use the extra cash.

Somehow, I'm not in any pain from all my injuries. I've broken both legs, but never a femur. I've broken both bottom leg bones, my ankles, some toes, both arm bones, wrists, shoulder blades, collarbones. And I've had concussions. If I'm real stiff, I take Tylenol. But I keep my muscles going. I keep moving. One knee pops out occasionally, but that's the knee I injured in football. Cold days are the worst for me.

Oh, oh, my high school graduation picture. At that time, I was seeing stuff that was right in front of my face. I wasn't looking down the road, thinking of my career, and was I going to get married and live in Palo Alto or Menlo Park. None of that stuff. It was the immediacy of a few weeks.

I wish my first marriage had been "Happy Days" or "Ozzie and Harriet," and we would be holding hands in old age, petting our dog by the fire, knowing our kids loved us. But human nature isn't that way. People grow in different directions. Now I've got two wonderful grown daughters with wonderful grandchildren, two wonderful stepchildren, and a beautiful, wonderful wife. I guess you could say my life has turned out wonderful. I also have two great dogs and a nice home. No worries.

The pilot's widow

Diane Sullivan

★10★
The Eternal Ant

Diane Sullivan Gayer Reynolds was among the prettiest and most popular girls at Menlo-Atherton. She wed her high school sweetheart, a Navy pilot who was killed during the Bay of Pigs. A second marriage ended in divorce. Though guided by a strong social conscience, she has had terrible luck with men.

I look at my childhood in Menlo Park the same way an ant sees an ant colony. In an ant colony, ants all have a job. They dutifully do it, and it's for the team. These ants must have a good attitude or somebody eats their head off. I'm an ant. I've been an ant all my life. I'm still doing my ant job.

How did I become an ant? It started in a field near my house. Julian Unger, myself, and a couple other kids spent the summer with a spoon, digging these holes. There were all these ants, carrying their little eggs. We'd dig and wreck things and the ants would start all over again. They were so unique.

To know the person I am, everything interests me. I've had a chance to touch everything. I've been a wife, a mother, a grandmother. I've painted, taught, fought injustice, excelled in sports and dance. I was married twice, and I was a widow at twenty-four. But my purpose in life is to make life better for myself and other ants.

I was shaped as a person, in part, by something that happened during my childhood. Menlo Park was like Pleasantville. Here were my mother and father, very secure. Then the husband of my mother's best friend down the street turned in a wonderful neighbor who taught at Menlo College—turned him in for teaching communism. The FBI came out. It was horrible. I saw what happened. I saw the people interviewed. The accusation turned out not to be true, but the teacher died under the stress. It was so evil.

Years later, my boy friend, Fred Gayer, and I were in a pizza parlor in Menlo Park. We saw this same neighbor man, the accuser, with some woman who wasn't his wife. They were groping, kissing, hugging. I was shocked. What is this? It was another reason for me to break out of Pleasantville.

I was defiant about this kind of behavior. Yet my mother showed similar behavior regarding the garbage man who lived across the street. He had a lovely house and two lovely daughters. Once in a while, his pickup truck, which was very clean, was parked in front of his house. My mother would say, "Isn't that awful. What if I was having a tea party?" My mother never had a tea party. Everything was a facade in those times. It mattered how things looked, not how things really were. I began to see this inequity and I'd get so mad. Something was boiling inside of me, a need to make things right.

My family was very mild-mannered. They didn't carry any spears or torches, like I did back then and still do. My parents were born in San Francisco of Irish backgrounds. Being good, old Irish families, they smiled, danced, loved and drank. We had these huge, fun, family units. People I come in contact with today, young people in business, don't have those strong family units. Families are separated; they don't know who they are. Either the families are broken apart or they've moved apart. With my Irish heritage, we carried that close family feeling with us, knowing how strong that family support group was. It molded us into how we turned out to be.

My dad, David Sullivan, worked for Bethlehem Steel during the war. He then went to Kaiser Aluminum near Cupertino, where he worked for the rest of his career. He was a manager for Kaiser and retired in that position. My dad could do anything. He could build anything with his hands. He also was a closet drinker. We had this Irish-Catholic drinking family, although I didn't turn out to be a drinker. I saw enough drinking in my childhood.

At night, after dinner, I'd go out in the garage with my father and make miniature trains. My father holds a world speed record in small boat hydroplane racing. They don't have that engine size any more, so his record's still good. He did this before marriage, then my mother wouldn't let him do it any more. That kind of broke his spirit. He had this little twinkle in his eye, but he was no longer a competitor. He did stuff by himself. He didn't have a lot of friends. He was a great guy who had a big effect on my life.

My mother, Alice Chapman Sullivan, was a homemaker. I was an only child, for a couple of reasons. I was very sick when I was born. In my first year, I was almost lost many times. Because of the Depression, all of my immediate family had only one child per family. My mother didn't get up with us in the morning, so I didn't see her until the evening. I had breakfast every morning with my father. Both of my parents are gone, but I just realized this recently: I really didn't know my mother.

As a young girl, I had a lot of spirit. That's who I am to this day. You could see that spirit in Girl Scouts; I was the only one who wanted all the badges. Everyone had one or two badges; I had twelve of the fifteen. So the others didn't like me, and my troop leader didn't believe I did the actual work. I was able to prove that I did. I was just doing my ant job.

In high school, I joined every committee, every team. I was the ant. I wanted to achieve. Work and reward: the ant philosophy. I got the M-A block letter and the star, which meant ultimate recognition. I was good at swimming, basketball, tennis, softball. I was very good at modern dance. Today, I might have gotten a college scholarship for swimming. I swam in college without one.

I earned a golden key, which meant good grades. I had A's and B's, graduated something like thirteen in a senior class of about three-hundred and sixty-five students, even though I struggled because of dyslexia. My teachers really took the time with me. They made sure I got into special things academically. I couldn't work hard enough for them because of their friendship. More work gets more reward.

I did feel protected in Pleasantville. I rode my bike with other kids down to the Park Theater, paid my ten cents to watch the matinee, and felt as safe as can be. It was a totally safe community. The first time I did-n't feel safe was in high school. I had my folks' car. I think I had been to Sue Erstrom's, and then I went to Foster's Freeze. A car full of Mexican boys followed me. I became afraid and drove into a stranger's driveway, where there were some lights. Those boys drove off and I hurried home.

I've always tried to be fair in judging people, regardless of their eth-nic backgrounds. In the early years of integration at Menlo-Atherton, two black athletes came over from Ravenswood School in East Palo Alto, a community heavily populated with blacks. I was called in as one of the student leaders and was told, "We've got to make this work. Be sure you get the (white) kids out there to accept the black kids and not cause any problems."

I couldn't imagine why we would have a problem, though I was naive about racial issues. I said, "What are you talking about? These are nice kids. Let 'em be." It started me looking at what was right, what was wrong. In Pleasantville, everybody was nice, everybody did their job. Entering high school, I saw that people were jealous. That didn't fit into what I per-ceived to be the correct pattern of life. That particular time had a lasting effect on me. What I've done throughout my life is to wield my sword and fight for the right to....My kids, to this day, say, "Oh, God, here it comes." It's the inequities of life. Somebody's not being treated right, I try to help. That's who I am. My daughter now carries the same sword.

Being the ant, I've had jobs since I was twelve. In Menlo Park, I worked at the pharmacy, the dime store, and the gift store, where the owner wouldn't pay me at my work station. He wanted me to go up to his office to get the check. I wouldn't go. Dirty old man. There was this loving pharmacist who taught me how to use a cash register. He'd say, "If men come in and want to buy condoms, you just say, 'Oh, they're in the back.' Then step back, and I'll come out, so you don't have to deal with that."

Was I a good girl in high school? Oh, yes. Absolutely. Sex? Oh, no. Other girls did it. They definitely did it in the car while I was there. I sat with my hands folded. Then I fell in love in high school. This is what I wrote in my diary about the night it happened between Fred and me:

"It was a sudden look across the room at a party. A life connection was made. It was the summer before our junior year at Menlo-Atherton High School. We fell so in love and had so much fun. We swam, snorkeled, danced, laughed, and were best friends. Many dates were spent with best friends or making pizza and watching TV with his mom and dad. They were great, too."

We were supposed to go to Oregon State University together, Fred on a football scholarship and me to study scientific illustration towards a science art degree. Fred ended up going to Menlo College for football. He came up to Oregon on the train to visit me once a month, staying with his grandmother.

After our freshman year, Fred and I transferred to San Jose State. I joined a sorority and became its president my second year, but the two of us were inseparable. It wasn't a real surprise when Fred signed up for Navy pilot's school. He loved to fly, he already had his pilot's license, and he'd take me flying over San Jose. He did wing-overs; my mother would have died if she knew that. The two of us were in heaven, literally and figuratively.

While walking hand in hand on the San Jose State campus, we saw a sign on a trailer: "Fly Navy." A week later, Fred dropped out of school. He went to Navy training school in the South, and came home for the holidays. He'd fly his jet to Moffett Field, where I'd pick him up. He looked so handsome in his Navy uniform. The following Christmas, he asked me to marry him. We picked out rings and had our names inscribed. We were married in 1960 when he was an ensign and I had finished college with great grades....the same ant work.

Going into that marriage, I clearly knew Fred. He was as advertised: He was fabulous. He was that perfect person, totally complete. We were so in love, it was ridiculous. I didn't even think of the life I was going to live as a Navy wife. Before we moved to Key West, Florida, Fred just wanted to fly jets. Then he saw the Navy as a career thing. He hadn't made a final decision, though. We were still young.

We were married almost two years. His job was top gun stuff. Then came the Bay of Pigs. Fred's job was to protect the air space between Florida and Cuba. One day he came home and said, "I've got twenty-four hours until I have to be in Norfolk, Virginia. I have to be gone three months and I can't tell you the destination."

He was gone a month and a half, flying the F-FD Sky Ray fighter interceptor, the hottest, fastest plane at the time. Then, suddenly, it was over. The XO's wife told me, "Diane, Fred's lost. We don't know where he is." They never found Fred or his plane. I have no idea what happened. I still don't.

But Fred was gone, and you just, just, go to a level that's not like real life. It's like walking a foot off the ground and the sound is different. I was in that state for a couple of years. I looked at Fred as an early gift for the life I was going to live. It's a funny thing. You never lose this, do you? (Her eyes grow misty). Other people I've lost, even my parents, have never affected me like losing Fred. Terrible pain. I never got over him. (She starts to cry). I still think about him every day, forty-two years later.

At the time, I didn't know any young person who had lost anybody. And I didn't know how to sever my ant chain. What do I do? My mother flew out. She was very supportive. I came back to Pleasantville, moved in with my parents. That lasted a week because of my mother's would-you-do-this-like-a-good-girl kind of thing. I moved into my own apartment in Menlo Park. Fred's parents lived just down the street. The support was there, too, especially from Fred's mother. She invited me to go to events. (Further tears).

I was in this blur. I had forty-four thousand dollars in insurance money, what I was paid by the government for Fred's loss. In those days, that was all the money in the world. So I didn't have to worry about money. But I was the ant, so I started working for an interior decorator. I couldn't even think about my next step. I wasn't in the real world, and if I saw someone who looked like Fred, I'd do a double take. When President Kennedy was assassinated, I thought, "Here's another young person who's gone."

Then Chuck Reynolds came back into my life. I had known him since I was four. His father was my father's boss, so we had to interact. Chuck was four years older. I dated him for a while when I was a high-school freshman and he was in college. I told him, "Why don't you date girls your own age?"

Now it's ten years later and Chuck says, "C'mon, it will be good for you to go out." I know him like a brother, right? At the time, I didn't think much of him because he was scandalous. He always had five girl friends. A rogue. And he was so full of himself. He'd always been this award-winning athlete. He was a huge star who had made it to Triple-A in pro baseball.

Now he's come back home and selling paper for this company. I started going out with him. My mother asked, "What are you going to do with your life?" I'm floating around. Chuck's friends offered a comfort zone. But they partied, and I don't drink. Then Chuck asked me to marry him. I assumed he was going to be the heir apparent to Fred, even though I knew what Chuck was like. But I was just expected to be married, right?

So I re-married a year after becoming a widow. I wasn't in love with Chuck. Nothing was the same—relationships, nothing—after Fred had died. Chuck was a friend. I said, "How bad could this be?" Then I found out how bad. Two weeks before we got married, I found out Chuck had been unfaithful to me all along. Chuck said he was sorry. So sorry.

Fred was looming in my heart. So much so, I threw away our wedding pictures. I felt I had to do this to break the bond we had. Chuck was a new life. I stood at the garbage can and said, "I've got to do this because I can't make it with Chuck the way this is going." So I threw them away, not knowing my mom had a second set. Well, Fred didn't go away. He didn't go away....ever. (Continued tears).

I was married to Chuck twenty-two years even though he was never home. He was at work, teaching and coaching at a local high school. Then he'd stay out late at night drinking with his friends. He'd come home at 2 a.m., get up at 6 a.m. and go to work. I really didn't see him. On the weekend, he'd go play golf. Right around when we married, I got a teaching job working with disadvantaged kids. I did some fabulous things with them. I threw myself into my work to fill the void and to keep myself busy as the perpetual ant.

Married to Chuck, I tried everything to attract him. I wore Frederick's of Hollywood's things, which weren't my style. The warmth from him still was missing. Then at two golf tournaments Chuck played in, we got thrown together with Chuck's good friend and his wife. I said to the wife, "I want to have a baby." She said, "I'll take my husband away so you two can be together. Just grab him." And that's how I got pregnant. Both times. We didn't have a normal sex life. He was never there. Never home. And he was so drunk, he couldn't have sex with me.

We had two children, a son, Charlie, and a daughter, Teri. Both of them, I say proudly, grew into extraordinary ants. Chuck was there for Charlie's birth, but only a few minutes before he left. When Teri was born, he wasn't there. He was at a golf tournament or somewhere. After she was born, he made it to the hospital.

We stayed together for the kids. They're great kids, but they were so scarred by his behavior. He was never there for them. He never came to one of our daughter's basketball games until I told him he had to go. He walked in for ten minutes, then walked out. My daughter won all these equestrian awards. He came to only one horse show. She won this big award. But he left before she received it, saying "This is boring." She accepted the award while crying her eyes out.

Chuck and I made good salaries. I had that government insurance because of Fred, so Chuck and I bought five houses. I painted those houses, fixed the plumbing, did the gardening. I designed the home in Saratoga where the kids grew up. We had a nice thing going in terms of property investments. Unbeknownst to me, Chuck bought a bar in Santa Cruz with another drunk friend, who had no money. He was the bartender, but the bar was in Chuck's name. Well, the bar didn't go over and they lost all the money. My money. I don't remember the exact amount, but it was a lot....thousands.

I was the ant going along. And I was the super mom, doing all the activities. I got into new academic doorways, like teaching the gifted program, first through eighth grades. I started writing programs, writing grants, winning awards. Starting on a career, I learned if you got more units, you'd get more money. So I took every science course at San Jose State.

I also was a professional artist, painting everything you could imagine, selling lots of paintings, and loving it. I joined a paint group that was mind-boggling. I got my science students into extensive projects. I showed them they had power as people. I connected with NASA to work on special national education projects, connecting kids to actual scientists. Another school project was studying Saratoga Creek. I received many different awards for my environmental efforts and for my NASA curriculum work.

I found out San Francisco Bay was being used as a depository for a toxic substance that helps take out cancer-causing carcinogens. I called the regional water division manager. I said, "Instead of putting that substance in there, why don't you stop the carcinogens in the first place?" He said, "Listen, lady, why don't you go back to your kitchen and let your husband deal with the things that are important? This is too important for you to worry about."

I said to him, "I happen to be a school teacher, and I have two hundred students a day. And we're all involved with this national award-winning curriculum, which I wrote. They're very concerned about the environment, and our focus is San Francisco Bay and Saratoga Creek. Because you're in charge of those things, you better talk to me a little differently because those students are so angry about this that they've started writing letters to appropriate people. And their parents are senators, superior court judges."...Suddenly, changes were made in both the bay and the creek.

In my science class, a new kid from the East Coast put lab chemicals in my coffee. Other kids told on him, but the school tried to cover it up. And that's not how you teach a kid that he's going to get into trouble. So I stopped teaching that class.

At different times, I had five to nine kids living in my Saratoga home, none of them my children. This social conscience of mine developed from the inequities I saw as a child in Menlo Park. I had a law suit against the title company I worked for, challenging them on their treatment of seniors.

I'm so sick of men from having to fight for everything as a woman. I don't know how women do it. It's sickening how men treat women. With men, it's the Marilyn Monroe syndrome. Men want the assets.

They don't want your brain. They want a trophy on the couch. They want food and sex. Making chocolate cookies extends your trophy power. They want to be friends with their buddies.

And if you close your eyes, they like to grope other women. Chuck's good friend tried to get me to go to bed with him for years. I've refused him, though Chuck didn't know anything about it. Another man approached me at a party, very drunk, and said, "You're so beautiful. You've got such big boobs." He lurched forward and put his hand down my dress. Everybody was stunned. Chuck was at the same party. I told him about it; he did nothing. He was always drunk. But the guy was kicked out of the party.

Toward the end of my marriage, I smelled perfume in the house that wasn't mine. Chuck was off gambling, drinking, whatever. I didn't know what he was doing. Our kids hated Chuck. Finally, they said, "Mom, divorce him." I now was disenchanted with marriage. I saw other men not taking the ball. I saw other divorces. My family came first. I was working. I didn't have the time for this, so I left Chuck.

After the divorce, a good friend said we needed to get out. We went to a place called the Blue Pheasant. You didn't have to drink, but men do want to dance. I made up some rules. Specifically, you don't want to get hooked up. I had a two-dance limit with every man.

Then I met someone at the Blue Pheasant and thought he was the one. It turned out he was in my graduating class at Menlo-Atherton, although I didn't really know him or anything about him. He was shy back then, and short, and his father wouldn't let him participate in any-thing. He and his sister had to be home right after school to work around the house. He finally spread his wings in the Army. He grew up, acted crazy. When I met him later in life, I thought this was destiny. Here was a guy my age, from my school, my background. This must be right. I even lived with him. He wanted the whole thing, so he gave me an engagement ring. I said OK, but I wasn't going to marry him. It's a good thing, too, because I finally saw his violent side.

One day, he was taunting his daughter. She argued back and he went over and grabbed her by the throat. They were screaming and yelling, running around the house after each other. I had never seen anything like that. I got up and left. The next day, I came back to get my school stuff. He was so sorry. Then he and his daughter are screaming at each other again. So I got out, telling him I can't handle this any more. I stopped going to the gym and to the Blue Pheasant, because he was following me. Like a stalker.

He came unglued. He tried to attack me. He broke my car window as I tried to get away. He stalked me for a year. He went to my work place and parked outside. He called or e-mailed me at work. He e-mailed my bosses. He'd leave dead plants on my driveway. He wasn't working, so he followed me around. I filed reports with five police departments to get it all recorded. One of his ex-girl friends then told me that she left him because of his angry side.

The stalking ended, finally. He was out of my life for good. I've been with enough men to know there's this control thing. My daughter said, "Mom, there are good men." And I said, "Thank goodness for Fred because I wouldn't have thought so." I do know lots of good men who are good friends. I didn't pick any of these other men. They picked me. I've had fifteen marriage proposals, one from a married man.

Two years ago, I got cancer; a growth in my uterus. The surgery on March 1, 2002 lasted seven hours. I chose to have the surgery over chemotherapy, because I don't believe in ruining cells to catch a cell, which leaves you with nothing. At my age, no thank you.

Some ant philosophy: You know how if you put soapy water in front of an ant, the ant just doesn't sit there, it starts taking different roads. I don't know why I'm like that ant, but the determination to succeed, to get the reward, is there. I can beat cancer. I can do anything.

It's been a wonderfully extraordinary life. I had chances that other women didn't have. The diversity of life is what I've loved. If I had been born sixty years earlier, I would have been a suffragette.

I look at my senior picture in the Menlo-Atherton yearbook and I think, "That's the girl." I'm the same nut I was then. I know that rewards get me rewards. I am an ant. I'm still doing my ant job. Somehow it's a great relief to say this: "I haven't changed a bit and I like it."

Memory's lapses

Gordy Plaisted

⋆ 11 ⋆

The Challenged Brain

Gordon Plaisted has been through two failed marriages. He's dealt
with estrangement from his two sisters and his first child. He has built
a long, loving relationship with his third wife and their children. But
life's latest obstacle—Alzheimer's disease—is troubling his already
worried mind.

There is no sign of Alzheimer's in my family. Doctors haven't told me
what is causing what I have. A doctor gave me some pills that are supposed to help me get a lot of my memory back, but it hasn't worked yet.

I don't want to get to the point where everything is gone mentally,
like my getting in the car and then having a problem getting to wherever we are going. When you mention high-school names to me, I've
forgotten them. If I didn't have the problem I have, I'd always remember
names. I don't remember my first wife's name or the name of my first
child, by my second wife.

Velma and I have been married thirty-six years. Today is our anniversary. We talk about how I can remember things. Sometimes that works.
Oh, it's terrible, I can tell you that for sure. It drives me crazy. When
you're talking about....what did Velma say I had? Right, Alzheimer's.
The thing that's always worried me about Alzheimer's is I've known
people who had it, and as they continue to get worse, if they walk out the
door and they come right back, they can't remember where they were
supposed to go.

The thought that really gets to me, though, is why I forget so many
things. So many simple things. Some of it does come back to me. For

the name of a restaurant, I'll grab the....right, phone book. Stuff like that, I don't remember until you mention it.

I've had this problem for two years. My life hasn't really been that bad except for the last two years and my retirement from the National Park Service. I worked for them twenty-four years. It was good work and I was making fairly good money when I retired. But the money I thought I was going to make in retirement turned out to be a third of what it was going to be. That's why I'm working now as an after-school janitor here in Tulare, to get our financial situation better.

I'm very happy in my third marriage. What do I like about Velma? Everything. I have no problem with her whatsoever. Velma also had been divorced twice when we married. People predicted our marriage would last six months, but it has been thirty-six years. She had a daughter, Sandra, from a previous marriage. I adopted her when I married Velma. Then we had Gordy, Jr., together. I have excellent relationships with Sandra and Gordy, Jr.

When my father passed away from a heart attack in 1962, that's when things really started happening differently. There was a five-year period where my older sister, Marilyn, wanted nothing to do with me. I called her six months ago and she wouldn't even return my call. She likes the girl I was married to before Velma. I haven't talked to my younger sister, Margie, in twenty-five years. The (second) divorce had a lot to do with it. The last time I called her, she hung up on me.

How hard has this been for me? It's not hard at all anymore. I told my wife that when I pass on, I wouldn't put down my sisters' names (as family). So it would be like having no sisters at all.

After Velma and I got married, if I wanted to spend time with my mom, I would call her and she would make sure neither of my sisters would be there. My mom eventually accepted Velma. After my father died, my mom met three or four men who were nice. Both my sisters told her there was no way she could be married to anybody else. They would not let her do it, and if she did, they wouldn't accept it.

When my mother died, what's the name of my friend from high school....? Right, Bishop John-David Schofield. He gave the eulogy. There was a reception at Marilyn's house in Visalia, but I didn't talk to my sisters or Sally, my second wife. There were a lot of people there. Sally was on one side of the building and I was on another. My first child was there, but there was no interaction. I can't remember her name. It's Linda or Lydia (Laurie), something like that.

I haven't seen her since. I'm not even sure where she is. One time, when I was working in the Grand Canyon, I went to San Francisco for some training. I found out where she was....San Carlos, I think it was. I took her out to dinner. I had some pictures of Velma and our kids. It was very nice. At that time, (Laurie) wasn't really happy with her mother. I told her that I would get back in touch with her. That was, at least, fifteen years ago. Every time I wrote to her or called her after that, I never got any response.

When my father was around, everything was fine because my sisters couldn't predict him as they could their mother. I think he would have put a stop to all this (family acrimony). It has been so many years since he died, but every day when there's something on my mind, I think of him because he was a wonderful, marvelous guy.

My dad, Guy Plaisted, was born in New Hampshire. My mother, Mildred, was born in Indiana. Dad was married previously. His first wife and their newborn child both died in childbirth. My mom and dad married shortly afterward. She was his secretary at General Electric. He was transferred from Indiana to New York and then to San Francisco. He didn't want to live in San Francisco. He found a house in Menlo Park for sixteen thousand dollars around 1950. Five years ago, I heard it sold for nine-hundred-thousand something.

I have no bad memories at all about high school. I think I was listed No. 82 in our graduation class of about three-hundred and fifty people. I sang in the school chorus, and there were four of us boys who would sing together. I should remember who the other three were, but I can't. I played football, but I only practiced. I never had a uniform at game time.

In high school, everything seemed to go well. I was very happy. Four of us were good friends, but, you know, I don't remember their names

(Schofield, Mickey Pierce and Richard Parks). And you and I were buddies. I can remember dating someone, but I can't remember her name (Judy Patterson). And now that you tell me, I remember my first car (a green Willy's Jeep).

I applied to two colleges, one in Oregon and the one in Los Angeles (Occidental). The one in Los Angeles accepted three-hundred and fifty people, and there were two-thousand, five hundred who applied. I was accepted along with another M-A classmate (Wade Hampton and Susan Samuels). It was so funny, because when I went to college in Los Angeles, I started the first game on the freshman football team. I played in the line on both sides of the ball. I wasn't good enough to be invited back my sophomore year, but I have to tell you this funny story. I was on the bench and my family was there to watch me. The coach sent me into the game. As I ran on the field, I tripped and fell flat on my face. Talk about embarrassing!

After two years at the Los Angeles school, I was kicked out. I studied hard, but they said my grades weren't good enough. I did well on tests where I could expand on my answers, but if the test answers were A, B and C, I would get a D or F. I was told I could come back in a year, but they wouldn't accept any units from another school.

I went into the Navy for two and a half years. I was in Los Angeles....isn't that the south part of California? Oh, San Diego, that's it. They had this thing on TV you were just talking about ("Truth or Consequences"). Four of us from the Navy were accepted. We had to guess something about the gal who was there, a beauty contest winner, something about what she was wearing. I don't remember what it was or who she was.

After getting out, I went to this school (Foothill Community College) with the thought of finishing up at that college in San Jose (San Jose State). But each time that I applied, I was just below what I needed to get in. I never got in there. Years later, in Coalinga, I'd work all day then drive seventy-five miles to take night classes at Fresno State. I finally finished up my college degree in the late 1970s.

Anyway, after the Navy, I started dating Sally, who was in nursing school at Stanford. Then I met my first wife. Like I said, I can't remember her name (Barbara) or how I met her or how it was. But we started dating a little bit and she worked out better than Sally, so I married her. I was working then, but I can't remember where. We were married only a few months, and I don't remember exactly what it was that broke us up.

I went and found Sally and we started dating again. Did it take a lot of forgiving on her part? Without a doubt. We got married in 1963 or 1964. She had finished nursing school. We had a little girl, and that marriage lasted three years. I can't remember exactly what it was and why it didn't work, but it sure didn't. So I left her. She was very happy that we were divorced. She hasn't ever remarried.

I was married to Sally when we bought the babies' clothing store in Visalia. I'm not sure why I got into that kind of business. A year later, Sally moved back to Menlo Park. Velma worked at the full-grown clothing store next to our baby store. I wasn't dating Velma while I was married to Sally. But after Sally left, I hired Velma. I had the store for about five years, but it just didn't work out.

I wasn't nervous about getting married a third time. I just wanted to make sure it was going to work out right, and it seemed like it would. And it has for thirty-six years.

I was unemployed two years before I went to work for the National Park Service, first at Sequoia National Park, then at a park in Santa Fe, New Mexico, and finally at the Grand Canyon. I had an office job working on contracts. I'd get to work at 8 a.m. and wouldn't leave for home until 8 p.m. I'd also work Saturdays, because there was so much work to do.

We lived right at the canyon. I was there eight and a half years. When the boss I worked for left, and the guy who replaced him was a jerk, that's when I decided to retire. So we came back to California, first to Porterville and then to Tulare, to be closer to our two children and four grandchildren.

Coming back to California hasn't been easy for us financially. As I said, my park service retirement wasn't what I thought it was going to be. That's why my car was repossessed; the payments were too high and

I couldn't make them. We have a less expensive car now, and the payments work out better.

Then on May 1, 2006, my birthday, I had a big surprise. My older sister, Marilyn, called to wish me happy birthday. She promised to mail me a thousand-dollar check from something—I forget what it is—that she had kept over. I talked to her for about ten minutes, then Velma talked to her for about fifteen minutes. We have talked to her a couple more times since. It has really been wonderful, and I hope it continues.

Looking at my high school graduation picture, I don't look a helluva lot different than I look now. At that time, I was thinking about what I was going to do. The goal was to get to college and get something done that way. I didn't know what I wanted to be. I didn't expect to be married three times.

My life? Right now, all the basic stuff, like driving to Los Angeles, I can do fine. I don't have any problem with that. It just affects me the most when I try to remember things, like names. So many names that I used to know totally, I just don't remember at all.

But when I do remember things, I feel great.

★12★

The Mind's Eye

Anything men could do, Lynne Kramer McCallum could do better, like riding a horse or driving a dragster. Adopted at birth, overweight most of her life, legally blind from diabetes, and now fighting kidney failure in her late sixties, she pushes onward with a spirit that is both dauntless and inspiring.

I've learned every day has a new miracle. I open my eyes and I can see the sun. That's a miracle because it's still there. I open my eyes and I'm still here. That's a miracle. Life has become very precious. Every rosebud, every blade of grass has a meaning. I don't take anything for granted.

I went blind overnight in 1989. It all started when I just physically collapsed. I could hardly walk. I was going downhill. I told this respiratory doctor I thought I was going to die. Then I passed out in his office. My whole system had shut down—kidney, thyroid, everything~. It turned out I had E. coli poisoning. I was in the hospital fifteen days.

Then my eyes had a massive hemorrhage. The doctor said it looked like a battlefield in there. I had the diabetes under control, then the hemorrhaging happened. I was shocked. I was scared. I had laser treatments immediately to stop the bleeding in my eyes. Then I had a choice to make: To sit there and feel sorry for myself or I could get on with life and face it. So I took charge of the situation.

I now have ten percent of my eyesight. Looking at people close by is like looking through a spider web. I say "hi" to everyone because I don't know who they are. It doesn't bother me. I meet a lot of nice people this way. I have no depth perception. I can't see the stairs and I can't

Seeing with her heart

Lynne Kramer

see sidewalk indentations when I walk. So I've fallen a lot. I've always moved at a fast pace. I had to train myself to slow down, to make sure I have something firm under my footing before I take the next step.

I've had fifty-eight treatments in one eye, fifty-four in the other eye over a six-to-eight-month period. Three, four years ago, I had some cataracts removed and a lens inserted that gave me two-to-three-percent eye growth. That was major. I came out of surgery, turned to my husband, and said, "Oh, my God, you've aged." But I could see color. Real color, like a road sign. And a rosebud, which has beauty, softness and a meaning of perfection.

There's still a chance I could lose my eyesight entirely. If that happened, I'd cope the same way I do now. I'd have anger days. Some days, I really get ticked off, like when I burn myself or drop things. My hands aren't operating quite as well anymore. I can't open things like I used to.

Then five years ago, I began having kidney failure. I've managed so far to make it without dialysis. I'm doing alternative medicine; herbal blood pressure medication. My blood pressure is fantastic. Shouldn't be, but it is. The kidneys are going, though, and, eventually, I'm going to be on dialysis. But I'm not giving into it.

Am I worried that my life could be shortened? Nope. I take every day as it comes. I absolutely believe that we are what we are at the moment we're doing it. I never had great expectations in life except for getting married and having two girls, and I've done both.

Dale and I haven't made much money in our lives, but we've had a lot of happiness. We've enjoyed life to the utmost. We've done expensive things when we could afford it, and even when we couldn't afford it. We sailed boats in the Caribbean. We've camped and we've stayed in some of the best travel places. When I die, I'll have the feeling that I've done it all.

I can see through my grandson Brian's eyes. He has fantastic wisdom at fourteen. He's very intuitive, has a scientific mind. He and I have really bonded. He comes by every day after school. I help him with homework. I can see with magnifying glasses. I can't read small print, just the large print.

My eyesight is starting to get hazy again. There is scar tissue building up around the lenses. It could flare up again and I could lose my sight. Dealing with it, that's who I am. When I was a little girl, I'd ride the merry-go-round at the Santa Cruz boardwalk. I'd try to reach the brass ring, but I was too small. My mother told me to always reach for the brass ring in life, whether you can reach it or not. That's what I'm doing today.

The hardest part was giving up reading. I love to read. I didn't love television before, but it has become a good friend. I get nothing out of books on tape. I've turned a lot to my music, the music of the Fifties. I love it because it speaks to you, telling beautiful, sad and wonderful stories. The words have such meaning. I listen to the oldies station. I listen to country music. My favorite country singers in the Fifties are still my favorite singers: Eddy Arnold, Patsy Cline, Hank Williams, Conway Twitty, Faron Young, Roy Orbison. If it's pop music, I like Gogi Grant, Theresa Brewer, Patti Page.

Did I tell you I'm a kareoke singer? I'm very well known here in the town of Paradise. I sing in different bars three nights a week. My drink of choice is water and lemon. No ice. My voice has gotten low, very husky. So I do primarily ballads. Since I can't read too well, I practice at home. I sang in the choir at Menlo-Atherton and loved it, but I hated doing solos. I'm not afraid to sing in public anymore. You kind of reach a stage in your life where it doesn't matter. There's one thing in life I'd still like to accomplish: I'd like to be a lounge singer in Reno.

The Fifties were a great time to grow up. We had it made. There was an openness. We didn't have the drug scene there is today. We didn't have television telling us how to live our lives. We could use our imagination. When traveling with our parents, we noticed things. Remember the Burma Shave signs along the road? Kids today, with all their electronics, don't have what we had. We grew up exploring. Today's kids know all about sex. There's no exploration left.

We didn't have the pressures kids have today. We went to school, did our jobs. Today there's such pressure to get kids into pre-schools when they're three years old, when their brain cells aren't fully developed.

Today there are restrictions. Everything has a label. We could say things in the Fifties without offending anyone. There were rules and lines to be crossed that were identifiable without the ACLU coming in to decide your rights or my rights. Our rights back then were fine as long as they didn't infringe on anyone else's. That's why the Fifties were fabulous. We were free.

Everything now is in computer language. There isn't the flow in language that you and I had, the same vocabulary. Today it's all initials. There's some beautiful music being written, but with rap, there's no decorum left. When I was a young girl, we had dinner around the dinner table. That's when we discussed things. You don't see that as much anymore. I told my daughters I wish they could have been raised in the Fifties. Today, there are so many ways to raise kids. There's ADD kids, bi-polar kids. We didn't have that back then. It's so much tougher today.

I remember Marquard's, the local drive-in on the El Camino Real that was the M-A hangout. Such a neat meeting place. My girl friends and me had a great time cruising Marquard's in my baby blue Dodge. I think it was a 1948 model, a heavy boat with a three-speed stick shift. My dad picked it out, so there was no way I could get into trouble. What he didn't know couldn't hurt him: I could out-drag most cars from a standing start. These guys pulled up next to me at a stoplight and revved their engines. My friend, Jackie Burris, said, "Are you going to do it?" And I said, "You bet." I knew how to pop a clutch, which most girls couldn't do. After I won that first time, that set a trend. I only dragged a short distance, but enough to make me feel great.

I was competitive. I loved sports. I got a block letter my sophomore year at M-A in basketball and in volleyball. Most girls didn't get their letters until they were juniors. In basketball, despite my size, I handled the ball. Even though I have trouble with my weight today. I'm still competitive.

Looking back on it, we were the "Happy Days" kids. Absolutely. We didn't realize it then how good we had it. But in talking now with close friends from that era, we realize we were fortunate to grow up when we did. We had those lazy, hazy days of summer. We could grow up to be who we wanted to be, and we had choices. A lot of professions were opening up at that time, to men and to women. There were some women, the brainy ones, starting to get into engineering, studying to be doctors. I never felt left out by not going to college. My parents told me I'd be taking up space needed for men coming back from the wars. I was raised to go to work, get married, and have a family.

I never knew my real mother or father. And I wasn't curious to find out more about them. I only know my birth mother was a prominent woman in her forties in southern California who had an affair with a very prominent judge, an extramarital affair for both of them. I was the result. My birth mother came up to Oakland; that's where I was born. The couple I consider my real parents had made arrangements to adopt a boy. They were told there was a girl they might be interested in. I was lying there, an instrument baby with a scar high on my forehead. My mom turned me over, and she said there were these blue eyes that looked up at her and smiled. I was blonde as well as blue-eyed, and that did it. They walked out with me.

I never had an abandonment issue. I was a special child, my parents told me, who was chosen by them. That's why I never grew up feeling different from anybody else. When I had my first child, I was interested in finding my birth mother, but only for medical reasons. My adopted mom said OK, but when my father walked in and heard us talking about it, I don't think I could have hurt him more. He took it as if I didn't love him.

In those days, you didn't tell anyone you were adopted, because there was a horrible stigma with being adopted. My best friends in high school didn't know it, even though my parents were much shorter than me. I reached my full height of five-foot-eight in the sixth grade. I was around nine when my parents finally told me I was adopted. The reason they did: we had a neighbor, a girl of eighteen, who found out she was adopted and went berserk. She moved away from her family, wanted nothing to do with them. She felt betrayal.

My daughters wanted to know about my birth parents. I said to them, "Why? I don't want to open up a can of worms." I have diabetes and kidney failure that could be traced to someone in the family. But why would they want to know if there is some other treacherous disease out there for me? If it happens, I told my girls, I'll face it then. They dropped the idea.

But I never had any doubt who my parents were: Ben and Norma Kramer. They married in Wisconsin at age nineteen, then drove across the country. My dad found work in different towns to pay for the trip. They reached Oakland and worked in the Works Progress Administration camp before the San Francisco-Oakland Bay Bridge was built. They adopted me in their late thirties. I was their only child.

My parents worked as a chef and waitress at the Belmont Dog Track, just below San Francisco. They lived in Belmont before my dad became a painting contractor. They moved to Redwood City and then to Menlo Park, where there was enough space to have horses. It didn't cost much to keep horses back then. How else could they have afforded it? After yet another move, to a home in Menlo with six acres, we kept three to twenty horses at various times. Both my parents rode horses. And horses became my life.

I rode my first pony at two and a half. I have recall of events from the time I was eighteen months old. And I've proven that my recall was true. I was a year and a half when my family took the train trip back to Wisconsin. A black porter on the train read me books. He had a white jacket and one of those little porter caps they had at the time. He was the most wonderful man. I was in his pocket, walking up and down the train car with him. And I could name the books to my parents, so they knew exactly that it happened.

I remember the train stopping in Montana or Wyoming and seeing my first snow. I had a white rabbit-fur jacket. I remember that vividly. I also remember my aunt's house in Wisconsin, hiding under the crib in one bedroom. When I was sixteen, we went back to Wisconsin. I walked into my aunt's house, went into this one room and said, "My crib was in this room." An older cousin said, "Oh, my God, she does remember."

I remember when Pearl Harbor happened. We were lying in front of this same radio console that you see in my living room. I was looking at the Sunday funnies while listening to them being read on the radio. That's when I heard the news about Pearl Harbor, that we were at war. I was three years old.

My dad was on mounted patrol, patrolling the beaches. And he was head air raid warden in the neighborhood. We had these black shades, and it was always our light that was shining in the neighborhood. That's because I had to lift the shade to see what everyone else was doing. I've always been very curious about life, and it started at a very young age.

My father didn't want me to be a helpless female. So I could change a tire on a car before girls ever did things like that. I knew how to put oil in a car. I could pull a horse trailer when I was sixteen. I showed horses, even "backyard" horses against the twenty-thousand-dollar horses at the annual Grand National at the Cow Palace in Daly City. I won my first trophy at the Menlo Circus Club when I was nine. I thought I was good. I was so cocky, my father took me off the horse and told me if I didn't learn to be a good winner as well as a good loser, I wouldn't show again.

I rode all through high school because you only stayed a Junior until you were eighteen. We'd gather in Woodside and ride all day long. There were trails all along Sandhill Road. We'd head down Walsh Road, say hi to Sue Samuels, then cut across all these beautiful estates. I showed horses all over the state of California. I did a lot of horse training as well.

I remember arguing with my father about his old-fashioned business ways. Everything by handshake. I took business classes at Menlo-Atherton and told dad he had to have contracts. I over-stepped my bounds in his mind. When I was sixteen, he lost his painting contractor's business. He had worked for two brothers who were building housing tracts. One brother told my dad to go buy all the painting materials he needed for this one project because he had the job. But the other brother hired somebody cheaper, and that cost my dad his business. If only he had a signed contract, he could have sued the two brothers. But you didn't do that back then; you were a man of honor.

That's when I learned the harsh reality that the world could be cruel, so you better take care of yourself. My father sold three of our six acres to pay his bills. Losing his business kind of crushed him. He had a very strong ego, probably pride more than ego. He became a handyman at Rickey's Hotel in Palo Alto. My mom had to go to work, waitressing at the Menlo Country Club for nineteen years. My father started drinking more than usual. In those days, you didn't say someone was an alcoholic. But looking back, he was an alcoholic.

In grammar school, I started hearing comments about my weight. People called me "Fatty" and said, "Are you going to eat again?" They said I was lazy, which irked me because I could do rings around these people. But it was only their insecurities showing. They had to point out differences in someone else so that they'd feel better about themselves. My absolute best friend was a horse I called Chickie. I could tell her anything. If I was crying, she'd get these big tears. I kid you not. Horses are non-judgmental.

My weight problem was really frustrating because I'm not a big sweets eater or a soda drinker, the things you associated with gaining weight. In fact, I don't eat much at all. It's never been an eating thing with me. I've always been very active, but it's just who I am. I don't think I have any metabolism issues. I'm a bear. I don't eat and my body stores.

Some M-A students were cliquish, some were snobby, some were as down to earth as you can get. Some of the older students were very nice. As a freshman, somehow I got my locker right in the middle of the senior block. I never got any hazing. I was "Sunshine" to all these senior guys because I was always smiling. I even got along with the pechukos, the rough guys.

A lot of money at M-A came from the Atherton side. But there also was the delusion of money. I swept driveways in Atherton to earn money. My father managed to survive when his business crashed, but two Atherton families I worked for crashed financially and had a difficult time recovering. Their kids didn't fit in anymore, couldn't find their spot. That was like a tragedy, another of life's lessons. Those you climbed over on your way to the top are the same people you're going to fall over coming back down. One of those displaced Atherton kids later had a bunch of problems, including drinking.

Our Class of 1956 was special in that we didn't stand out as a group in a bad way. We were a class that bonded. Everybody mixed well. I never felt we had one outstanding person in our class. We had a lot of outstanding persons. We had super-brainy people, and people who were really unique in other ways. Maybe they weren't going to make a million dollars, but everybody was pretty content within themselves.

My father was very strict throughout my high school years and even beyond. If I was one minute late for my curfew, he would ground me for a month. That meant I couldn't ride my horse, my car was taken away from me, and I couldn't go out on weekends. One time, I had to be home by midnight. Well, at 11:40 p.m., I had a flat tire. I had someone call my father to tell him I would be five minutes late because the tire had to be changed. I got home six minutes late, and he took my car away. No excuses.

So I was never going to be this spoiled kid. My father waited up for me every time I went out. He'd sit by the front door, and if I was in a car necking with some boy, he'd shine a spotlight on us when the clock hit midnight.

Then in my senior year, I became engaged to a person three years older, a skin diver who swept me off my feet. He gave me a diamond engagement ring on my birthday. I was primed to get married. I wasn't going to college. That's when I got into French kissing, which was new to us. We called it the "pearl divers club."

I was runnerup Miss Redwood City Rodeo right out of high school. I lost out to Bette Pervis of M-A. As part of the queen's court, I had a lot of activities. The guy I was engaged to was upset that I wasn't spending enough time with him. He pulled me out of this gathering at somebody's house and told me that since I was engaged to him, I would do whatever he said. I ran back into the house crying. My friends said, "I told you." So I took off the ring and threw it at him. He was possessive and I didn't want to be possessed.

Then at the wedding of Sally Seaver, an M-A classmate, I met this nice-looking man who was six-foot-five. We started dating, it became serious, and we got married. It was a fairy tale dream. He wanted to be a doctor. I was going to put him through school. But not all fairy tales have happy endings. It turned out to be an abusive situation. He hit me. Then he dropped out of school and wouldn't get a job. So I was supporting the two of us. He wound up pumping gas and hanging out with some low lifes. I found out later that they had been in jail and would beat up gay people for money.

Sexually, it was bad on our wedding night and it didn't get any better. Finally, all his anger came out. He slugged me in the arm as I was getting out of the car. Then he peeled off with my hand on the door handle, pulling me and spinning me around. I went to a pay phone, called my father and told him to come and get me. My dad was fabulous, absolutely fabulous. I said, "I can't get a divorce." And he said, "Oh, yes you can." A divorce meant a one-year waiting period before you could marry again. Just what I needed. I didn't want to make another mistake and marry the first bozo that asked me.

I moved back home, a terrible mistake. I still was under house rules, with curfews and the whole bit. A girl friend and I got this job with Remington Rand in San Francisco. We took the train to work. Coming home on the train one day, I passed out. I had gotten mononucleosis, which put me in bed for three months. I'm sure it was a reaction to the whole divorce thing.

I couldn't work for six months. My dad got me a job with the phone company in Palo Alto. Through a friend, I joined the Palo Alto Ski Club. That's how I met Dale. I got invited to a Halloween party at his house. I made him call me to invite me. I didn't ski, but it was a good social club, and Dale was a top-notch skier. So I decided to learn how to ski. Dale and I had six dates before I fell head over heels in love. He was cocky, but really sure of himself. He knew how to have a good time, but he had a serious side, and we both had a sense of humor. You hear the term soul mate. Well, I admit it, I skied to catch Dale, and after we got married, I never skied again.

I married a second time just before my twenty-second birthday. Dale's an inch and a half shorter than me, but that never bothered either one of us. It has been a fantastic marriage of forty-four years. We have two daughters, Kim and Lori, who are in their forties. They've had their own traumas, but they're doing OK. Both my childbirths were difficult, but I wanted two girls. I've really enjoyed being a mom. I'm not a baby person, but I love my girls. We're very close. And Dale, a wild playboy when I met him, has been an excellent father.

You've put my high school graduation picture right in front of me. I know what she looks like. My hair style's about the same, isn't it? She looks happy, looking forward to life as it came. I had a great feeling back then. I don't think I've changed much since then other than the added maturity.

I think that girl would be real happy about the choices she made and how she lived her life. There were mistakes made along the way, but that's how you develop into who you've become.

I don't have any regrets. They're a waste of time. It's all part of life. That's why I say if I drop dead right here, have a party. I want a kegger. I want people to celebrate my life, and to take the page from my life that says if there is something you really want to do, make it a priority.

13

The Abused Child

Joe Parodi always had a ready smile and a wisecrack in high school. His happy-go-lucky demeanor was a facade, hiding the abuse he endured at home: continual physical punishment and the denial of such children's needs as toys, teams, friends. As a father, he had to learn how to give to his own kids.

When I was at Menlo-Atherton, I'm sure nobody else at that school was living like I was living on a day-to-day basis. My parents had no idea what to do with kids. They thought strictness was the best policy for me and my two older brothers. We were never allowed to play. We never had toys. They didn't believe in that crap. I played with dirt and rocks. Those were my toys.

You know what I remember about Christmas? My next oldest brother, Alfred, didn't like beans. So he opened up his gift and it's a big bag of beans. My oldest brother, Richard, and I got a gift to share. We shook the box and it sounded like a ball. We hadn't had a ball before. Can you imagine the excitement? We should have known better. It was a turnip. Richard and I didn't like turnips. It's a wonder all of us boys didn't wind up in jail one day.

Abuse was a daily thing, you just didn't know when and how. I've been hit with about everything you could imagine. Pitch fork. Garden hoses. Tree branches. A razor strap was a piece of cake. My mom got me with a big brass sprinkler in the forehead. That opened me up pretty well; I still have the scar. My dad had these big brick boots. At the dinner table, he'd kick me and knock me clean out of my chair. I learned

Laughing the pain away

Joe Parodi

to wrap my legs around the chair, so when he kicked me, he'd kick the chair. I'm now an adult, but I'll catch myself at the dinner table, still wrapping my legs around the chair.

The way child abuse is looked at today, my parents would have been locked up long ago. My brothers and I knew that sometime during the day, we were going to get hit. It could be a slap in the face, a kick, getting whacked by tree switches. We took it in the morning, afternoon, whatever. We lived in daily fear, but we became very accustomed to it, and we adapted. We built up an immunity to it after a while.

My sense of humor obviously was a defense mechanism. God must have given it to me. How else was I going to survive that environment? Nobody at school knew what I was going through. I wasn't allowed to invite kids over to my house and I was forbidden from going to their houses. People invited me to parties, and I'd say, "Can't make it." I didn't want to tell them why. It's kind of embarrassing, saying, "My parents won't let me come." I didn't go to my first party until graduation night at M-A, at Carol Stickney's house.

My kind of humor was making analogies. Kids get a big kick out of that. I like to laugh, to show that life is good to you. At M-A, I would look for windows or opportunities to slide in a word. I knew what the other person would say before he'd say it, then I'd say something and knock their socks off. I was way ahead of them, including the teachers. There was this drafting teacher, a hard ass you couldn't get to smile if you gave him a thousand dollars. I said something one too many times and my counselor said, "Joe, I got to get you out of that class before the teacher kills you."

I didn't go to the Junior Prom or Senior Ball. I didn't have one date in high school. I thought Patsy Adams was a cute little girl. I wanted to take her out so bad, but my parents didn't believe in parties and dates either.

All three Parodi boys were excellent at sports, but our parents wouldn't allow us to compete. I could have run track at M-A; I could run like a scared ape. My mother drove by the school one day and saw my brothers playing ball. They weren't supposed to do that because it would screw up their shoes. She got them home at night and hit them over the head with their shoes. One Sunday, my parents tied my brothers to a post in the garage for the entire afternoon, while I went with the folks for a Sunday drive.

We had a very unusual childhood, to say the least. The way we were raised, we weren't supposed to make mistakes. My mother sent me to the grocery store to get some milk and a loaf of bread. I came back three hours later, beat to hell from playing with my buddies. My mother stepped out of a side door and got me with a broom handle. The bike went that way, I went this way, chewed to hell after I hit some gravel. And the milk and bread went in a third direction.

Like I said, nobody knew what I was going through. I'd ride my bike from East Palo Alto to M-A, then home again. I knew only two directions. As soon as I got home from school, there were chores to do. We had two acres of tall weeds to knock down. I still have the hoe I used back then. If my dad came home and saw roots on the stems, he'd take a switch off a tree he was pruning and whip the shit out of me. This went on for years. And, boy, those switches hurt. Richard was eleven years older than me, and Al eight years older than me. So after they left home, I was the last dog to kick.

We had this family doctor, a nice man who'd give us gifts. He brought me this tiny machine gun for Christmas. I'd never had a toy in my life, so could you imagine me with this tiny gun? I woke up on a Saturday morning and my toy was gone. Nobody's saying anything, and if you're smart enough, you don't ask. So I go outside and the kid next door is playing with my gun. My parents gave it away.

My father and mother were just old Dagos. Both of them were born in Italy. They got along with each other. They argued once in a while, but they took most of their frustrations out on us. Sometimes, they were clueless. When Richard was eighteen months old, he couldn't walk. That's because every time he cried, my mother would feed him. He was as big as a house.

We took our abuse for screwing up, only it never seemed to stop. One of my brothers was building a toy gun. He cut out a piece of wood from this brand-new sheet of four-foot-by-eight-foot plywood. Only he cut it out of the top corner, where my dad could see it. He came home, saw the plywood and, boy, he gave my brother a couple of whacks for cutting off a piece of wood and a couple more whacks for making a gun.

One summer, the blood dried on my back from getting hit with a switch, making it hard for me to peel off my T-shirt. If someone wanted to take me on at school, they'd better pack a lunch. For this was an opportunity to vent my frustrations on someone else for a change. This one guy always tried to pick a fight with me. One day, I had enough. Remember those five-minute periods between class? I unleashed and laid him out flat. He never bothered me again.

At M-A, I enjoyed taking craft classes. I never did any homework because I didn't have the time. I had chores at home, and I'd work in my dad's shop until ten or eleven at night. To pass my book reports, I would take an article clipped inside the book about the book, then I'd read the book's ending, and write a full-page book report. I was good at it. The only time I got caught, my teacher had actually read the book. He called me in and asked where I had found it. I told him on a shelf in the school library. He said, "Well, I've read it, and it's not at all like you wrote it." It was a gamble, but I cheated any way I could to get my grades going. Did it work? Well, I graduated, didn't I?

Until the day they died, my parents never apologized to the three of us for all their abuse. We realized later on they did the best they could. So we mellowed towards them. They didn't know all that much. My mom, Maria or Mary, was from Genoa, Italy. My dad, Martin, was from Savona in northwest Italy. He came to this country in 1921 with a cardboard suitcase, a bottle of cognac in one pocket, and a seven-millimeter Luger in the other pocket. Who knows why. America was a foreign land and he didn't know anything about it.

Dad was in the first World War, fighting for Italy against the Austrians. He got deathly ill and lost most of his hair, which he never regained. When the war was over, a military buddy invited him over for dinner and introduced dad to his sister, my future mother. My dad had a sister living in Mountain View. My dad's mother was there, too, after she had abandoned her family in Italy when my dad was nine. She was some animal that woman. I don't know what they fed her, but she had pretty sharp teeth.

After my dad came to America, he sent for his friend's sister and they were married here. My dad opened an auto mechanic's shop in Mountain View. He was doing pretty well in his new business when the Mafia showed up one day. This was Prohibition, the Mafia ran booze, and they wanted my dad to build a couple of tanks they could fit inside their car doors to haul the booze. Dad did quite a few cars; it was good money. Then they came in one day wanting to take him for a ride in their fancy Cadillacs. They took him to some vineyards on Route 152, then walked him out to the center of the field. He thought this was the end of him. But they opened up this wooden trap door and there was this big complex underneath where guys were making the hard stuff.

My dad belonged to a motorcycle group; I still have pictures of him with his Harley Davidson "hog." He was a tough guy who was made of steel himself. He was soldering a neck on a gas tank in his shop, but needed someone to hold the neck still. You can't ever get the fumes out of a gas tank, but the guy he had found to hold the neck did so with a stick, which slipped and hit the soldering iron, which caused a spark off the wood. The tank went off and a chunk of gas tank hit my dad across the chest and knocked him across the room and against a wall. A settling tank fell over in the process, breaking the neck off, and the whole shop was in a blaze.

My dad was in a hospital for a year. He was scorched with a couple of broken ribs. Doctors told my mom he wasn't going to make it. But he mended and stayed on in the auto mechanic business, working for different dealerships and opening up another shop in San Francisco for a while. The post office in Mountain View offered training classes in English, including speech and writing. My dad took them and became an American citizen. My mom never got her citizenship. She was one of those Dago housewives who stayed at home doing the cooking, the washing and the sewing.

By my senior year at M-A, I was in the Navy reserves. As soon as I graduated, I was good to go. I would be gone for three years. My parents didn't care. They probably were out of sticks. In August 1956, I left for Navy boot camp. I thought I had died and gone to heaven. Other kids were crying over how much they missed being away from home. Were they crazy? I thought this was great. I never had it this good.

I went home on leave in my Navy uniform and mom took a swing at me because I had gotten in one night after midnight. That didn't set well. I grabbed her wrist, got her up against a wall, and said, "Don't ever hit me again. You've done all the hitting you're going to do to me. This is your last shot." My dad never raised his hand to me again either. Once I was in uniform, that was it. The time had past.

With the Navy, I got to see the world. I wanted to be on a destroyer; the Navy gave me one. We did a lot of cruising—four-hundred and fifty-thousand sea miles in three years. We were stationed out of Long Beach, where I did a lot of plane-guarding. But I also spent a lot of time in the Formosa Straits, which has a lot of typhoons. I experienced nine of them.

I grew real fast. I'd put down a case of beer at night, then get up and walk away. We had wine at the dinner table when I was growing up, so I'd stuff away these Navy guys right and left. Women were all over the place and I had my share. I certainly sewed my oats. Melbourne, Australia, that was a helluva time down there. But I was scared to death to take a date to a restaurant. I'd think about it for days. I had no previous experience doing that. I'd probably been in one restaurant by the time I was eighteen.

Coming home on leave after a six-month tour, I was walking down the driveway of my parents' home, wearing my uniform, when Carol Barton saw my reflection in her bedroom mirror in the house next door. She was sixteen; I was four years older. My uncle Joe said, "She's a nice girl. If you marry her, I'll give you five bucks." I told my uncle, "For five bucks, I might do anything." Carol and I had a few dates, then after I came home on another leave, it started getting serious. I got out of the Navy in 1959. We were married in 1961.

Carol got a mixed bag of a husband. She has done a lot for me. Her childhood was directly the opposite of mine. She worked hard to tame me. One of the most difficult things for me was watching our three kids get away with things I would have gotten killed for as a kid. My daughter left her skates laying around. I told her, "I never had skates, but if I did, I'd never leave them laying around." The next day, the skates were still in the same place, so I threw them into the garbage. That's the last time I ever did that, and I still feel badly about it even now.

It was extremely hard for me becoming a parent. Our kids definitely had toys. They were able to go out for sports. We allowed them to date. They did whatever they wanted to do within reason. It was good to see, but I still had to make a serious adjustment on how to become a father. Carol adjusted my mentality. Kids are kids, but I couldn't remember anything but work as a kid.

As a father, it was a whole different way of thinking for me on what children are all about, and what they need, and how they're raised.

My son would say, "We're going to a Sadie Hawkins Dance." Carol would have to explain to me what that was, the boy and girl dressing alike for the dance. I had ignored all that stuff in high school. If I couldn't participate, I didn't want to hear about it. My kids know about my childhood. I think their reaction is if I screw up, they know where it's coming from. They understand their dad didn't have the best examples in the world, so we'll have to roll over on that one. I've raised my hand to them once in a while, but just spankings. My grandkids got to sit in a corner. That worked. Carol reads our kids very well and understands them. I've learned a lot from her.

In the Navy, I had considerable experience in electronics. After getting out, my first job, though, was at an employment agency, working with these secretarial women, trying to get them jobs. A lot of them had history degrees, but what were they going to do with those back then? They didn't want to teach, so they became secretaries, when they were really looking for their "Mrs." degrees. Well, I hadn't placed anyone in six months. Then this wonderful woman, Freda Daniels, invited me down to see her company. I did, but I didn't know that she was interviewing me. A couple days later, she called and said there was an opening as a technician. My first break.

I spent the next three years as a senior tech, building big monster transmitters for the military. Then I moved up to supervisor. In 1963, with Vietnam about to break, I got a call from someone at Applied Technology, which was developing the radar homing and warning systems for the Air Force. I needed a new challenge, so I became a shift supervisor at Applied Technology, building "black boxes" so we could save these pilots who were falling out of the sky. We started up the "Wild Weasel" program, whose purpose was to pick up missile sites and destroy them.

After eighteen months with that company back in Lincoln, Nebraska, I came back to California and went to work for International Video in Sunnyvale. Then I went through a whole slew of companies in Silicon Valley. Outside of Hewlett-Packard, none of them knew how to treat employees. I'm not bragging, but I always had people who wanted to work for me, partly because of my humor. I worked at Amdahl for ten years. As a production operations manager, I had three-hundred and seventy-five people working for me over three shifts. It was a good sharing relationship. When it was time to get tough, or to draw the line, I had no problem doing that.

I also used humor to keep things moving along. Humor depends on the individual; you really have to know your folks. I'd use small accusations. I'd accuse somebody of something to spark them. When they'd come back at you, you'd succeeded, you'd won their hearts. Because if they don't come back at you, then you've got a problem. You've got to read your people. I was never trained for it, but I was good at it.

I got laid off by Amdahl in 1990. We were downsized big time; they got rid of seven hundred personnel. Silicon Valley was in the toilet by 1990. I knew body work, so I opened up Old World Body Shop in Redwood City. I made the same move in 1973 when I needed a break from electronics. Second time around, I was with the auto shop for seven years. Then I had a heart problem. I had two stents inserted in 1997. They haven't rusted out, so I guess I can keep working. I had pneumonia really bad after that; I've had pneumonia four, five times. I'm not sure why. But I've been doing good the last couple of years.

In 1998, I was back in electronics, in field calibrations, for three years.

Then I got a call from Menlo Park Presbyterian Church, which needed a director of security. I had spent time in the Atherton Police Department reserves. That church job ran three years, then came another lay-off. Carol and I raised two grandchildren for a couple of years until our daughter could get through some personal issues. So I took on odd jobs, like delivering flowers, before landing my current job as engineer at the Hyatt Hotel in Burlingame.

I'm the only one left from my first family. My parents are gone. Both my brothers passed away in their high fifties.

What was I thinking when I took my M-A graduation picture? That I could hardly wait to get the hell out of town, to get out of Dodge, because I had had just about enough of Dodge. The Navy was the vehicle that was going to do that for me. I wanted to go ride the high seas, and the Navy took me away.

Looking at that same kid now, and seeing how his life has turned out, I guess he would say he's taken his fair share of hits, had his ups and downs. But he dealt with them the best he could, and he still was successful, able to raise a wonderful family together with my wonderful wife in the process.

★ 14 ★

The Activist

Susan Samuels Drake had an affluent childhood before joining her minister husband in California's migratory fields, assisting Cesar Chavez in his quest to unionize farm workers. Her marriage failed, she wrote a book about Chavez and herself, and then found her true calling as an activist.

I believe Cesar Chavez was one of the great American heroes. I don't know why his life's work wasn't included in the end-of-the-century news stories and television documentaries, the same way Dr. Martin Luther King, Jr.'s life was reviewed. Both men championed change by using nonviolent tools such as boycotts, sit-ins—Cesar had pray-ins—and voter registration. Cesar not only organized the successful United Farm Workers, AFL-CIO, he remained a continuing role model in his persistence for social justice for millions of people in our society, especially Latinos, even posthumously.

I knew Cesar for thirty-one years, from the time (1962) that my husband, Jim, first took his ministry into the fields to help California's farm workers. Cesar trained Jim to organize people to work together in solving such common problems as getting safe housing and improved water service. In little towns up and down the San Joaquin Valley, they talked about how to improve conditions in the fields. Later on, I became Cesar's personal secretary. My book, "Fields of Courage," describes what it was like for this girl from wealthy Atherton to live among the poor people who feed us.

Hail, Cesar!

Susan Samuels

. I must admit, it took me a while to see Cesar as a powerful leader. He appeared very quiet at first. When I attended the Friday night meetings in Delano, where the movement's leadership met with the grape strikers, I saw Cesar's magnetic, persuasive charm. He was very genuine, though earnest might be a more descriptive word. He wasn't tall—about five-foot-five—and he didn't have what I would call movie-star classic handsomeness. He had this kindness in his face that made him very attractive. When you met him, he smiled, listened, really focused on you. He made you feel special; his handshake was sincere. He wasn't a B.S. kind of person. His magnificent charisma, though, didn't come across to me until his first food fast in 1966.

I grew to love him; he was so much like my father. It was really hard for me when Cesar lapsed into small-mindedness, or other times when he was very critical. I wanted him to stay perfect and positive, but he was human. Cesar introduced me to astrology. That's when I learned he and my father were Aries, a sign that is charming, yet can be cruel in its selfishness. I'm the same astrological sign, Cancer, as Cesar's mother. So in the big picture, maybe we were meant to know each other, to work out some parental thing. Because I had parental issues when I was a girl.

Growing up in Palo Alto and Atherton, I thought everyone lived in homes like mine in the Fifties, only perhaps in happier homes. We were very sheltered, though. We didn't have crime. My father was financially responsible for the family. Much of my victim-hood was self-imposed, thinking I wasn't good enough or pretty enough. My father drank pretty heavily, but I didn't know how alcoholism affected some friends' families. The only scandal I remember was when some fathers got busted at the Menlo Park train station for watching porno flicks, although I don't think anyone went to jail.

Where I really thought our home was different from other homes: My parents' relationship lacked respect. Their unhappy marriage shaped my confused impression of what love within a marriage is like. Mom told me it was understood that men would have affairs. I read a lot about Henry VIII and his women. I thought dad was like Henry VIII. The drama of his affairs, even his sneaking around, fascinated me. The dilemma: Ozzie and Harriet vs. Henry VIII. I thought about sex a lot in high school, and yet I didn't experience any deep-down hormonal urge until college.

I was just boy-crazy at Menlo-Atherton. By then, dad was running his law firm, and I stopped being daddy's little darling. He had less time for fun things with me. I argued with him more, and I replaced his male attention by getting crushes on boys and even my teachers.

My father, David Lilienthal Samuels, grew up in San Francisco in what was known as the "Jewish ghetto," though he wasn't raised in that faith. He flunked out of Stanford summer school because it interfered with his social life. At least, that's the family myth. He got into Hastings Law School on the promise of maintaining a high grade average. In 1946, he opened his solo law practice in Palo Alto, where he had our first home built. His firm became one of the most successful in town, which is true even to this day, although the name of the firm has since changed. Dad's success made it possible for him to buy property on Walsh Road in Atherton. He had our next home built there, which put me in Menlo-Atherton's school district.

My mother, Katharine Marie Bireley, was a cousin of the man who started the Bireley's soft drink company. However, the three Samuels children weren't allowed to drink carbonated drinks except at parties. Mom was an art student at Mills College when she met my dad at a San Francisco speak-easy. She was shy, but my father made her entertain a lot. "To maintain his clientele," she said. We had Hewlett and Packard—Bill Hewlett and David Packard—over for dinner. Russell Varian, too. Mom and dad were gracious hosts, which rubbed off on me. I, too, enjoy having parties in my home. Mom's creative outlet was painting watercolors. Dozens of her well-done art pieces were stashed in the rafters of our house. They remained unseen by anyone but her teacher and fellow classmates until after she had died.

The Samuels weren't considered high society, but I grew up in a fishbowl. Mom knew that my friend, Jacqueline Cook, and I walked around Menlo Park on Sundays in between church and Sunday school. She would tell us, "You better behave because people know whose daughter you are."

My dad was tolerant racially, probably because of his Jewish background. Mom kept any prejudices to herself, but she wouldn't let me wear purple because it was "colored people's color." I turned fourteen and started getting a clothing allowance. The first thing I bought: A purple dress. Mom wanted this sweet little girl. I know how to do that, but it's not comfortable. I can't help swearing. My nails look pretty good right now, but they usually have dirt under them, and the nails are all different sizes.

I was raised with a prejudice for lazy ignorance and acting stupid. My two younger brothers, Bob and Perry, and I were criticized for what we didn't do and for the poor choices we made in our parents' eyes. The three of us longed for more praise for the good we felt we did.

Respect for money was important in our home. My parents could have afforded to be extravagant, but they rarely let themselves spend on luxuries. A new car was about it. I learned to be careful with money, which was a good thing because I never earned much working with the farm workers and even beyond. Maybe that's why I shop at clothing consignment stores. I love clothes the way my label-conscious mom did, but I refuse to pay the going price for new things. The jacket I'm wearing right now belonged to my dad. I wasn't about to send a Harris tweed to Goodwill, not when it fits me so perfectly.

I had a love-hate relationship with my father. It lasted for decades, and all because he chiseled away at my self-esteem. But I'm glad today I'm more like him than my mom. Mom didn't speak up enough, didn't let herself blossom fully. When my parents split up for three months, just before I went to college, dad moved out. But he kept his horse on our property. He would come over once a week for a horseback ride after dropping off his clothes at the house. Mom would have his clothes washed, dried and ironed by the time he came back from his ride. I thought that was what marriage vows meant, that no matter what your husband did, you accepted it.

At M-A, I met Mr. Douglas Murray. He's Doug now. We bonded

instantly and flirted constantly. Thank God he never made any moves on me; I might have given in. However, I was such a prude, I probably would have avoided being seduced. He'd tease me when I wore my hot pink dress. Then he brought his wife, Barbara, to a school dance, and all of us saw how happy they were together. Even a more devious girl probably wouldn't have interfered there.

Mr. Murray believed in my writing ability. And he cared about my opinions, unlike my father who used to tell me, "Nobody wants to hear what you have to say." Mr. Murray got me a two-year job at the Palo Alto Times as a weekly columnist reporting on M-A activities. He appointed Jerry Juhl as editor of the "Bear Tracks," M-A's weekly newspaper, and appointed me managing editor our senior year. I felt Jerry got the job because he was a boy. That really hurt me. But Jerry made me feel that I was the co-editor. I still value Jerry as a friend. Doug, too.

It took me a long time to think of myself as attractive to boys. Mom kept telling me I was pretty. With freckles and glasses, I thought she was just saying that because I was homely and also because she thought nobody else would say I was pretty. It wasn't until years later that I looked at my early pictures and saw that while I wasn't pretty, I was cute. Now when the late-blossomers from our class, a small group of female friends, get together for periodic reunions, I see how we've bloomed into women who enjoy being kid-like, even more so than during our teenage days. There is grace and fun in our faces, and we're taking good care of ourselves. Good for us.

At Occidental College, I plowed into being a Psychology major. But my grades dropped, a lot of C's after only one C in high school. My writing faded except for lots of letter-writing to friends and family. Jim Drake and I met about the time I let passion surface a little more. He was a year older, tall, good looking and shy. Because he was pretty quiet, except when he discussed philosophy with other guys in our group, I made him up in my mind as the perfect father and the attentive husband, like Harriet's Ozzie. Midway through my sophomore year, we began dating. By spring, we began petting. I thought we should marry because I wanted to have all-out sex, and marriage was the only way we could do that.

That's how I believed, and Jim felt the same way. I had bought into that Fifties bit about "finding your other better half." The flip side was that I felt I was nothing without Jim.

We married at the end of my junior year, June 21, 1959, in the Menlo Park Presbyterian Church. I dropped out of college thinking I would finish one day. However, a degree hasn't ever been important to me, given my wife-mother goal. Only after I married did I discover that Jim was fantastic in a room of twenty to two-thousand people, but you put him in a room with one woman and he had a rough time dealing with anything but practicalities. There were problems right away. I can easily over-focus on relating, while Jim preferred to act rather than to analyze such things. The more I expressed dissatisfaction, the more he didn't want to talk about it.

In the bedroom, problems arose, too. I thought married people made love every night. All my saved-up preoccupation with sex embarrassed Jim. We made love once a week. In between Saturday nights, I was "over-sexed and underprivileged" as the saying goes. Depression dogged me off and on, and not only for sexual reasons. I wanted to believe I could be a good wife, and yet I failed at imitating my mother's genteel, acquiescent behavior.

But in spite of the disappointment of our marriage, I am grateful that Jim took me into the lives of farm workers. Any hesitation I may have had about living among the most impoverished segment of America's population dissolved immediately. I liked being with Mexican, Mexican-American, and Afro-American women in Goshen, California, a fly speck along Highway 99 near Visalia. Some of the local high school kids came to our house after school for tutoring. That way, I partnered with Jim, who was organizing the community toward building a recreation center. I was proud to be the wife of such a highly respected man.

However, being on my own more often with two little boys, I began looking for male attention. I not proud of this, but it was a fact. One night at somebody's house, I had a little too much wine—maybe a full glass instead of my usual sip or two—and started gyrating to Jose Feliciano's "Light My Fire." Jim was mortified. He hadn't seen this side of me. I hadn't seen it either. I was ashamed afterward, having added sexy dancing to the list of things I did wrong in the marriage. And Jim did little to correct my impression that our troubles were all my fault.

In 1968, we moved to Delano, the heart of the labor union. I fell for a Franciscan brother by the name of Andres. We became very close. He was handsome. Jim had put on lots of weight. Andres sang to me and played his guitar. He took me rowing. He also was committed to serving the farm workers' movement, but he wasn't always busy like Jim was somewhere else. Andres and I ran a teen club together. Several months after we met, we finally admitted our mutual attraction. We parted with a hug, nothing more than that, not even a kiss. He left the brotherhood shortly afterward and married somebody else.

Jim knew of my feelings for Andres. I don't think he ever trusted me again. I began commiserating with a male co-worker whose marriage also was rocky. He said, "You're on the verge of having an affair. It might as well be with someone who loves you. Me."

Right at this time, Cesar was invited to the centenary celebration of Mahatma Gandhi's birthday in New Delhi, India. Cesar's health wouldn't permit his going, so he asked Jim to go in his place. The Migrant Ministry found a ticket for me to go along. I dislike traveling, but I went only because I was afraid that if I stayed home, I'd go to bed with this co-worker.

India was a fantastic experience. I led a march on the American Embassy there to inform President Nixon that this group of seventy-five marchers from the Gandhi Peace Institute's seminar on non-violence wanted the United States out of Vietnam. Jim was nervous about my setting this up. But I pulled it off, and it's the thing I'm most proud of, politically, in my life.

Jim and I didn't get along well most of that trip. The day we returned to Delano, I called the co-worker and we began many sneaky nights of romance while Jim was away. Neither of us would leave our spouses. Sometimes my lover reminded me of my father with his impatience. Still, I treasure that experience for several reasons: The man loved me without question, he helped me explore love-making, and he made me feel pretty.

If I could fast-forward through twenty years of post-divorce relationships until 1993, these learning experiences, all together, didn't make a pretty sight. Then in the local newspaper, Andres' ex-wife read an article I wrote about Cesar when he died on April 23rd of that year. She phoned to talk about our years working with what was now the United Farm Workers. Andres was by this time a former Franciscan. I asked her to tell Andres that I'd like to see him again.

He called and we set a date to get together. He arrived holding a yellow rose and looking like a million dollars. We were so polite getting reacquainted. Secretly, I wrote poem after romantic poem about him. He wanted an athletic woman; that isn't me. By 1995, after taking walks and going to occasional movies together, I said to him, "I tell my friends that you're my anchor." And this usually shy man said, "I'd rather be your fireworks."

Twenty-seven years after we first fell in love, our fireworks show would beat out any Fourth of July brilliance. All those disappointing years of running around, looking for something that lust alone doesn't provide, were over with. Then, sadly, after nearly ten years of making each other happy, and unhappy, we parted after realizing a life-partnership would be too constraining for both of us. Friends again.

My ideal relationships, friends or lovers, are partnerships where both take the initiative to plan work and play. I like people who express their individuality passionately in ways that unfurl who they are in their core. Could be writing, painting, stonework, something creative. These people aren't easy to live with, but I enjoy them a lot. Most of all, I want Word People in my life, people who play with words, phrases, puns and quotes—and ideas and curiosity. It's clear that I'm not ready to partner-up....yet! I have more time to devote to my writing, and to political causes.

And to think of Cesar Chavez' influence on my life.

After eleven years of working with the farm workers' movement, and nearly three years as his secretary, Cesar fired me in 1973. I completely misjudged how he dealt with opinions different from his own. He sometimes saw them as criticism and disloyalty. I informed him in a letter, so that I would sound logical and level-headed, that I thought he was taking the union down the wrong path with strategy he was using. Other people high up in the movement agreed with me, but I had hurt Cesar with what he perceived as betrayal. He then rehired me, but only for a month so I could help put together the union's first convention. However, by his firing me, I also felt betrayed. It was only my loyalty to the workers that led me to redirect Cesar. Thirty years later, a co-worker hauled out my letter to Cesar and put it on the list-serve of former UFW staff, to show others that I was right after all.

A couple of years after being fired, I went back to Delano for the dedication of a building on the movement's land. The event hadn't begun when I saw Cesar standing alone on the platform. I went up to him and yelled above the noisy crowd, "Can't we be friends?" He put his arms around me and held me tight. He couldn't say the words, "I'm sorry." But if you didn't insist on rehashing or verbally resolving the situation, he could be a steadfast friend.

And we did become friends. I moved back to my birthplace, Palo Alto, to raise my two sons, Matt and Tom, along with the help of my parents and brothers. I went to work for Palo Alto Co-Op Markets as the management team's secretary. Co-Op, by the way, supported the farm workers strongly. Cesar would come to the San Francisco Bay Area, always traveling with a bodyguard after having a threat made on his life. The two sometimes stayed at my home. There I got to see Cesar more as an individual than as a famous leader.

He'd arrive late usually. I'd go to bed after a few minutes of catching up, and he'd stay up to watch Johnny Carson, who was his favorite. In the morning, we'd have breakfast together. I nearly dropped dead that first morning when this famous leader, who had his face on the cover of Time Magazine, was doing the breakfast dishes. Now when I buy a postage stamp with his face on it, I have to pinch myself—this was the man who washed my dishes.

My drug of choice is writing, and I've always had a creative mind. When I was a young girl, I wanted to write Queen Elizabeth after her wedding and invite her to come to Palo Alto, so we could have a parade and I could wave to her. My mother told me we didn't have her address, and she likely wouldn't come. I was so disappointed. In the second grade, I got a one-hundred score on my first report, about bees. That planted the writing seed, which I carried through high school and continued to explore into adulthood. I've written poems, short stories, memoirs, features and interviews, mostly in newspapers and magazines in the Santa Cruz area where I now live. My interview with Dolores Huerta, co-founder of the United Farm Workers, was assigned by two national magazines: "The Progressive" and "El Andar."

The book I wrote on Cesar—the full title is "Fields of Courage: Remembering Cesar Chavez & The People Whose Labor Feeds Us"—has been well-received and continues to sell. I've heard one comment, third-hand, from one of Cesar's in-laws that I was "too honest." In the book, I showed Cesar three-dimensionally, his warts as well as his leadership. I was just as up front about my shadowy side, showing myself pushing Cesar's buttons. There were plenty of times, I admit, when I could be annoying and exasperating. The best compliment about the book came from a guy who works to get kids out of gangs. He said it was the one book that shows Cesar as fully human, a realistic person whom a gang member could learn to be like.

After I left the union, I continued some social justice activism, mostly for the farm workers' benefit: Fund-raisings, picket lines, letter-writing to legislators. More recently, it is the farm-worker experience that pushes me to fight for causes—causes that shape how I spend my money and time. I continue to make occasional public appearances to rally support for changes in the farm workers' working and living conditions.

There is a big hurt inside of me. Maybe it's betrayal. I thought America was the perfect nation, especially during President Eisenhower's years. Of course, it has been imperfect for a long time; it's just that my awareness has improved. In June 2004, the Praxis Peace Institute political seminar I attended was so moving that I decided to work four hours a week to get Democrats elected. I've kept that commitment. It's now 2005, and for the 2006 election, I want to have a better understanding of the various political points of view, in hopes of somehow working together for common interests: Health care, education, Social Security, the environment.

How will this country survive if we're not educating people to be intelligent and cooperative about managing challenges. I believe if Americans stay alert and pressure Congress to act on behalf of what we want, and not what mega-corporations or fringe groups dictate, there will be change. We can't blame political parties or our presidents. We need to look at our own apathy. I believe we can recoup and maintain Constitutional freedoms, and make America a place that respects all of its citizens.

My life-long struggle to find self-respect seems to be over. I'm really enjoying my senior citizen years. I like setting my own agenda. I feel more generosity of spirit not being in a man-woman relationship.

Jim died of cancer in 2001. There were five memorials around the country celebrating his life, showing the kind of impact he had in the ministry. We divorced in 1973, and he married several times after that. I haven't remarried. Jim wasn't good at marriage, but he was a wonderful man and a wonderful father.

What do I see in my M-A graduation picture? Someone hopeful. I don't see worry. She looks as if she has a sense of being pretty now that her hair is peroxided. A lot of people knew who I was, teachers and students alike, and they depended on me. It took a long time to appreciate that honor.

If that girl was looking at me now, she'd think that all her childhood dreams did come true: Wife and mother, writer, and the romantic, exciting life of Henry VIII's mistresses. Thankfully, I only figuratively lost my head.

That same girl wouldn't be surprised that I am still interested in organizing things, for fun or for political purposes. I think she'd be proud of me, that I have grown from trying to be a "Yes, dear" woman to making my own way. She'd say, "Right on."

★15★

The Cool Dude

Dan Tapson was an anomaly in the 1950s, a child from a broken home. That difficult upbringing led to his independence, and his swagger. "Curly Dan" was among the brightest students in the Class of 1956, always with an eye on the ladies. Then this cool-breeze kid set the world of radio on fire.

I do believe I am a composite of coolness and swagger. This means easy going, poised, smooth, an air of self-assuredness. And maybe I'm a bit cocky.

This aura was a necessary part of my makeup. Otherwise, I might not have achieved the success I've enjoyed. A lot of only children, like myself, become somewhat introverted. But I turned out just the opposite. In business, I was often in high-profile positions and situations. There were times when I caused heads to turn in bars and restaurants. But while rock 'n' roll was part of my life, I never felt the need to be a rock star.

Coming from a broken home—my parents divorced when I was in junior high school—I developed that swagger because I had become independent so early in life. I had done things most kids at Menlo-Atherton never did. They didn't have to set pins in a bowling alley. They didn't have a paper route at 5:30 in the morning. These experiences and others caused me to grow up a little faster, and I didn't feel any less of a person because of them. In fact, they taught me responsibility and self-confidence at a very young age.

I realize my attitude was, very possibly, a defense mechanism for not

Curly Dan, ladies man

Dan Tapson

having a father around. My mother and I lived in an apartment in Menlo Park. All of my friends lived in homes. Let's face it, Menlo Park and Atherton were pretty affluent areas. A lot of kids had their own cars by the time they were sixteen. I walked to school.

As for coolness, at that age you're still trying to impress. I wasn't totally mature. I did a lot of immature things in my growing-up days. Actually, this lasted a little bit past high school. But I felt good about myself; that's key. Maybe I thought I was cooler than the next guy. I had good grades. I was chosen for Boys State. I was on the Student Council. I was on the basketball team. I was in the social scene. I had no problem getting dates. I went out with the boys and found a six-pack of beer. I ran for senior class president and lost to Bill Brodie. But life was good.

And, to think, I didn't live in my first house until I had become a husband and father. My parents lived in a small, one-bedroom apartment in San Francisco, 2145 Larkin Street, before the move to Menlo Park. There were two beds in the bedroom, and a Murphy bed in the living room. I slept on the Murphy bed except on those evenings when my father drank too much. Then he would sleep in the Murphy bed. He drank a lot, and spent a large percentage of his paychecks in a bar, so that very little of it came home. During World War II, we'd use coupons to get food. At a young age, I learned to be frugal.

My father was an outgoing, heavy-drinking, cigarette-smoking Catholic Democrat with a good sense of humor. My mother was a very frugal, tee-totaling Christian Scientist Republican who was a bit introverted. Put those two together and you're going to have some sort of conflict. As best as I can piece together, my mother's mother set them up and they got married. I believe I was born shortly thereafter. I'm not sure if my mother was pregnant when they got married. I was never privy to the marriage certificate. Gloria was pregnant when we got married, but that turned out to be very positive.

Daniel Victor Tapson Jr., that's me. My dad, who went by Danny, was a semi-professional baseball player, a third baseman who was very fast, turning doubles into triples. He went to spring training with the Detroit Tigers and New York Giants, but never got past minor-league ball. Unfortunately, chasing a pop foul, he crashed into a fence and severely injured a vertebrae in his back. That ruined his playing career, but he did become the youngest manager in organized ball with the Wheeling, West Virginia, Stogies before I was born.

My mom, Winona Van Kuren, was a telephone operator who grew up in Kankakee, Illinois. She met my father in the Chicago area. I was born in Chicago. A year later, we took a train to San Francisco, where my father was born and raised. His father, my grandfather, and my dad's brother still lived there, Because of my father's broken back, arthritis set in and he was physically challenged. He couldn't lift his head up too high or turn from side to side; thus he couldn't get a driver's license. He was unemployed for a while. My mom wanted to be a stay-at-home mother, devoting quality time to my upbringing. As a result, funds often were low. I had to take on some responsibility at an early age. We were late with the rent check almost every month. My parents would send me down to the landlord's apartment with the check figuring a kid wouldn't get eviction threats.

My father got work at Hastings Clothing Store in downtown San Francisco. He remained with them thirty years, selling suits and sport coats. It was difficult for him because he was so hunched over and in a lot of pain. We didn't have a car so he took public transportation to work. He later became a store manager, with a big raise. He told me he now made a thousand dollars a month. That became my goal, a thousand dollars a month. But my dad's thousand didn't go very far, being consumed by the things I mentioned earlier.

The summer of 1952 was a growing-up period. I was 13 and going into the ninth grade at Marina Junior High. My parents and I took a bus to the Marin Town and Country Club in Fairfax for the weekend. On Saturday night, there was a dance band. While this was an adult affair, I was eager to see if I actually could dance without my peers watching. There was one teenage girl in attendance, so there wasn't much choice. I found out later that she had her learners permit to drive, so she was at least fifteen and a half years old. We struggled through a couple of dances and then sat down to talk for a bit.

Soon afterwards, her parents said she had to leave. She said to me, "Let's meet at the pool tomorrow." We did that and spent the day together. The local movie theater was located on the main street in town, and could be accessed on foot via a trail around a huge picnic area, a baseball field and a wooded area. We had parental approval to attend the movie that evening. As we walked to the trail, it dawned on me that this was a date. I had been to birthday parties where there were girls. I went to a couple of Saturday afternoon matinees with girls. But this was my first unchaperoned date.

We sat in the back row of the theater. Before long, kissing was the primary activity as opposed to movie-watching. She whispered, "Have you ever gone all the way before?" My bold reply was, "Yeah, sure." She said, "Let's go." We were out the door and on the trail. She led me into the wooden area where in a small clearing, I lost my virginity. Hers had been previously lost. As we walked in the moonlight past the baseball field, I laughed to myself as I thought of the phrases I heard older boys use about getting to first base, etc., on dates. I wanted to go step on home plate.

We arrived at her cabin right on curfew time. That night, as I lay in bed, I felt a sense of relief. It was over. There was no more mystery about sex. I was anxious to try it again, which I soon learned would be no easy task. But there also was an empty feeling. Even as this young age, I thought at some level there must be more emotion involved with this activity other than hormonal release. My family caught the bus home early the next morning. I knew I would never see her again.

In retrospect, there probably was some lasting impact to having this kind of experience at this age and in this manner. Casual sex could have its place in my life with no hangups or guilt trips. On the other hand, I learned there was more to sex, and it encouraged me to make the act of true love-making a much more meaningful experience. This was ful-filled in my marriage to Gloria years later.

Back when I was very young, parents might have stayed together for "the kid's sake." In retrospect, my attitude was "Don't do this for me, folks." One day, my mother said, "I can't live like this much longer." I had been prepared for that day a long time, so the divorce wasn't all that traumatic. In many respects, it was a relief. My mom started doing phone solicitation work. She set up bowling lessons, which is how I got that job setting pins manually. It was the most physically exhausting work I have ever done. Those pins were heavy and I had to jump up on a railing to keep from getting hit by the rolling ball, while working two lanes at a time.

My mom saved up enough money to get a used car. She got her driver's license and then sold encyclopedias door to door. I'd go with her and sit in the car. She sold enough to get by, but she was very devoted to looking out for what was best for me. She decided it was time to move. I don't know how we ended up in Menlo Park, but Menlo-Atherton had just opened up and it was a good school. We moved into an apartment on Laurel Street. People might say I came from the wrong side of the tracks, and I'd say, no, I'm right on the tracks. You see, the railroad tracks for Southern Pacific were just on the other side of our back fence.

Starting at M-A as a sophomore, it took me about a semester to assimilate. Grades became important because they would determine where I would go to college. Once again, school came easy. I did a lot of partying at M-A, as did the people I knew. Though my father missed on alimony payments and child support all the time, I was content. The divorce was behind me and there were no more arguments. And Menlo Park was a very nice area to live in. I had my swagger and self-confidence. If you liked me, we could be friends. If you didn't like me, I could go another way. I tried to avoid cliques.

After my junior year, I was selected to Boys State in Sacramento, where we learned how government works. I went with two classmates, Jim Reinhardt and some guy we called "Lips," who didn't graduate with us. I was elected "sheriff" in the "county" in which we "lived." I felt sure I was the coolest guy there. I applied to Stanford and was accepted. But I didn't get the scholarship I applied for, and that was the only way I could attend there. My mom and I didn't have a savings account, even though I worked every summer vacation. A California state school was the only option for me in spite of graduating number five in the class of '56. I did receive a Peninsula Volunteers scholarship, a true blessing as it covered many of my expenses, and not just books and tuition. I wasn't at all disappointed to go to San Jose State. My goal was college, so San Jose State was where it was going to be. And as a bonus for my hard work, there were pretty girls and lots of parties.

That first semester, I commuted from home. The second semester, I got an apartment in San Jose with some other guys and joined the SAE fraternity. I made a lot of friends there that I stay in touch with even today. School was no problem, other than finding a major. I was encouraged by counselors to pursue engineering. But after three and a half years of exploring various types of the engineering curriculum, I came to the conclusion I didn't want to be an engineer. I changed my major to industrial technology. This was perfect as I used all my technical credits from engineering and then took a year of business courses. I was liberated from the slide rule and exposed to what made corporations tick. I liked that.

My philosophy was "work hard, play hard." If I got my school stuff done first, then it was time to play hard. I had some crazy times at San Jose State, even while working. Scholarship or not, my appetite for fun required additional funding. So I was a dishwasher. I worked at a cannery. I was a clothing salesman at Hastings in San Jose; my father got me that job. I mowed lawns. Worked as a lifeguard, sold screen doors and patio enclosures door to door, worked in a machine shop. But there still was time to party. I graduated in four and a half years. I had that important piece of paper, a Bachelor of Science degree, the first step in my goal to make a thousand dollars a month.

The military was an obligation I wanted to resolve as efficiently as possible. I enlisted in the United States Army Reserves; this meant six months of active duty followed by five and a half years of monthly reserve meetings and weekly summer camps. I was stationed at Fort Ord in Monterey. After my basic training, along came the Berlin crisis. My ordinance supply unit was activated, and my duty was extended for almost another year. I was not happy with this turn of events. I became the company clerk, an envious position compared to others in a field supply unit. When it came time to be released from active duty, my job was to type up orders for the men in my unit. I personally took myself out of the reserves completely, then put myself into a control group with no meetings or any possibility of future active duty.

By then, my father had a second family. Shortly after my parents divorced, or maybe during the divorce, he met another woman. They got married and had three children. I only saw my father once or twice a year, and now with another family, it made things awkward. I had to consider my mother's feelings. My father continued his smoking habit until he died from emphysema at the age of sixty-eight. By then, he had divorced again.

Long after I left the nest, my mother remarried a retired Navy man who had a gambling habit. He was a very generous man when winning. When he lost, he became nasty and mentally abusive. He had told my mom she wouldn't ever have to worry about money after he died, because of his Navy pension. When he died of a heart attack, we found out my mom could not collect on his Navy pension. So she lived for many years on minimal assets. We looked after her until her early eighties. Near the end, we placed her in a nursing home. She lived about another year before passing away.

After the military, I had to go to work. My goal, remember, was to make a thousand dollars a month. I got a job at a San Jose corporation that made tanks. It was a boring six months, so I made a life change. A couple of friends had gone to Hawaii to be beach bums. I decided to join them. In order to accomplish this, I became "homeless." I gave up my apartment and put my worldly possessions in my car. To save money, I'd show up at various friends' places to spend the night and occasionally enjoy a nice meal. Some girl friends were involved, too, but every paycheck went into my pocket. I was "homeless" eight to ten weeks, but had enough money for a one-way boat ticket to Hawaii. At the sending-off party at the dock in San Francisco, several buddies came to see me off. So did three, four girl friends. I had to do a little finessing.

My friends in Oahu lived in a hut right out of "Animal House" just a block from Waikiki Beach. There were sleeping bags on the floor and a couple of chairs around. My friends had no money, no jobs, no transportation. They told me about this old taxi cab with a jumper seat for sale down the street. I said if it will make it to and from the liquor store to get a case of beer, I'll buy it. It did, and it cost me one hundred dollars. We'd take the vehicle to the dock or airport, find some young girls getting off the boat or plane, and give them a free ride to their hotel. That's how we'd meet girls and get dates. I also was a male escort for a dating service that catered to divorcees coming over from the mainland for a fling. But these divorcees were looking for slightly older, richer companions. Still, I made a lot of tips.

I soon ran out of money. Hawaii had just achieved statehood, so I applied for and received unemployment. I panhandled near the big hotels and resort areas. I moved in with a girl friend who had a good job waitressing, which meant no rent and my not going hungry. I moved out after about a month, then drew on my Hastings experience and got a job selling clothes. Finally, reality set in and so did "rock fever," a condition that eventually hits all visitors who come to the islands. With "rock fever," you want to get to where the real action is, which meant the mainland. I had been in Hawaii for one year before realizing I had to get on with my life.

Then more wanderlust set in, unexpectedly. Another friend visiting us in Hawaii was going to Navy flight school in Pensacola, Florida. He asked if I would like to come along, because he was first heading for Mardi Gras in New Orleans? Would I! Hooking up with four other guys in San Jose, we partied all the way to New Orleans. Mardi Gras isn't something I would do in my sixties, but it was great fun in my twenties. After Mardi Gras, my friend still had a few weeks left before reporting to flight school. So we decided to hit the East Coast. That's how I wound up in New York City, arriving in the middle of winter with a golden tan. Talk about swagger, I was looking good.

New York was exciting. We met up with an old college friend and stayed at his apartment. We were going to parties every night and meeting people, mostly ladies. When it was time for my flight school buddy to leave, I decided to stay in New York. I moved into an apartment with two other guys. This is when I met Gloria, through an acquaintance of ours. Gloria and her roommate were invited to a party at our apartment. By the time she arrived, there were four other guys and ten women. It was a quick "Hi, Gloria, I'm Dan." That was it; I was working the room. The next day, my roommate and I looked up Gloria and her roommate, a redhead whom we heard really liked men. I wanted the redhead. My roommate did, too, so we cut cards. High card gets the redhead, buys the beer, makes the phone call. The other guy gets the brunette and free beer. My roommate got the redhead. I don't want this to sound like Gloria was a second choice, other than the fact that the redhead was known to be loose.

While the other two were having a good time, Gloria and I sat there, drinking beer and talking. We just kind of hit it off. There was a chemistry that hadn't happened in my previous experiences, even though it's kind of interesting that your first date with your future wife was the end result of cutting the cards. We dated fairly steadily for about six months, then decided to get an apartment together. Gloria was told she could never have children, so we didn't use any precautions in our relationship. We discussed marriage, but I had put that idea quite a way into the future. Because even though I was working, I had no career stability or any assets at that time. But miracles do happen: Gloria became pregnant. We looked at that as a blessing, because if it didn't happen, would we have gone through life without children? We got married.

It had taken me about six weeks after arriving in New York to get a job. My roommates both worked at advertising agencies, which sounded like a really cool business. A large agency, Dancer, Fitzgerald & Sample, hired me as a media trainee at a hundred dollars a week. I went from trainee to media buyer and then senior buyer within six months. I was told I was on the fastest track of anyone who had ever worked there, and I would be a media supervisor soon. But even with a twenty-five percent raise, I would make only sixty-five hundred a year. Hardly my goal of a thousand a month, but I was paying my dues.

However, I was doing a big dollar ad business with all these sales people, which didn't take me long to see where the money was being made. Several guys pulled in one-hundred thousand dollars a year. This was the direction I wanted to go in, so I interviewed with this large media conglomerate, Metromedia. A little short guy who ran the sales division in New York told me I wasn't ready for the "big time." But there was a sales position opening at the company's Philadelphia radio station that offered nine thousand dollars a year guaranteed. I took it. My first year there, I made more than thirty thousand dollars in commissions. A thousand a month, and plenty more.

I was able to convince people to buy advertising because No. 1, I'm a good listener. People like to talk, to talk about themselves, their interests and their business needs and problems. I listened for the hot button, the trigger. A good salesman needs an engaging personality, trustworthiness, and believability. It also doesn't hurt to have a good product. What came back to me was "It feels good to do business with you." The vacuum salesman who has his foot in the door, is that a pleasant buying experience? No. You have to make the buying and selling relationship enjoyable. Never leave someone scratching his head and saying, "Why did I ever buy that?" I worked a lot of twelve-hour days, calling on restaurants at 10:30 a.m. and car dealerships at 9 p.m. The more contacts you made, I discovered, the more sales you make.

We were in Philadelphia a year and a half. I was not only the largest sales producer at the radio station, but the youngest. Then I got a call from the little short guy in New York. He told me I now was ready for the big time. He sold me on going to work for him at Metro Radio Sales. I moved my family back to an apartment in Manhattan. I sold advertising time on selected radio stations across the country to the big ad agencies in New York City. After two and a half years, I was the top revenue producer in that organization by a big margin. But it was a pool commission arrangement, which meant whatever commissions I generated were being shared by the rest of the sales staff. I felt like I was over-contributing, although the money and the recognition made up for that easily. You always hear, "If you can make it in New York, you can make it anywhere." I was about to choose "anywhere."

We bought a house, my first house, in New Jersey. But commuting did not agree with me. It went like this—drive the car to the train station, take the high-speed rail to a subway station, then to a second subway station, and then walk the short distance to the office, a three-hour round trip. Then in the winter, snow-covered driveways and walkways had to be shoveled. In the summer, the huge lawn had to be mowed and things always needed fixing.

California here I come!

My general manager in Philadelphia was promoted to the head of the radio division of Metromedia. Through him, I got the job at KNEW radio in Oakland. KNEW was in dire straits, living in the red and lacking a good reputation. I was thrown in as sales manager without any contacts in the local business community, and minimal revenues besides. We had the Oakland Raiders games to sell and not much else. We bought a home in Moraga and I went to work, stumbling upon a good idea. In Los Angeles, I happened to hear a radio sex-talk show. I thought that was interesting and told my boss about it. He listened and liked it. That led to "California Girls," which started on Sundays and then ran Monday through Friday in prime radio time. KNEW's ratings went way up and its sales soared. "California Girls" promo parties were pretty provocative. It was high profile time for KNEW and its staff.

My next career move was this little-known San Jose hard rock station called KOME. A New York company was being formed by people I worked with there. They purchased KOME pending FCC approval and then approached me to be the general manager. The only way I would agree, I told them, is if I got a percentage of the company. They said, "We can work that out." But I had to take a cut in pay first.

One of the loneliest days of my life was arriving at KOME to start my new job. The station was located in an old house. I found holes in the carpet, plaster coming off the walls, toilets plugged, and the station operating with the most outdated equipment imaginable. You could smell marijuana on the premises. The station's ratty carpet had urine spots; that's because one of the DJs brought his dog to work. It was an absolute dump. You couldn't bring an advertiser into this place, though we hardly had any advertisers. No one could have imagined this dump becoming the beginning of Infinity Broadcasting.

The first thing I did was clean up the place. Six months later, we achieved a break-even position and never looked back. With the help of a graphic artist, we created the soon-to-be-famous KOME decal, which received national recognition as the most successful decal campaign anywhere. You'd see all these young people driving around the Bay Area with a black-and-yellow KOME triangular decal on their cars. The station became extremely popular and financially successful. This was the 1970s. What could be more fun than running a rock 'n' roll radio station, especially with my "work hard, play hard" philosophy? I was respected as an industry innovator/leader. I served as president of the Northern California Broadcasters Association and also president of the Santa Clara Country Radio Broadcasters.

Ten years after I took over, Infinity Broadcasting was the largest radio-only company in the United States. KOME was its first entity, generating millions of dollars in cash flow; this enabled the company to buy radio stations in such major markets as New York, Los Angeles, Philadelphia, Chicago, Detroit, Boston, Houston, Chicago, San Diego and Seattle.

I made a very good living, but I'm not into excessive material things. I'm frugal and budget-oriented. I'm not a "car guy," wanting a Corvette or Porsche, though Gloria had a Mercedes for a while. I'm self-confident by nature, but I was humble when praise was extended. And I was quick to credit those who worked for me. Thus business accomplishments were "we," not "I."

Infinity had become a big corporate company similar to Metromedia. I didn't want that kind of bigness again because of the corporate mentality and its politics. It just wasn't fun any more for me. So after eleven years at KOME, I declared my independence, appropriately, on July 4, 1984. I said to my partners, "Show me my money." They were not real excited about cashing me out, so I had to force the issue. Finally, they went to the bank.

After the settlement, Gloria said to me, "You're forty-five. You only worked twenty years." Yes, but I had set bowling pins, had a newspaper route, and washed pots and pans prior to that. Well, I didn't stop working entirely. After Infinity, I did some consulting work. Then with some free time, at last, Gloria and I traveled extensively over the next several years. We covered a large part of the world with trips to Europe, the Orient, Australia, New Zealand, Tahiti, South America, and to most of the good old USA.

It was in Australia that we finally told Debbie she was a miracle child. It was a three-week trip, and I kept putting off telling her until the last day. I was nervous and kept thinking of new ways to present the full story of the circumstances surrounding her birth. Then I drew upon my salesmanship and, in an upbeat manner, I truly made her feel special.

She is special. We set some funds aside for her under the "uniform gift to minors act." At eighteen, this money was hers to use as she saw fit. She acted in a very responsible way. She bought a modest used car and went to UC Berkeley, joined a sorority, and worked summer jobs to supplement her trust fund. She never asked for financial help during that four-year period. Not all kids could handle this responsibility, but she did with flying colors. And enough funds were left after college for her to spend a summer in Europe.

Then I realized I was too young to be retired. My friends were still working. Two years after leaving Infinity, an opportunity was presented to me to purchase a Visalia radio station. I investigated, made an offer much lower than they had expected, but it was eventually accepted. I did not get bank, venture, or private funding for this project. My only partner was Gloria.

We wanted to get the station going financially. We hired a manager to run it. My first trip to the station after the closing, I found the place stripped bare. No paper clips. No toilet paper. No scratch paper. Also there was minimum revenue coming in, and the accounts receivable had been compromised. I rolled up my sleeves and went to work again. Advertising revenue started coming in, and the break-even point was attained quickly enough so that I didn't have to feed it. The station began to show significant ratings in Fresno, which then enhanced its value.

After a year of long, hard work, we accepted an offer to sell the station for a healthy profit.

I still wasn't officially retired. A friend of mine started a little advertising and promotional company in Los Gatos together with a former San Francisco 49ers player who had multiple Super Bowl rings. My friend felt my expertise would be valuable, so I offered myself as a consultant with the understanding that he could pay me whatever he wanted. A promotion we developed for US AIR and the Lucky Supermarket chain gave birth to a whole nationwide industry that specialized in customer loyalty retention and development. This idea and subsequent airline/supermarket promotions generated huge revenues for our company. My name was now on the front door as a full partner. After three exciting years, we divided the assets and moved on.

I was now fifty-one, the same year Debbie was married. Still not fully retired, I entered the high tech world, starting an Internet Service Provider company when the Internet was in its embryonic stage. I guess I was burned out on "start-ups," for a year later I sold out and retired for good. Gloria and I moved from Los Gatos, where we had lived twenty years, to San Luis Obispo. We built a house built near a golf course and took up golf. It was time to give back a little bit, so I took a course from H&R Block and volunteered my time doing taxes for lower income people. I also served as president of my homeowners association for three years.

After seven years in San Luis, we moved up to Monterey County to be closer to our family. Our daughter and her family live in Los Gatos, while my half-brother and his family live in Carmel. I have a good relationship with my father's other three children. Gloria and I have two grandchildren, and I enjoy them in a more relaxed manner than I could my own daughter at that age.

Looking at my high-school graduation picture, I remember exactly what I was thinking when that photo was taken. My mind was on where I was going to college, how I was going to get there, will I be able to make a thousand dollars a month, and who is having a party tonight?

At this current point in my life, I feel very content and comfortable. I cannot think of anything I would want to go back and change as far as life experiences. I have enjoyed life to the fullest, and for that I feel very fortunate. I have traveled down many interesting paths, and would hope that those I encountered along the way would feel good about our relationship.

Being a cool guy turned out to be an OK thing.

★ **16** ★

The Doll Lady

Carolyn Gerbo Scherini had domestic issues to overcome as a child and again as an adult, including family tragedies. She found the strength to cope with her grief through her faith, her doll collection, and by aiding others as a care-giver. Now a senior citizen, she continues to grow as a world traveler.

Dolls are my friends. My mother was a harsh disciplinarian. So when my world started to cave in around me, I would go into my closet, close the door, and play house with my dolls. It took me to another place. At that time, I didn't realize it, but I was very depressed and insecure.

I guess I put on a good act in front of people, trying to be liked. But, inside, I was crying without tears. Many times, I would go home and cry about this deception, because I wanted to be natural and not put on a show. It became a big strain on me even as I got older.

Dolls helped me through that difficult time. Dolls still are a huge part of my life. I have about two hundred dolls in my house. They are friends and pals to me. What can I say: I have a doll fetish. It is like a drug you always need, a fix every now and then.

My parents were like the Archie Bunkers. They were so negative, and they made fun of things that were important to me. In my day, parents had funny ideals. They thought if you complimented a child too much, they'd become spoiled and swell-headed. My parents never really gave me too much positive feedback, even if I got an A grade in school. So I never felt real joy in receiving that A. There was always a negative with a positive.

Learning to cope

Carolyn Gerbo

I took dance lessons because my mother thought I was clumsy, when, in fact, I was pigeon-toed. I danced with the "Stars of Tomorrow" in Redwood City. We danced at the Opera House in San Francisco, but my dad thought I was too fat, so I had to quit. We also did parades, and we entertained military veterans in hospitals. Then my parents felt I should quit that group altogether, even though I wanted to stay. It was another loss in my life.

Unfortunately, my sister and I had to do everything our parents' way. We were good girls, so our parents bragged about us to others. But I didn't know the true me, and I cried a lot because I didn't like the feeling I had. Maybe I had a good time when I was a child, and maybe I didn't. I put on a good show. When I finally told my dad in my thirties how much his teasing affected me, he was sick about it

I was very close to my sister, Louise, and I still love her to death. My father liked to tease, though his mother, my grandmother, always told him he teased too much. As a young man, he lost an eye because of a BB-gun accident. He was very conscious about it. When we'd have pictures taken, he'd cut his face out.

My parents met in a factory. They were factory workers at the time. I was born in a boarding house in San Leandro, California. My grandmother had a boarding house in those days, and my parents lived in it. Not only was I born there, but a fire broke out at the same time. It was all in the newspapers, a stork bringing in a baby and playing fireman, too. I came in with a bang.

When I was four or five, we moved to the Peninsula. My dad bought a truck and started hauling vegetables to different restaurants. Then he and his brother bought the Menlo Cab Company. My dad drove Shirley Temple Black around. She lived close by in Atherton. My dad owned the cab company through my high school years. He even worked on his own cabs as a mechanic.

My dad's name was Harry. My mom was Gerhardine. Everyone called her Gerdine. My dad worked, my mom stayed home, and we made a living. We were just middle class. My dad's first love was hunting. He hunted deer, elk, ducks. Twice a week sometimes, we'd go with him to the San Jose hills, past Milpitas. He'd hunt and I'd milk cows. There was also motorcycle racing. We visited our friends at this ranch. I have very fond memories of that entire experience.

In general, I had a fear of doing things because they wouldn't be perfect. Like I said, I had a very bad insecurity. I was called "Blimp," because I was chunky, and "Purple Cow," because I had such fair skin. When I got to the eighth grade, things changed. I now looked more like a woman than a girl, and boys noticed me. I was only interested in Barry Manheimer. He loved Diane Sullivan. But when no other girls were around, he knew I'd be there.

I liked the families in Menlo Park. Everyone went to church. There weren't divorces, although there should have been. Most families stayed together in the neighborhood for years and years. So you got to know your neighbors. They were kind of like family. That lifestyle is gone now. Everyone moves around. Or they work. Back then, we played "Kick The Can." And "Hide And Go Seek." Remember that?

We didn't need a lot of money. We knew how to make something out of nothing. We knew how to use our imagination. Kids today don't. They've got computers. I collected acorns and made designs. I've tried to instill that imagination in my grandchildren. I made things out of ceramics and sewing. That's what I mean by simplicity. It was good to be a child back then. They're not children anymore. By kindergarten, they're reading. They just don't seem to have the fantasies we had.

Park Theater in Menlo Park had Saturday matinees. Oh, boy. Parents always shipped their kids there. During the matinee, the movie would be stopped and there would be a game. I remember winning this popcorn-eating contest, to see who could toss the most popcorn into their mouth. I had a big mouth, so I got this flashlight, which I thought was so great. At the Park, you'd see Hopalong Cassidy westerns, which were very popular at the time, and newsreels showing everything that was going on in the world.

Carol Stickney had a very nice house. Her parents had lots of parties. Diane Sullivan had such neat parties, like on Valentine's Day. I loved her mother and father. Yvonne Layne had parties. Some I was invited to and some I wasn't. I wasn't in the "in" group in grammar school, which was Yvonne Layne and Andy Schwarz, Suzanne Baughn and Bill Augenstein, Diane Sullivan and Bob Perry. I was with a group of girls who weren't popular. I was so hurt when I wasn't invited to those parties. So my mother had a party for those girls who weren't invited.

It was exciting going into a new high school. All of us who went to Menlo-Atherton grew up together. So it wasn't like going to a strange school. It was a happy experience—the dances, the activities, homecoming, the football games. Everyone liked to go to the dances. I was on the Social Board. All that was about was planning dances and decorating. I was in the Tri-Y, which was going on ski trips. I also was on the Student Council, which was just sitting there and listening if anyone smoked on campus, or if they littered, or if they zoomed their car engine. The punishment we gave out was to do so much yard duty. The council just had to determine how many hours.

My best friends in high school were Frances Lum for a while, and Diane Sullivan for a while. Diane gave me the nickname "Corky." The Fifties were all about cruising in our cars. That's all it was, cruising and cruising. I remember as a senior telling my mother that I was going to get drunk. We all got in Carol Tait's Cadillac and went up in the Stanford hills after buying every kind of booze there was. We ran all over the mountains and I got sick. Then I was driven home. Because my mother knew I was going to do it, she thought it was OK, this being my last year of high school. I was always honest.

Remember the Fifties styles: crinolines, buck shoes, the rolled socks? We'd sew in Miss Forbes' class, then have a fashion show for the seniors and their mothers. We modeled what we made. I think even some of the football players sewed. The Lantz dress was very popular back then. I cut apricots, thirty-five cents a box, all summer long so I could buy a Lantz dress. It was hard work, but I made enough money to buy one, though I had cuts all over my hands from the apricots. I still have a Lantz skirt.

Cashmere sweaters were "in" back then. I remember wanting one for Christmas, because there were a lot of wealthy girls in school, and everyone had them. My mom got me one made in China, because they were cheaper. It wasn't what I really wanted, but she tried. Probably nobody knew it was even cashmere.

It didn't bother me that a lot of kids at M-A came from wealthy families, because these kids were so sweet and so nice and so caring. The ones with the money shared everything—their homes, their cars. They invited me to parties, like the one Stewart Morton had at his place on New Year's Eve, with a big band. It was very nice. Those kids were just so great. The wealthy don't have to prove anything. They were popular and didn't feel threatened by anything. The ones who weren't really rich, and let it go to their heads, were not as sweet or nice or caring. Some thought they were hotshots.

I didn't have any longterm relationships with boys. I went out with Larry Sautter, Don Genasci and Bob Hatch, who was a year younger. There was somebody else I dated as a freshman whose name I can't remember. He gave me a ring, which wasn't much of a ring. And he waited for me everywhere, even outside the bathroom. I couldn't stand that. I needed to be free, so I broke it off, and he threw the ring. I remember putting my hair up in "spoolies," or curlers, after necking on dates. I didn't want my mother looking at me after I got home. I still have those curlers, and the bag they came in. Why? Memories.

We weren't totally innocent in the Fifties. I smoked. I rolled my own when I was ten years old. But I didn't get into any trouble. I was naive, really naive. I thought a monkey bite was horrible. I've always had this religious thing in me. I was the Virgin Mary until I was married. Or else my folks would have killed me.

I'm still not mature even now. Some people think I'm crazy—or just abnormal. They're kidding, but I am a kid in my heart, and I love it. I laugh when I think of us driving around in Carol Tait's Cadillac, picking up stuff on construction sites and throwing it on Bill Brodie's lawn because he was popular. After that, we'd drive to Marquard's. We drove around a lot, cruising. Carol used up a lot of gas.

High school, though, isn't always a good time. You're changing. Everything's changing. It's harsh in a lot of ways. There were kids who were made fun of. Somebody you liked didn't like you. I don't think I'd want to go back to being a teenager. But I've always said, "When it's time to be peaceful and placid, it's time to say good-bye." You know, going to the Guy in the sky.

Leaving M-A, I had nothing planned. My dad got me a job that summer working at Dinker Donuts on Santa Cruz Avenue in Menlo. I made donuts and waited on tables. I've always loved serving people. Why, I don't know. Maybe it was a way to get away from serious conversation. When I go out even today, I don't want to be serious. I want to be light-hearted. Life is serious enough. But by doing the dishes in the kitchen at Dinker Donuts, I didn't have to sit around and talk to people. I could be by myself, just like I am with my dolls.

I decided to go to college, to the College of San Mateo, a local junior college, in order to become a dental assistant. I went for a year and a half, but I wasn't doing too well in chemistry. I did make the swim team. I had done aquacades in high school, so I joined aquacades at San Mateo. But I didn't really follow through. I discovered college wasn't my cup of tea.

So I quit school and went to work as a receptionist at a pediatrician's office in Redwood City. I worked there a year and a half, and found I work better by myself. I like to be in control. And there's that thing about other people's feelings. I didn't like dealing with that, because I have a hard time letting those feelings go. I'm a very sensitive person, although most people wouldn't guess that because I'm always so upbeat. But, again, when I'm by myself, I feel safe, the same way I feel with my dolls.

Working in Redwood City, I met this man who was twelve years older. I met him through the family and thought I was in love with him. But he was totally controlling and broke up with me. I thought I'd never be in love again. Then I met my husband, Remo Scherini, and that was true love.

Remo's real first name is Villy, because his mother wanted to name him Willard. But she's Italian and couldn't pronounce it. Before I met him, he had legally changed his name to Remo. His father had started calling him that.

I knew Remo through my parents' friends. When I was a teen, I'd baby-sit his daughter, Susie, either at my parents' home or at Susie's aunt's house. I made Susie a skirt in Miss Forbes' class. I met Remo again when I was working. He had come out of a bad marriage. His first wife had flown the coop. Remo was seven years older than me and working in the auto parts business.

I don't know what attracted me to him, but sometimes you just know. It's just there. He was mature. He knew what he wanted. I guess anybody would love anybody after being taken out for dinner and given two Manhattans, a glass of wine and two Grasshoppers. And I didn't even drink, well, except for that one time in Carol Tait's Cadillac.

On our first date, Remo told me he loved me. I lived at home until the day I got married. Maybe that's why I'm immature, because I never got out there and lived on my own. And I wasn't going to tell anyone I truly loved him until I really knew for sure. It didn't bother me that Remo already had a child. My mother thought Remo would give me a good life. You would think my parents wouldn't have wanted me to go with a man who had a child. But they really liked Remo and approved of him.

My parents had a fit, though, because Remo bought a house before he gave me a ring. We first dated in August of 1957. He gave me an engagement ring in November. The fool. He could have given it to me at Christmas. We were going to get married in May, but my future mother-in-law died a few days before. We buried her on our wedding day. Then we were married a month later at the Presbyterian Church in Menlo Park. I was twenty. My dad had told Remo he couldn't marry me until I was twenty.

I found that being a wife and mother was the right fit for me. But it was only because I was so in love with my husband that our marriage was the perfect place. That sums it up. I wasn't always a patient mother, but my husband always made it all right for me. My marriage was very devoted, very caring. We made it through tough times without splitting, which showed we had a strong marriage. We always gave what the other person liked. We always tried to please each other. My husband told everybody that the best way to have a good marriage is to understand that the woman's always right. But it was always there between us, in the eyes. Always there.

Susie was five when we got married. My mother told me to bring her in and treat her as my own. And that's what I did. Susie never felt unwanted. Her birth mother hasn't ever played a role in her life. I adopted Susie. Legally, I'm her mother. Elouise was born in May 1959. It was supposed to be Eloise, but I didn't know how to spell it. I had Raymond two and a half years later. I guess I just like dolls. My husband said, "OK, OK." Then after a span of five years, I told Remo I was going to be bored if I didn't have another baby. He said, "OK, OK." So we had Bill. Then the last one, Ann. Ooops!

Now I had a house of eight people. Remo's father lived with us for twenty-five years. We first lived in San Rafael, where Remo worked, and where he had bought the house. Twenty-two years ago, we moved to my present home in Petaluma after first renting in town. Buying my current home was a good investment. The San Rafael home sold for $170,000. This one cost $169,500. Upstairs in a box is the $75 wedding dress I wore when I married Remo. All three of our daughters and daughter-in-law wore that same dress when they married. Now we all have wonderful memories together.

But the reason we moved out of San Rafael was because Raymond had died and my other kids didn't want to live there anymore. Raymond had a difficult time almost from birth, with a hearing problem and a cleft palate. Maybe he wasn't just right up on top, but in Marin County there was access to free drugs. There was lots of money in Marin, and kids would find drugs. Raymond got into drugs, LSD, things like that. I think later on that he became schizo(phrenic). I really do.

We tried to get Raymond therapy, but there was no help at that time. I'd get on the phone from morning to night and nobody would help me. They said it was the parents' fault. I'm sorry to say this, but a lot of school counselors at that time were smoking marijuana. And the parents were being blamed for everything. Drugs had just come into being during that time, and there was no knowledge on what to do for Raymond.

He cut his wrists. I went to Marin General Hospital and begged them to keep him there. They said no. They didn't see anything wrong, whatever, and wouldn't keep him overnight. When he got really bad, we sent him up to Grass Valley, but the school there wasn't equipped to handle him. He went on a starving binge and said he wasn't going to eat until he could come home.

I remember being in court, pleading with the judge. I was afraid of my life because Raymond would take weapons and throw them around. He'd kick in walls and sneak into our room, try to get our keys, so he could back out the car. He was becoming dangerous, not only to himself, but others.

He lived in and out of our home all the time. I was told my only recourse was to call the cops. It was like a living hell. I didn't know where to turn. We never gave up on him. We did everything we could. For the five years or so that he was on drugs, we felt like prisoners in our own home. I'd get him away for a while. He'd have his own apartment. Then I'd tell him, "Raymond, it's time you come home."

He came home that last time and went upstairs. That's when he tore up all his baby pictures. He told me, "Mother, you know what I'm thinking." Or "Mother, I want my ashes scattered on a hill." But the Lord told us that we couldn't handle Raymond. And Raymond can't handle life, so it's time to go.

Raymond made a sawed-off shotgun. He also made explosives. He was brilliant. He went into a lot and shot off the gun with the explosives inside, like he knew what he was doing. Only it backfired. The coroner said it was suicide. But Raymond could have been experimenting with the gun, and then it backfired. We aren't sure to this day.

Remo was on the road when Raymond died. Because it was a firearm, two detectives came to the door. I said, "What's wrong?" They said, "It's your son." And I said, "I had a feeling." The police checked the whole house and the grounds outside for bombs. Because of the explosives, they had to check for bombs.

Raymond was nineteen when he died. He couldn't go on the way he was going. There was a time when I couldn't even think about his having died, because it was painful in every way. But if you asked me today if I wanted him back the way he was then, I would say no. He's at peace. I don't mind talking about this if it helps people who've had a similar experience. It helps to know you're not alone.

Everything had changed in the 1960s and 1970s. I didn't know how to handle these kids, and the way they thought about things. A lot of kids' mothers weren't home at dinnertime. So some of these kids had no routine. As I said, everything had changed. They even had the wife-swapping era then. It was a different world from the one I was brought up in.

In those days, it was up to the woman to be the disciplinarian, because the men were off working, supporting the family. Remo acted asleep when the kids talked back to him. He wouldn't even recognize them. This was a problem when I became the villain. People used to call Remo "a snail without salt" in Italian. He was slow motion, a thinker. He kept everything inside. I never knew about his thoughts much.

I'm a strong person—a very strong person to go through all that I've gone through. My father took his life. I don't want to say how, but he died before his sixtieth birthday. He couldn't go hunting because he was starting to have heart attacks. He thought he would use up all his money medically, and he didn't want to do that to my mother. He told me if he couldn't go hunting, he didn't want to live. He told me what he was going to do, and how we were supposed to act at his funeral, and where we would sit. And we weren't supposed to see his body, although my mother did see it. He told me how to grieve for him. So I've never grieved for my father.

After he died, my mother became a party girl. My father didn't dance, and she loved to dance. She went wild. She found a boy friend. It was like she was let out of a cage. Later on, she had a heart attack. So my sister had her to handle. We put her in a convalescent hospital to try and rehabilitate her, but she went home and broke her hips. I put mom back in the hospital and took care of her needs for twelve years. About that same time, my father-in-law got Alzheimer's, and we put him in the same place as my mother.

Near the end, my mother had a stroke. She always said, "Don't cry for me when I go, but treat me good when I'm here." I did. My mother was seventy when she passed away. We didn't have a final conversation. She just said, "I always loved you."

After my father-in-law died, I was finally able to take care of all my grieving that I didn't have time for before. Needless to say, I was in counseling for about three years. I always had to live by my parents' rules, and really never knew who Carolyn Gerbo Scherini was. Which made me depressed. For the first time, through counseling, I really saw life. And it was exciting, a whole new world. I felt exhilarated.

My last family crisis started with ulcers, only Remo didn't know he had them. When he got to the hospital, he was nearly bloodless. He received a bunch of transfusions to stop the bleeding. Then he wasn't able to hold his food down. That's when doctors found out he had the ulcers. A big piece of his stomach was cut out, giving him a normal-sized stomach. He liked to eat. But after his surgery, his complexion turned yellow.

So we got him a CAT scan. The doctor came into the waiting room afterward and said, "I'm sorry, he has (pancreatic) cancer. He's not going to make it." Just like that. My daughters became hysterical. I told him, "You can go. I'll be OK." His last words were, "No." So he never said good-bye. He lasted about seventeen months with this cancer, and he was determined that he wasn't going to die. But it didn't work. He died in July 2001. He was seventy. We had been married forty-three years. Near the end, I was in a daze. But I get strength from my faith. My main objective was Remo, making sure that he was comfortable, that he was clean, and that he would die with dignity. That was a full-time job. I didn't have time to think of him dying.

One of the loneliest times for me now is driving home from an event—alone. I am alone in a huge world that I really have nothing to do with. It has been four and a half years since Remo died, and I am just learning how to be independent. It is a very hard adjustment. There is a saying: Something good comes from something bad in time. I am really grateful for my three grandsons. God took my son, but He gave me three back.

The best thing for me is to keep busy. If I'm not going to die, and I don't want to be a burden to my kids who have their own lives, I must build a new life. My life had been raising kids and taking care of my husband. But you won't know what this new life is like until you go through it. Because you are basically alone, even though my children treat me like a princess, just like my husband did.

But I'm not going out there to look for a man, because I'm not interested in any man. And you know men die first. There are more women than men. It's not so easy to find a man. Going on the Internet to meet guys? No way. If it happens, it happens. But I'll tell you one thing: I'll never marry again. Part of me likes my independence. And why get involved with another family? I don't want to combine my money with anybody else's. So that's it.

I'm doing OK. I own some commercial real estate in San Rafael. It was my father-in-law's, a one-hundred-year-old building that is one side of Marin General Hospital, the part where they keep records. That's what's carrying me, financially. My husband didn't get much retirement. His company stole most of it. I have another piece of property that hasn't been lived in in two years. There's good property rental in San Rafael.

I'm very fortunate. I have so many activities and friends that I don't feel bad going anywhere socially by myself. It's no problem. I've traveled extensively to China, Cuba, Italy, the Caribbean, Hawaii, and I just returned from an eight-day safari in Kenya. I saw lions, giraffes, hyenas and rhinos. It was amazing. I felt like I belonged there—a piece of land with no one around me, seeing all these wild animals so free. I let a giraffe pick food, or pellets, out of my mouth. What's to be frightened of? His tongue didn't even touch me, but I washed my mouth afterwards.

In a Masai village, I met one of the chief's seven wives; he has thirty-seven children because no one there uses condoms. AIDS is a serious problem there, with millions of deaths. The young kids go to school in uniforms, but they're hungry. That's the sad part. The children have flies all over their faces. The girls get castrated at eleven so they won't feel sexual pleasure; only the men are supposed to feel sexual pleasure.

Families eat veal and lamb, and drink cow blood and milk together as part of their diet. I saw a dead goat in the yard. I asked the chief's wife about removing the goat, which really smelled. She said they leave it for the dogs to eat. The villagers build fires, which they put out with cow dung.

Since coming back from that safari, I've been talking to a friend about going to Egypt, to see the Pyramids, and to go down the Nile. All my life, I've felt like I lived in Cleopatra's time.

Even at my age, I guess I'm still trying to grow. But what's keeping me going is the church. At Christmas, I've sewn the whole nativity scene, made all the costumes. I cook for the priest and for those who take communion at Easter. I'm a Eucharistic minister, going into rest homes and giving communion to the sick. Like I said, I've always liked to give. My mother always gave gifts because that was her way of apologizing. I give because I want to give.

I think I've done all the goals I wanted to do in my life. I feel I've done everything that's exciting. However, in Germany, they have a doll tour. You tour the old factories that made those porcelain dolls in the early 1900s. I hope to do that sometime.

I've picked up dolls, fixed them up, and sent them to orphanages. I made custom-made doll clothes and sold them. It's like my house is a hobby house with all my dolls. When I push some dolls in a certain place, they sing. I can do a lot of fun things with dolls. I've written notes on them, saying where they came from, sentimental things.

I belong to two doll clubs, both non-profit organizations. We have fund-raisers, with the money going to the YMCA battered children's home. We've donated more than sixty-thousand dollars to that home. I have been to many national doll conventions. Because of my dolls, I've been written about in a local newspaper, and been interviewed by a local television station.

Over the course of my life, I've been given dolls. Or I've bought them at doll shows, gotten them from friends or from people who've passed on. I've bought them on eBay. Doll collectors, I've found, are nurturing and very kind.

My children like dolls, but not like their mother does. I use to give my dolls names, but not now. My brain is fried—fried from life. I don't talk to my dolls, but do I kiss them and change their clothes. My rule is that they all have to have underwear. Dolls have modesty, you know. Now that all of this is coming out, I need that little man in the white suit to come get me.

My dolls bring me happiness. But so do my children, my grandchildren, my friends. I've decided I don't want to live longer than eighty. My body is tired. Really tired. Right now, I'd like to rest. I'm not afraid of dying; I'm afraid of how I'll die. I've been talking about death all my life, because, after all, death is a part of life. I'd like my ashes strewn over San Francisco Bay. Remo's ashes are there. At first, I wanted Carmel. Remo and I used to go there every New Year's. Only they don't spread ashes there. But Remo and I just loved the ocean.

When it's my time to go, just remember all the good things about me. But when I'm gone, I'm gone. Reincarnation? Who wants to come back? I mean, it's OK, but say there's no God, say there's no Jesus. We all wonder. Because what you don't see, you don't....but when you die, there's no more pain. That's your heaven.

You're showing me my M-A graduation picture. I was very happy then. I got a lot of attention—graduating, parties, my aunts giving me stuff. I like to be the center of attraction. Everybody looks happy there in their graduation pictures, don't you think?

But that girl who's me would look at the woman she became and think, "She's lived all she could live. She gave all she could give." In a novel I read, the woman tells about all the tragedies in her life. Someone asked her how she made it through them. She said she had endured.

And so have I endured.

The one who leads

Andy Schwarz

★17★

The Searcher

Andy Schwarz was Menlo-Atherton High's student body president in 1956. After graduating from Stanford, he started a construction business that took him north to Alaska. Learning and adventure feed his lifestyle. He's a non-stop reader and an outdoorsman who travels to the remotest parts of the globe.

My wife, Ann, and I share this love for the outdoors. We've have logged more than fifteen-hundred miles of running rivers together above the Arctic Circle. Ann loves to ski, she loves to travel, she loves the beach. She scheduled a trip around the world by herself. We rendezvoused in Guam, then traveled to Yap and Palau, a group of islands in the western Pacific. We were diving in Palau long before anyone had heard of it.

Ann and I had three separate honeymoons. The first was on the Haul Road from Fairbanks, Alaska, to Prudhoe Bay in northern Alaska, where an oil pipeline was being built. Ann was a sole source contractor for the state of Alaska for five years. She was asked by the state to follow the Haul Road all the way to the Yukon River and then file a report on what was going on. I went along as her driver. We had a great time. Ordering cherries jubilee for dessert after a really nice dinner, I commented to Ann about the expenses. She said, "Listen, buster, the oil companies are paying for this, and they pay for everything!"

On our second honeymoon, we flew from Anchorage to Fairbanks to Bettles on the north fork of the Koyukuk River. A bush pilot then flew us to the Alatna River, located in the Brooks Range. He dropped us off and flew off. And there you are. We portaged a quarter-mile, put our little boat together, paddled across the river, stashed the boat, hung a bunch of stuff to keep the boat away from the bears, then backpacked into the Arrigetch Mountains for four days. Hey, you're out there, right? After coming back to the river, we floated two hundred and eighty miles to our pickup point.

For our third honeymoon, we went to Nairobi and chased around for a while. Ever hear of Maldives, a country in some islands off the west coast of India? We went there from Kenya, had this guy drop us off on this uninhabited island for four days. It's an island you can walk around in twenty minutes. This was 1978, our first Thanksgiving together as a married couple. We have our tent, some water, some papayas and bananas. We're naked, but it's just the two of us on this island. We went from there to Sri Lanka, where we spent a couple of weeks. Then we went to Bangkok and Hong Kong and back to Alaska.

Ann and I spend a lot of time hiking. That's what we do. In Durango, Colorado, where we live, we hike in these beautiful mountains sprawling with all kinds of flowers. And there's a lack of people around. We day-hike when we're home, but we do a lot of camping elsewhere. In the Brooks Range, you get on top of these mountains and you can see two hundred miles in every direction. And there's not another pair of human eyes around. We've seen eighteen grizzlies in the wild. We've had bears in our camp. There's good fishing. We've also seen moose, a wolf, a musk ox and eagles. We were so high in the Arrigetch, we were above the mountain sheep.

If I had to pick a perfect day, though, it would be a day hike in Utah, probably Capital Reef. I'm a desert rat and have been ever since Ann introduced me to that way of life. There's a restaurant in that Capital Reef area, Cafe Diablo, that has food as good as anywhere you can find in the Southwest. Ann and I have a solid marriage—the second marriage for both of us—and that's because we have absolute trust. Ann's really attractive, and really bright, and I like bright women. We're reading books all the time. We have a tennis court on our property. I play, three, four days a week. We're close to skiing, and rafting, and hiking. Durango is a cool little town.

I spent seven years in construction in Alaska, 1975 to 1982. Alaska's where I met Ann. Then Anchorage got to the point where it was too gray. We both wanted the sun. I came to Durango when I was forty-four. I had just finished a sub-division in Alaska. Ann and I built a house in Durango on some property she bought with money from her divorce. Then I realized I didn't have to work again if I didn't want to. I have this philosophy that if a person has a chance to really do what he wants to do, then go for it.

I was never in the construction game for prestige or recognition or to see how much money I could pile up. But I had reached a point where I was self-sufficient. This has given Ann and I a chance to thoroughly enjoy life. For my last act in construction, I built the Durango Arts Center, a wonderful way to transition out of being in business. That art center is thriving today.

My first real travel experience happened after my freshman year at Stanford. Bill Augenstein and I worked that summer on Wake Island as laborers. We got six hundred dollars a month, which was big bucks in 1957, plus free room and board, and free transportation and laundry. We started out working six ten-hour days, but we worked so hard that we got it down to five-day work weeks. We lived in a hut. Although there was no social life for kids our age, we had a great time. We skin-dived every day after work and organized a basketball league. There were old bunkers left over from World War II; the only evidence of what had happened there a decade earlier.

Bill and I are cousins and lifetime friends. Everyone calls him Augie, but he's Bill to me. We went to grammar school together in San Francisco and Menlo Park. We swam and played water polo together at Menlo-Atherton. We were both all-league in water polo in 1955 when M-A was league champions, the first undefeated team in any sport in the school's history. Bill's mother was my dad's baby sister. Bill's dad worked for my dad in construction. Every summer except for the one on Wake, Bill and I worked for Hayman Homes, which employed both of our fathers. After a summer of working, Bill and I were happy to get back to school. We both knew that we didn't want to pound nails for a living.

Nevertheless, when I was born, my life was laid out for me. The boss at Hayman Homes told my dad, "Someday your son will wind up doing for my son what you're doing for me today." Lo and behold, that's what happened years later, although the relationship didn't last all that long. That's because I had a background in leadership. In the eighth grade, I was class president and "boy mayor" of Menlo Park for one day. At M-A, I was Commissioner of Welfare, the equivalent of student body president. The only part of leadership I didn't like was speaking in front of assemblies. I liked the small meetings where you could sit around and discuss different things. But after being student body president, I had no fear of being in charge.

To do a job right, you have to be a leader. I really think, though, that I learned leadership from my father. He was tough, but he wasn't mean. He wasn't touchy feely either. The highest compliment I ever got from him was "That's not bad." When I was an Air Force lieutenant, I was the boss and had to take command. When I became an entrepreneur, it was the same thing. I wouldn't have made a good corporate man with all the in-fighting, people competing against people for a position. I just like to do my own job, and if I'm recognized for it, it's not a big deal. I loved building; it was never work. And I never let work become all-consuming. I love to play, too. Life should also be about fun.

It was a thrill going to high school. I was a decent student, I had good friends, I was out for sports I liked, and I had some really good teachers. I was attending a brand-new school; M-A was called a country club at the time. I had a good time all the way through, no regrets at all.

And I had a girl friend, so I wasn't looking around. Yvonne Layne and I went together from the seventh grade all the way through high school. We were kind of opposites, but she was comfortable, a very nice person with very nice parents. After six years of dating, I wanted to get out of the relationship. It would have been a major thing if we broke up then, because I really cared for her personally. After she went to San Jose State and I went to Stanford, that made it easier. We dated a couple of times and that was it.

Then I dated Bonnie Jane Russell for four years. She was two classes behind me at M-A and a straight A student all through high school. My classmate, Bud Varty, was dating her. After Bud went off to college at Whitman, I stole my buddy's girl friend. Bonnie Jane then went to Stanford. We contemplated marriage two different times. One time, I asked her and she didn't want to. Another time, she asked me and I didn't want to. But, looking back, I went with two girls for a total of ten years.

In the Air Force, I changed my relationships with women. I was twenty-one and I wanted a good time. I had a series of girl friends, but nobody I cared to have a long relationship with. After the Air Force, I ran around San Francisco and had a good time as a bachelor. I was twenty-seven when I got married the first time, which was kind of late for people from our era.

Ruth was a good-looker, a graduate of the University of Michigan. We dated three months and got married in 1966. She was a teacher who then taught for a year and never taught again. She was a stay-at-home wife before she was a stay-at-home mother. She was interested in social climbing, flitting around and going to lunch. Pretty soon we were involved with what I called the cocktail-party scene in Menlo Park. I didn't want to participate because I found it artificial and superficial. Ruth disagreed, so we fought. After five years of marriage, we divorced when our adopted son Rush was three. Ruth was a good mother then. But after Rush grew up, got married and became a father, she wrote him a letter resigning as his mother. It was a very nasty letter.

I did work for Hayman Homes, so the prophesy of my birth was fulfilled. My dad's boss turned over the business to his son, a good guy but not as smart as his father. The company had an impeccable record under the father. My dad disliked working for the son, so dad retired after thirty-two years with the company. Then I decided I had to get out of there. It was either work for someone else or do it myself.

So I bought three lots near a Hayman construction site that we had built. Hayman loaned me a carpenter, let me use some of their construction plans, and things started out great. We were framing the roof when I sold the first house. We were still working on the first house when I sold the second and third. So I was out of the blocks pretty well.

But there weren't that many choice lots around, and that's what drove me north to Alaska, a state that rewards talent. I was rewarded there because I was a good builder who sold my houses for nice profits.

I'd build for seven months a year in Alaska, then I'd winter in Palo Alto, where I kept an apartment. I remember the first time I saw Ann. She was in a mail room in Alaska, wearing a green raincoat. I said to myself, "Who is that woman?" Then I wanted to marry her. I did and we've had a great life together.

I was thinking when my high-school graduation picture was taken that I had a lifetime job awaiting me. When I got it, I didn't want it any more. But my life has turned out great, superb, couldn't be better. All phases of it.

Some times haven't been good, but you have to get through them. Ann and I had back surgery the same year. I told her, "You have to look at it like we're a couple of old cars. So we've had a flat tire. We'll just fix it and keep rolling on."

Clockwise from top left: Nina Carson, M-A Class of '56, gets a kiss from Elvis Presley after The King's Bay Area concert that same year; Senior Ball queen Merry Davenport is crowned by class president Bill Brodie, while princesses Gerrie Keely (left) and Mikel Ann Edelen look on; Diane Sullivan and Dayle Barnes ham it up at Menlo Photo; Jerry Juhl (center), editor of the M-A's school newspaper, Bear Tracks, is surrounded by (left to right) staff members Gerrie Keely, Josephine Booth, Jim Chandler and Susan Samuels; (left to right): Jerry Terhune, Carol Stickney, Merry Davenport, Sonny McNitt on a double date.

Clockwise from top left: Bill Lawson, wife Bernadette (far left), and Patsy Newhouse celebrate his recent birthday at Oasis hangout in Menlo Park: clockwise from top left: Menlo-Atherton class-mates Dave Newhouse, Andy Schwarz, Wayne Chan and Bill Augenstein fit in a phone booth at the Oasis; Menlo-Atherton High School, home of the Bears since 1951; Susan Erstrom Thomas (left) and Barbara Boucke, best friends at M-A, reunite at 50th class reunion

From top: Menlo-Atherton's Class of 1956 holds its 50th reunion at a country club - what else? - with the banner donated by anonymous classmate, who was George Carr; Ann's Coffee Shop, a Menlo Park staple since 1946; Marquard's Drive-In Restaurant, popular M-A hangout in the 1950's, is seen left in its heyday and, below, where it once stood now is a construction site for the future home of an office complex.

Cop story

George Carr

★18★

The Watchdog

George Carr attended Menlo-Atherton. So did his late wife and their two children. Carr has resided in Menlo Park most of his life. He served twenty-six years in the Atherton Police Department. He loves his hometown, he loved being a policeman, and, with time and forgiveness, he grew to love M-A.

I'm the oldest M-A student around here. I never left this place and I never regretted a minute of it. M-A does mean something to me, even though I had a hard time there as a student. I looked around back then and saw a lot of kids who were really wealthy. Some of those kids were driving better cars than the teachers. I went to M-A with a chip on my shoulder because all of my childhood friends had gone to Sequoia High. I just wanted to get out of high school any way I could and go into the Navy. That was my escape.

But when I saw my school burning down eleven years later, and equipment being destroyed, and students going to the hospital, I couldn't deal with that. I did have to deal with it as an Atherton policeman, but it made me realize that I really cared about Menlo-Atherton.

When we went to M-A in the 1950s, life was simple, clean-cut. What we thought were problems weren't really problems. We had a few beer parties and we went to the coast by Half Moon Bay, but I can't ever remember seeing a uniformed cop on campus. You saw truant officers, guys from juvenile hall, but now they have a uniformed cop stationed at M-A day in and day out. And it's an Atherton cop because the school is in Atherton, although if you cross the street fifteen feet, you're in Menlo Park's jurisdiction.

Like I said, we had it a lot easier in the '50s. The 1960s were militant. The 1970s were anti-establishment, anti-police, anti-military. Military recruiters came on campus and they would be booed off. I don't think they have recruiters on campus any more. In the 1970s and 1980s, you walked through Menlo-Atherton and it broke your heart. Our beautiful school wasn't beautiful any more. Our school was in disrepair. Kids were tearing the bathrooms apart and breaking windows.

The school, physically, is looking better these days. They've built a new teachers lounge, a new gymnasium and swimming pool. They're building a performing arts center. To my knowledge, M-A still is held in high esteem academically, although you can bend statistics any way you want.

But M-A kids today are a long ways from the way we were. We had our music, dances or sock hops, drive-in theaters, beach parties and Marquard's, the local car-hop restaurant that was our hangout. We pretty much wanted to be together. You saw your cliques, but that was OK. Now you're seeing, unfortunately, gang influences on campus. By law, they can't fly their gang colors on campus; they'd get sent home. There are Hispanic gangs and Asian gangs. The blacks are kind of hanging back. The Hispanics are more prominent because East Palo Alto, once predominantly black, is mostly Hispanic now.

The Atherton element still is there on campus, but a lot of them have transferred to Woodside High, which was built after we left M-A. The strict school border lines back then no longer exist. Now you can attend any school in the Sequoia School District. The East-side element really came into M-A after Ravenswood High was shut down in East Palo Alto. A lot of these kids are living in poverty, so I imagine they have a hard time seeing uppity white kids driving around in their fancy cars.

M-A students react differently to teachers nowadays. There are sexual advances and indecent exposure on the part of students against teachers. There's a record of one case where a kid walked up to a female teacher, unzipped his fly, and laid his private parts on the desk. There have been assaults, kids striking or grabbing hold of a teacher. Kids are throwing things in the classroom. They're saying to their teachers, "If you do this to me, I'll do this to you." Teachers feel they can't retaliate because they'll be retaliated against by the student or the student's friends.

I'm a member of the Menlo-Atherton Alumni Association and spearheading an effort to resurrect our "class pillars." They were demolished in June, 2001 by then principal Eric Hartwig for no other reason than he did not like them. Now it looks like they will be resurrected in the center of the new performing arts center. Most of the alumni were upset about their removal. I can remember driving by when they had just finished the demolition. My wife was in tears. I can best be described as very angry. I vowed to do something about it. The process is slow, but we are getting there.

Recently, in meeting with a group of people on an unrelated issue, I said my assessment of myself as a Menlo-Atherton student was that I was an underachiever. I didn't want to do any more than I had to do to graduate. I did play football. I managed the track team. I sang in the a cappella choir. But I was in conflict with my counselor, Mr. Yeager, a lot. He wanted me to get into mechanical drawing. I didn't want to because I heard the teacher, Mr. Carlton, was really difficult. A kid from the class behind ours allegedly punched him in the nose. I finally took mechanical drawing and just loved it. I got into drafting, which benefited me later on. I flew through all my drafting courses, getting good grades.

But I was bit of a hell-raiser. I spent a good deal of the time in the principal's office for disrupting classes. Mr. Nugent was the principal. He got up at my first freshman assembly and said, "My name is N.M. Nugent, and if you want to know what the N.M. stands for, it's 'no mercy.' I hope you don't have to find out what that means." I was scared to death of him, though he turned out to be the sweetest man. He'd just say, "George, what have you done now?" Then he'd sign my slip and send me back to class.

Part of my problem at M-A was the stuff my parents were going through. I came from an interesting family, to say the least. My maternal grandfather, William McGarvey, had underworld connections. He came west from Chicago to get away from the mob, changing his name in order to hide. The mob wanted him because he knew a lot of what was going on. The authorities wanted him to testify. He was between a rock and a hard place. He ended up going out of state and living by himself because he didn't want to subject his family to any of this. He and my grandmother never divorced, and when he came home to die, he was fairly wealthy. The two of them are buried side by side in Palo Alto. We unpacked his bags after he passed away, and there was a snub-nosed .38, a blackjack and brass knuckles.

My mom was born in Chicago, the first of seven kids from a tough Irish family. All seven grew up to be good people. During World War II, mom worked in the Alameda shipyard as a pipe fitter. An original Rosie the Riveter. My dad, George Edward Carr, Jr., was born in Oakland. Then his family moved to San Francisco, where he met my mom at a dance hall. They married in 1936. I was born in 1938 as George Edward Carr III. My dad was a career Navy man who retired in 1961. He was stationed at Mare Island in Vallejo as the executive officer of the tug boat fleet while I was at M-A. I always loved being around my dad. On school vacations, I would go and visit him and live aboard the tugs. Because of my dad, I grew to love the Navy.

My parents divorced. My paternal grandmother had a lot to do with it. She wasn't a very nice woman, but neither of my parents could tell her to take a flying hike. The first time she met my mother, she said, "Oh, you're just shanty Irish." It was all downhill after that. My mom remarried in the 1950s, but I couldn't fit in my stepfather as a father figure because my dad was my hero. My parents weren't happy in their second marriages. Mom stayed in hers; my dad divorced. I really believe they still were in love with each other.

Discovering that I had completed all my requirements for graduation a few months early, I quit school and joined the Navy. Because of my dad, I got on the U.S.S. Bremerton, although he never admitted to pulling a few strings. I had seen the U.S.S. Bremerton and been aboard it during those vacations. I did well in the Navy, promoted far beyond my wildest dreams. My mother said, "You went away a boy and came back a man."

After my discharge in July, 1959, I was home for about three weeks, then decided there was nothing for me in civilian life. I contacted the Navy recruiter and learned I could enter the United States Naval Academy. My dream! I found out my high school grades would not help, but that my record of service would, and I could enter the academy via a prep school with the recommendation of my commanding officer. No problem.

One week before re-entering the Navy, I asked my dear friend, Dale Stopp, to introduce me to someone. He said, "I have got just the right person for you." On Aug. 13, at 328 Pope St. in Menlo Park, I met my beloved Jaye. Our love for each other was instant. As we say, the rest is history. I knew as the days passed that she was for me. I also knew that military life is hard on family life. So scratch those plans for the Naval Academy.

Dale, by the way, is an interesting story. As a kid, he jumped off a train, the train lurched, and he was thrown underneath. He lost one leg below the knee and the other leg above the ankle. I met him during summer school. I'd drive him to school, wheelchair and all. One year behind me in school, we became best friends.

Back to Jaye. She had a glow about her that was very genuine. As a sixteen-year-old high school senior, someone wrote in her yearbook, "Your personality will do you well for the rest of your life." Jaye attended the University of California at Santa Barbara, but didn't want to return for her junior year. She only went to college to please her mother. Her parents didn't like me. They saw me as an ex-Navy man who was loose and had no ambition to go to a higher university. And I was a Catholic. So Jaye and I eloped to Reno. Her parents had a fit, but it wasn't long before we became friends. Before their lives ended, they thanked me for being good to their daughter.

We got ourselves an apartment in Redwood City and wound up managing the building. The free rent helped us buy the house in 1963 I'm living in today. With my drafting experience at M-A, I was able to get several jobs. But I couldn't see spending my life on a drafting board. I was getting calluses on my elbows from leaning on drafting boards. And I was bored to death.

By that time, I was thinking of law enforcement. I liked the uniform, the regimentation and the challenge. When I told Jaye, there was anger and there was tears. She said, "Am I going to have to worry about you getting shot at?" But with her blessing, I joined the San Mateo County Sheriff's Reserves. I did not want to jeopardize my drafting engineering job, so being in reserves was a good way to find out if law enforcement was for me. I went to the sheriff department's academy and just loved it.

But with two children, I stayed on as a draftsman until just before LeRoy Hubbard, the Atherton police chief, hired me in 1967. Jaye was so happy, thinking Atherton wouldn't be nearly as dangerous as San Mateo County. Well, I came home the first day and dropped an empty shell casing on the table. I saw the blood drain out of her face. I had fired a round over the head of some burglars. Chief Hubbard told me, "George, we don't fire guns in Atherton."

I fired only one more round over the next twenty-six years. It involved a violent car chase. The guy had me pinned against the car. I fired a round between his legs and that was it. The M-A riots started about the time I was hired. That's when I realized how much M-A meant to me. I was walking down the main hall of the school, which was being destroyed. Literally. And I'm pissed off. This is my school, dammit! Cops were just on the edge of learning how to deal with riots. Even though I had had a hard time with the uppity white-collared kids I went to school with, M-A had done a lot for me. So I didn't want to see the riots continue. They eventually de-escalated.

The Atherton Police Department is a plush job. It's not like San Jose, where cops are going from call to call to call. In Atherton, you might have two hours between calls. But things do happen. The pay is pretty close to what the other departments make and the retirement is the same. There was just enough action for me. I never wanted for something to do. It might be a fight, trying to restrain a person. I was kicked, cut, spit at, punched....everything in the world. Atherton has a lot of swimming pools, so you have to know how to swim. Many times I've jumped in a pool and pulled someone out. We had to go over walls and we climbed ropes, so we had to be in pretty good shape.

One of the hardest things for a cop is children and babies who are injured, victims of accidents, abuse and other crimes. It's difficult not to show emotion, but I can assure you all cops shed a lot of tears in private. We're unable to hold back our tears. The first autopsy I witnessed was a young boy who looked a lot like my own son. Contrary to popular belief, cops have emotions just like everyone else. I'm one of those cops.

I wouldn't say I was fearful, but I was always thinking of the what-ifs. That's what kept me alive. If you get comfortable in your job and lower your guard, that's when you're going to get hurt. A lot of people don't understand it when you walk up to them at night with one hand on your flashlight and the other hand on your sidearm. They feel that we look threatening. Some people have said, "You look like the Gestapo."

They don't understand that it's called officer survival. You have to be mentally alert, focused on what you're doing, because all of a sudden, there it is. There may be a warrant out for their arrest. You don't know if they have a gun. You might get shot at or slapped. You don't know what's coming. It's called lag time. In other words, the other guy always has the advantage or the drop on you.

That "pig" stuff cops hear never bothered me. I was called all those names, but they're only names. I always looked at "pig-ment" as pride, integrity and guts. It's like someone asking, "Do you mind being called cop?" And I'd say no, because that meant either "Constable on Patrol" or the copper buttons on your uniform. Call me cop, and I say, "Thank you."

Most people don't appreciate what we do because they haven't been out there like us. Put yourself in a similar situation. When you're attacked, you want to survive. If a guy pushes you, there's no legal right for you to take out your firearm and shoot. You fend him off, use mace or a taser gun. If things escalate, you legally can do what it takes to get the job done. If he comes at you with a knife, you're justified in using maximum force.

Until you've been in that situation....I've had people who've taken off handcuffs and bent them. Taking PCB or acid gives them a tremendous amount of strength, and they don't feel a thing. I never felt the need to retaliate against a suspect. You've really got to restrain yourself. The hardest thing is refraining from using derogatory comments. Like they told us at the academy, you're only human, and after a while you can only take so much blankety-blankety-blank. After that, you come back with the same stuff. But I refrained from doing that.

Another thing you have to think of: A cop could be giving up his career and a wonderful retirement. Why give that up to thump on someone who really isn't worth the trouble? Then nobody will want to hire you. In court, I had judges stick up for me because they knew of my reputation. People lie about a traffic citation to get out of it. The judge would tell the defendant, "Don't you stand in my courtroom and lie about this officer, because I know who he is." I couldn't pat myself on the back, but I was proud hearing that.

A lot of that misunderstanding about a policeman's life turned around after 9-11. People developed more of a loving relationship, especially toward the fire department and the cops who died as a result of 9-11. One local cop died at the hand of someone mentally ill, a known violent person. When Ronald Reagan was governor of California, he closed a lot of mental institutions and said these people have a right to be on the street unless they're committed by a judge or they voluntarily want to be committed. Thanks, Governor Reagan. And remember, no cop who has been in the profession for any length of time hasn't been the victim of a certified crazy person. I'm one of those cops.

The people of Atherton absolutely love their police department. They'd have you stop by for a cup of coffee. Or they'd have a bag of oranges for you. There never was money under the table, except at Christmastime. It was an Atherton tradition to give money to the police, money that was divided up by seniority. I remember trucks pulling up at the station and dropping off cases of liquor and big boxes of candy and fruit. Then we got a new police chief who said we could no longer accept monetary gifts. Atherton people were really insulted. Our Christmas gifts ended except for fruits, nuts and candy.

Looking back, I dumped a lot of marijuana down street gutters. Or

I threw it into the bushes, scattering it around. It wasn't worth the time and energy to do otherwise. I don't see marijuana as that big of a problem any more. For what society gets out of that kind of arrest, it's not worth it. But if a guy has enough of it on his person to sell, you deal with those guys in a different way. A couple of roach cigarettes in his ashtray, and if he's got a good attitude, and he has a pretty clean background, and if I knew he would appreciate a break, hey, everyone deserves a break. Good-bye. I've had people months and years later come up to me and shake my hand to thank me.

I've never felt revenge coming from someone else. If I was in a grocery shopping with Jaye, and here came someone I had just arrested, I'd say, "Come on, dear, we're going down another aisle." She understood. I didn't want to involve my wife in a confrontation. If someone approached me and put out his hand, you didn't know what he would do. But it turned out OK.

In Atherton, I came into contact with parents of M-A classmates. One time, it was a shooting. The wife died and the husband shot himself. It was a pretty messy scene. I was just getting into law enforcement when my football coach at M-A went shopping for an automobile with his wife, also an M-A teacher. She became involved with the car salesman, and the two of them were found dead from gunshot wounds in the coach's house in Menlo Park. There wasn't enough evidence to indict the coach.

Some of the most violent crimes in Atherton involve people who have a lot of money. The only shootings I saw were suicides. You'd walk into a big mansion, with beautiful white carpeting and drapes, and there would be blood all over the place. Or people would jump in front of trains—wealthy people, older people. They wanted to end it. Drug overdoses were very prominent.

What's different, crime-wise, from growing up in Menlo Park and Atherton in the 1950s is the complexities. Domestic violence is much different. You didn't hear about those things back then. Now in Atherton, you have CEOs beating their wives, or vice-versa. In law enforcement today, if you get a call on domestic violence, you've got to make an arrest or lose your job. Before you might say, "Mr. Jones, come on, I'll take you down to the hotel. You spend the night down there, then you'll get back together tomorrow when you're more emotionally capable." Now you can't do that. Somebody has to go to jail. A red mark on the arm, a punch in the face, somebody has to get arrested.

Domestic violence is up because people are up tight and in a hurry, feeling the pressure to do well, to make money. Some people are doing too much cocaine or drinking. It all adds up. But when you get into heroin, that's the real money. A lot of the wealthy lose everything trying to support a heroin habit. I've seen it happen. A lot of the thefts in Atherton are by drug users. When I started police work, Atherton people didn't have safes. Toward the end of my career, alarms came in and burglaries went down. But Atherton continues to suffer from burglaries. People keep a lot of money and jewelry in their houses. Asians steal from Asians because a lot of Asians don't have trust in banks. And it can be a violent confrontation if it's Asian gangs. They have high-tech firearms. You almost hoped that they'd be gone by the time we got there. And most of the time, the bad guys were long gone.

I've met some famous people on the job. One of the nicest is Shirley Temple Black, an Atherton resident for many years before moving to neighboring Woodside. She is a great lady, extremely pleasant. She hasn't changed much since "Rebecca of Sunnybrook Farm." Same sweetness. I cited one of her children who had a bit of an attitude. I never heard a word. They paid the ticket. I was directing traffic one day and Shirley stopped by to chat. She was happy the road was being fixed. We exchanged pleasantries. She loved Edy's Candies in Atherton.

Willie Mays lives in Atherton. He's a terrific person. The key word with Willie is "kids." He's there for the kids, autographing baseballs and signing certificates after the Little League season. He'll stop what he's doing, anything for the kids. He's right there for you.

Memories? When I worked for the San Mateo County Sheriff's Reserves, we'd go up to Ken Kesey's cabin near LaHonda to see what he was doing. This was after he wrote "One Flew Over The Cuckoo's Nest." He had some wild pot parties, with sexual things going on. I always had to stand guard on the road, so I never saw what was going on. Ken was fun to deal with. He screamed so loud, but there wasn't a violent bone in his body.

Towards the end of my career, women joined our police department. I had a bit of a hard time with that at first. I still kinda do. There are very few women physically cut out to be a police officer. I won't say mentally, because I have respect for all women. But there's a place for everybody. Things I saw that happened to women wearing a badge weren't nice. They were taken advantage of by the suspect and physically hurt. And, emotionally, they couldn't cope with some of the things they saw happening.

I think Jaye had a harder time with that, seeing me driving around with these cute gals. She knew things could happen, because partners get close. It never happened to me because my love always was with Jaye. But her father and other male figures in her family were womanizers, so it was in the back of her mind that guys do these things when they're married. I saw it happen to guys on the force, and not just with women they were working with. Maybe the wife at home wasn't supportive of their job. Jaye was totally supportive of me in all aspects of my job. She knew I had to work weekends, holidays and nights. She kept the home fires burning, especially when I attended the police academy and got my Associate Arts degree. Dinners were always ready when I was working swing shift. Jaye wore the hat of dad in my absence as well as being the mom. She was the ultimate police wife.

I rose to the rank of sergeant. Jaye pushed the chief thing, but I didn't want to put up with the politics, dealing with the city council. I wanted to be out on the street with my people, where I belonged. That's why I twice turned down a promotion to lieutenant because that meant sitting behind a desk. I sat behind a desk as a draftsman. I retired from the police department at fifty-five because the time had come. After a while, you can only go over so many fences or get knocked on your fanny so many times. But my career, all in all, was very satisfying, and ninety-nine percent positive.

Menlo Park has gotten bigger since the 1950s. The county turned over some of its unincorporated land to the city. The population has grown to a little more than thirty-thousand. There are more schools. Menlo College has gone from a two-year to a four-year institution. Where I live, houses that went for ten-thousand dollars in 1949 now go for a million. And those are cheap houses. Some remodels in our neighborhood, Suburban Park, go for two million.

Our daughter, Jennifer, would love to live here but can't afford it. So she commutes from Danville to her office job at the Atherton Police Department. She's not a policewoman, but the chief's right-hand person. She handles the hiring, the training, the budgets. Our son, Chris, is a general contractor who owns his own business in Santa Rosa. Between the two of them, I have six wonderful grandchildren. Chris has four and Jennifer two. Both our children are college graduates, Chris with a bachelor's degree and Jennifer with a master's degree. They made Jaye and I very proud.

Everything I've become in my life, I attribute to Jaye. My mother thought I had become a man when I got out of the Navy, but I had a ways to go to achieve manhood. Jaye helped me get there by giving me the support I needed, and by making me believe in myself. I always gave her credit, but she'd say, "Honey, it was always there. I just brought it out."

Jaye worked as the City Clerk in Menlo Park. She received the Golden Acorn Award in 1995 for professional excellence. This happened five years before she retired, so she wasn't given it out of sympathy. When somebody was needed to talk to at city hall, they went to Jaye. They might be mad or violent, but Jaye was so good with people, she would smooth things over. When the city wanted a retirement dinner for her, she said that most of the people she knew couldn't afford to attend a retirement dinner. So the city had a retirement lunch instead and planted a tree with a bronze plaque in her name.

We found out Jaye's health was failing in the middle of 1999. We had dinner, then she sat down on the couch and said, "I don't feel well." She had an MRI, which showed a brain tumor. She had the operation, which turned out well: She had fourteen MRIs on the brain, and every one was a good result. Gone, gone, gone. Then in July 2004, at a reunion of some of her M-A classmates, she had a hard time walking. Jaye showed spirit. She put up with the pain, trying to be pleasant. By Christmas, she had developed a spot in her lungs that quickly went to her liver and kidneys. She decided to stay home. I took care of her.

It was June 27, 2005. I went to do some work on our forty-foot motor yacht. I was only gone fifty-five minutes, but Jaye said, "Honey, you can't leave me any more." That evening, sitting on the couch, she said, "Honey, I can't breathe." I called 911. The ambulance came and took her to Sequoia Hospital. She was there three days before passing away. The children and I were at her side. I held her in my arms when she took her last breath. She was sixty-four.

I had the best of the best in Jaye. I couldn't ever expect another woman to live up to what she meant to me. Our love affair will always be. What keeps me going is Jaye. She's still here. She'll say, "George, you got to keep going. Don't you dare let it go." I can't wait for the time when I see her again, and she, with her arms outstretched, as she often did, says, "Hi, sweetie."

Now you're showing me my high school graduation picture. What was I thinking then? Probably that I hope my picture turns out OK, and what am I doing in a suit, and is June ever going to get here? I'll be glad when it does, then I'll look forward to getting out of the area and my home environment. Because I wasn't all that happy. I was looking to go.

Looking at that same picture now, I'd say, "I never would have believed that you would be where you are right now, doing the kinds of things you've done in your life, being happily married, having two beautiful kids, and being a grandfather. This is more like a dream world, a fairy tale."

Life's a party

Barbara Boucke

★19★

The Dancing Queen

When rock 'n' roll arrived, Barbara Boucke Violich Rice cleared the floor when she boogied at Menlo-Atherton High. Smart, attractive, spunky, this party girl was an anthropology honor student at Cal. Now back to being Barbara Boucke, she's a principal fund-raiser for San Francisco's de Young Museum.

I was voted best female dancer in the Class of 1956. Donnie Day was voted best male dancer. Whenever there was a dance contest, we'd leave who we were with and dance with each other. We both were short, so that helped. We jitterbugged and we bopped. This was before "The Twist." We danced to "Rock Around the Clock," "Shake, Rattle and Roll" and "Tutti Frutti." We'd always win. Remember slow-dancing to "Sincerely"? The last song of every school dance was "Dream" or "Good Night Sweetheart." Remember?

Rhythm and Blues was played on the radio, but it didn't get played in high school, at least not at Menlo-Atherton. We were still dancing to Glenn Miller and Duke Ellington. But I listened to the R&B stations, to "Annie Had a Baby," "Work With Me Annie" and "Buick 69." That was pretty racy at the time. I still have those tapes somewhere.

I had a really good time in high school. I wasn't in the "in" group. I was on the periphery of that group, but I was pretty popular. What worked to my advantage was my name, Barbara Boucke, pronounced "Bookie." It's a funny name, a funny-smile name. Once you hear it, you tend not to forget it. Most people call me Boucke. "B BOUCKE" is on my license plates even today.

The people at M-A were really nice. We didn't have any bad guys in high school. We were pretty square kids. I was less rebellious than I wanted to be. That's what always bugged me about myself. I wanted to be a hippie, but I never quite made it. I don't know if it was guts, but I always wanted to be a good citizen. So that kind of kept me from going where I wanted to go. I mean, I told my mother when I was a high-school senior that I wanted to lose my virginity. I probably didn't mean it. If she had said, "Do it, Barbara," I probably would have run in the opposite direction. So my rebellion was more an annoying rebellion than a genuine rebellion.

I didn't do "it" back then, although you might have thought I would be the classic example, because I was a party girl. I was a virgin, in fact, until I met my first husband. But there was a division in those years, the Fifties, because none of us had access to birth control pills. That didn't happen until the early Sixties. My father told me when I was in high school that if I had sex, I would get syphilis in a week. He's gone now, but I still look up and shake my finger at him every now and then.

At M-A, I thought it would be cool to smoke. When I told this to my parents, my father said I had to learn that very night. They thought I would get sick and forget about the whole thing. So I sat in the bathroom all night, coughing, but I came out knowing how to inhale, saying "OK, now I can smoke, right?" I later got to a point where I smoked more than a pack a day. A cigarette in the morning? Ooooh. Smoking and sex were a great combination. Then I quit smoking cold turkey on my fortieth birthday.

As an M-A senior, I also announced that I wanted to learn to drink. So my father told me to stay home on a Saturday night, to have dinner with him and my mother, and they would teach me how to drink. None of my friends drank back then. My dad built a fire and made me Manhattans. I hadn't eaten much that day, so I was taking my first drink of alcohol on an empty stomach. My father said, "Drink it down fast, it will taste better." So I downed two Manhattans because they tasted so bad. Then I went into the bathroom and passed out. I didn't drink again until college.

I've always been a person who worked hard and played hard. Work keeps my mind going, keeps me engaged with people. I will always push myself, career-wise. But I also like to do wild and crazy things. Go to places I've never been before. Go smell the roses. Go out and kayak. Go find a good lover and have a good time. Go do things on a grand scale. I'd rather be a rose in full bloom than a rose bud—in full bloom where I can be as open as I want to be, even if there are a few bugs in there. A rose in full bloom is sensual and it smells good. I'm still trying to be this hippie earth mother, but I don't seem to be getting there.

If I had been an open rose at M-A, I probably would be a different person now in terms of my accomplishments. I mean, kids today have so much more to cope with. Back then, we didn't have computers and all the stuff you see now coming at you from every angle. We were able to sit and dream, read "The Fountainhead" and "Forever Amber" and envision what life would be like. When I was a teenager, life was a giant, romantic good place. There was not a Vietnam War. We had "The Loretta Young Show" and "Howdy Doody" and Ed Sullivan. We had singers like Nat "King" Cole, Frank Sinatra, Patti Page and Rosemary Clooney, and songs like "See the pyramids along the Nile....You Belong to Me" and "Sha Boom, Sha Boom, yadda, yadda, yadda, yadda...."

My expectations, then, were much more storybook. Go to college, get married, live in a nice house, have kids. Life would be forever after, fun and nice, fitted in a nice, neat little box. Well, it didn't quite turn out that way. Life has been pretty rough along the way. I've been divorced twice. But I've learned to take care of myself. It's my pioneer spirit.

My maternal great-grandmother came across this country on one of the first trains from Missouri. My maternal great-great-grandfather came across on horseback. He was an Indian agent who got to California's Feather River in 1848. This meant I had a direct descendant here before 1850, which means I am a member of the Society of California Pioneers, which started taking women about ten years ago. This is my first and only big snobbism.

My maternal grandmother, Julia, was the light of my life, the woman I loved most in this world other than my daughter. Julia was a sixth-grade school teacher in St. Helena. Her mother, the one who came across on the train from Missouri, was St. Helena's town librarian. My father was gone a lot during World War II. Working for Standard Oil, he built the Aramco Pipe Line in Arabia. We lived in San Francisco at the time, but my mother wasn't particularly a family-type woman. So I would go live in St. Helena, where I had this idyllic childhood up to the third grade.

My great grandmother, the librarian, kept these books behind her desk. St. Helena is where I learned to read. A rumor I'd like to believe is that the first book I ever read was "Celeste The Gold Coast Virgin," one of the books behind great-grandmother's desk. All this goes back to how I believe I was formed. I viewed myself as a pioneer woman, an independent woman who was molded by women—my grandmother and great-grandmother, who thought nothing of going out into the middle of the Nevada desert and looking for spokes from wagon trains. That's why I loved going back to St. Helena every chance I got. I learned how to take care of myself, big time, from those two women. I even named my daughter, Julia, after my fabulous grandmother.

I was devastated when my parents moved to Woodside, where we lived in a California ranch home on three acres. We never had horses like other homes in Woodside, though I didn't like horses anyway. But Woodside is way the hell out in nowheresville. When I came to Menlo-Atherton as a sophomore, all the action was with you guys in Menlo Park. I wasn't part of the Woodside set, which sent their children to private schools—the boys to Menlo School, the girls to Castilleja in Palo Alto. My mother wanted that for me, complete with the formals and cotillions. She had a reverse value from the women in St. Helena. My dad was now a Standard Oil executive. We had money, but we weren't old money. What mattered most to my mother was social status. She needed to get grounded in a social situation that my father couldn't buy for her.

Thank God I didn't buy into all that. I wanted to go to M-A even if it meant taking the bus. Later, I drove this little Mini Minor, red on the bottom, white on top. My dad bought it in London. The car had this funny "Bermuda bell" on the floorboard. Instead of a honking sound, it went "ding, dong" whenever I hit the button with my foot. M-A guys would pick up my car and park it over the logs in the parking lot. I didn't mind it; it was fun. But I had to go find some guys to lift it off.

My dad was a brilliant man. His premium on me: To do well in school and I better be bright. I was pretty lazy in high school because it was easy for me to get good grades. I wasn't intellectually challenged until college. I was fiftieth in my M-A graduating class, which wasn't good enough to get into Stanford. So I went to Cal, which only required a B average at the time.

Going to Cal, I discovered anthropology. And I loved it. I got A-pluses in that major and made the honor society. There wasn't another sorority girl near that anthropology group, which amounted to people who were hippies and had beards, or earth mothers who went to Java to study spear throwers and cannibals. I was a Delta Gamma, the quintessential sorority girl. I was cute, blonde, bubbly, popular. But I frequented coffee houses and drank wine from bota bags. I had this double life I loved, to the dismay of my sorority sisters. I also loved Cal. I still love Cal as an alumnae, Class of 1960. You've seen my Cal license plate frames. I still have season tickets to Cal football games.

Paul Violich graduated from Stanford in 1957. He's one of the best-looking, coolest of men. And a very macho guy, a frogman in the Navy. He looked like Sean Connery; he still does. We were fixed up on a date after he had gotten out of the Navy. We were married in 1962. Paul entered the investment counsel field and did well financially. But, as it turned out, we were happiest when we were poor.

We were certainly happy in New York after Paul got a job there and the phone company also transferred me there. I wrote speeches involving the World's Fair. After moving back to the Bay Area, I became restive because I now was strictly a housewife with a daughter and son. So I did a lot of charity work and got on different boards. We moved again to Marin County, where things got worse. Paul is a Republican. I'm a Democrat. Both of us are strong-willed. Both of us wanted to make all the major decisions.

Paul had this beautiful—to him—house built in Marin. Walking into it, I wanted to cry. It was a symbol of everything I didn't want to be, a house my mother would have loved. Paul bought me this big "V" diamond brooch—V for Violich, not B for Barbara—that I basically chucked into a drawer. I was too much of a challenge for him. We were married fourteen years, but we didn't establish that core of friendship I've seen in successful marriages. Paul asked for the divorce. Discussing the final details with our attorneys, he turned to me and said, "You'll always be Barbara Boucke to me."

Paul walked out of the house in 1976, when our Menlo-Atherton High School twentieth class reunion was taking place. I called Sue Erstrom Thomas, my best friend at M-A, and told her I was too devastated to go. She called Andy Schwarz from our class, someone I dated after college. Andy phoned me and said, "Don't be ridiculous. I'll pick you up and take you home." It was like throwing a life preserver out there. But what a great life preserver. Andy was divorced, too. Our relationship this time would last two years. He was building homes in Alaska. I visited him there often, then figured out there was another person in the picture. That's who Andy took as his second wife.

I went back to school and signed up for accounting classes. Then I took the Certified Public Accountant examination. I was among the six percent nationally who passed it the first time. That was 1982. There were eight big accounting firms in San Francisco. I got an offer from all eight. I went to work for Main Hurdman after being informed during the job interview that my ex-husband's financial records were in their files, and could I work there without looking at them? I never looked. I'm pretty proud of that.

I've been a CPA ever since, mainly a tax accountant. In 1987, I was hired as comptroller for the de Young Museum. Then I was promoted to Director of Development, or head fund-raiser, at the museum and also at the Palace of the Legion of Honor in San Francisco. I've been involved with the rebuilding of both museums. Lucky me. I'm the only CPA on staff. Dede Wilsey is President of the Board of Trustees. We've worked together ten years, two strong women, but entirely different. She's bright, funny, gets it, and she respects my opinion. We're not personal friends, on purpose, but we don't compete.

I have this habit of really liking bright, complicated men. I've been told that I'm waiting for Mr. Right. I've always said that I love Mr. Wrong. Denis Rice is a senior partner at the finest boutique law firm in America, located right here in San Francisco. He is brilliant, went through school on scholarships. He's a Democrat, right up my alley. He was mayor of Tiburon, then we ran against each other for an appointment to LAFCO, a county commission. Guess who got it? The boogie queen.

Denis' previous wife's occultist told her she should leave him. That same wife told Denis he should date me. We kept company for about ten years, then I told him I wanted to get married. We eloped to Yosemite in 1988. That's when I bought my present house in Stinson Beach, which would be my hideaway.

I wanted to be married, but my motives for this marriage were wrong. We cared deeply for each other, but, once again, we were fiercely independent. Denis, like Paul, wanted to make all the major decisions. But what tipped this marriage was when Denis ran for Congress. He put more than a hundred thousand dollars into the campaign, then lost the race. So he was frantic about money. Our marriage managed to last six years. It was easier being his friend.

I have two wonderful children—Julie, a professional cyclist, and Adam, a super venture capitalist. I love them very much and they love me. My kids knew I was a party girl. I used to smoke marijuana. I liked it as a relaxant. In 1982, my kids sat me down and said, "We're going to cut a deal with you. We won't smoke marijuana if you won't smoke it." They didn't like their mother getting stoned. I said, "That's a deal." For the most part, I've kept that deal.

Julie presented me with a grandchild, Luke. I absolutely love being a grandmother. I'm no longer interested in the institution of marriage. Financially, there's no reason, and I don't know if I could share my home 24-7 with somebody. I would prefer to have one or two men friends, and I wouldn't mind having a man here for the weekend. Or I would go to his place for the weekend. I'm not fast and loose. Just fast.

Look at my M-A graduation picture. Look at that little sweetie. I have no idea what she was thinking then compared to what she's thinking now. Her view on life back then was much narrower. She was an idealist.

She wouldn't think life has been tough on her, but that she's been tough on life. She's created some of her own issues. But even though she's had rough patches to go through, she's landed on her feet.

I'm just glad I didn't know all this back then, because I would have been pretty terrified.

The Sky's the Limit

Jerry Terhune was an M-A football star with an engaging smile. But his friendly face served as a mask, covering up his poor image of himself. The Air Force, marriage, and his second career as a therapist improved his self-identity. However, having served in Vietnam, he has similar doubts about Iraq.

Growing up, I had a very negative opinion of myself, which would have been diagnosed then as an "inferiority complex." Now they would call it "low self-esteem." It was very hard for me to accept a compliment. I'd make a joke about it or I'd think, "If you really knew me, you wouldn't say that." So I would generally put up a facade, cracking jokes and becoming the class clown, the idea being that if people are smiling, then they aren't angry or displeased with you.

This was all a projection: If I don't like myself, then you can't like me. So I played a role. I was a skinny kid, freckled face, red hair. I didn't like any of that. I wanted to be like my classmates, like Gary Grider with the muscles, curly hair, perfect teeth. Or Jim Bishop, a smart guy and a good athlete. Or Alan Sundquist, who wasn't afraid to talk about himself and who was so genuine about things. I would keep everything hidden and say that everything's fine. It was a protective camouflage.

I was an introvert besides. When things got tough or stressful, I'd get quiet and withdrawn. I wanted to remain private. I never self-disclosed. Often, I would fabricate. I might fail to turn in my homework and then would lie to the teacher. Even now, my wife, Ann, will tell you that after

Identity crisis

Jerry Terhune

forty-one years of marriage, when something's going on, I withdraw and get quiet.

As a teen, I had pimples, a case of acne, and I hated that. It added to the burden, drawing attention to me.I did feel good playing athletics. I tried hard in this area of my life. I wasn't the fastest guy or a Joe Athlete by any means. But I was competitive. My junior year, I was a starting end on the school's first championship football team. But when I would get a compliment after having played a good game, I'd think about a block I missed or a pass I dropped. There wasn't the freedom to really enjoy it. Conversely, I tried to avoid criticism from others, because it really bothered me.

My dad was a hard-working man in the grocery business. He took care of the family. As far as showing affection or affirmation or even spending time with me, I remember very little of that. I'd mow the lawn at home and no matter how hard I tried to do a good job, he would usually find some spot I missed. It got to where I didn't believe I was capable of doing a good job, so I would often try to avoid doing my chores. Maybe that is why when I'd get a pat on the back from someone, I wouldn't accept it. I would always feel I could have done better.

At Menlo-Atherton, needless to say, I didn't think I was a very handsome guy. And I was shy, especially around the opposite sex. I told Susan Holt at our fiftieth reunion that she had the most beautiful smile. She was one of the prettiest girls in our class. I would watch her walk down the hall. But I had great difficulty talking to her because I just knew she was only being nice and would not have wanted to date me. I was a chicken. I seldom got into any trouble. I was a close friend of Al Sundquist. Al and Jim Woodcock would always come up with these pranks to have some fun, maybe taking some risk. But I was afraid of getting caught and of the potential punishment. So I would stay close to the exit, ready to bail out.

I had one serious high-school relationship. I dated Carol Stickney for a couple of years. We broke up our senior year. Actually, Carol broke up with me. I was becoming too possessive, wanting to be with her all the time. The way I saw it, here was this girl from a successful family, and how could a schmuck like me be with such a wonderful girl? I wanted to be a part of that life, but I didn't have much to give in return. I was jealous of her. I think she felt smothered. When she told me we were breaking up, I begged her not to do it. I was in tears. Plus there was the whole aspect of sexuality. Not that we were doing anything, but your hormones are going. That's a difficult time for anyone.

I also was aware that most of my friends were going off to college and on their way to a successful future, while I didn't have a drive or aspiration in any particular direction. I harbored the dream of being Joe College and living in a fraternity. But my family didn't have the money and my grades were not that good. So I went to the College of San Mateo, a junior college, for two years. That was a very difficult time in my life. I was down, possibly depressed, without a whole lot of confidence. My grades suffered as a result. I was discouraged, had this fear of failure, and I really wanted to get away from home. I was in a kind of limbo, but sinking. I even felt that God must be disappointed with me.

Aviation always was an interest of mine. While in junior college, I learned of the Air Force's Aviation Cadet Program. I wondered if I had enough college credits to qualify for pilot or navigator training. I went up to Travis Air Force Base and took a battery of perceptual tests. My highest scores were in the pilot category, but there was a backlog of applicants awaiting entry into pilot training. However, I could get into navigator training right away. Because I was in a hurry to get out of my current sinking situation, I joined the Air Force's Aviation Cadet program in August 1958, with the intention of becoming a navigator. The day I left home, my dad was in tears. I was shocked seeing that as I hadn't ever before seen him cry. Looking back, that showed I really did mean something to him. And I had felt all of my childhood that I had been a disappointment to dad.

As an underclassman in the cadet program, I was harassed by upperclassmen. This was an essential part of officer training, testing my ability to take and carry out orders under stressful conditions, and to develop self-discipline. I found it easier than others to stay the course, probably because I was quiet and somewhat withdrawn. Thus I could take orders more easily. And I liked the military structure. You knew who was in charge and where you stood. A lot of cadets were weeded out, but I thrived. I also found out that if you did your job, you were commended for it.

I felt confident about being an officer and a navigator. I also felt free from the pressure of failure. I was succeeding, a different feeling for me, and it felt good. When I finished cadets and got my commission as a second lieutenant, my mother proudly pinned my bars and wings on me. I also felt approval from my dad, though he didn't express it verbally.

My first assignment was England, where I spent the next three years flying photo reconnaissance missions in the RB-66 aircraft. I wasn't thinking of an Air Force career at the time, but I didn't really have anything else to come home to, like some of the guys I knew who had a family lumber yard to take over or who had other career plans. On the other hand, I was driven to do my job, which was to complete the mission. When called upon, I was there, and I felt good about that as well as feeling important in my navigator role.

I still was relatively shy. I was stationed near Cambridge, a college town, so I would date. I felt better and was more mature in my sexuality, but I also learned to see and value the other person as something other than merely a sexual object. I was concerned with who the individual was as a whole person. Upon returning to the states, I was assigned to Dyess Air Force Base in Abilene, Texas. It was there I met Ann Presley in early 1964. She had graduated from Texas Lutheran University, had been teaching high school, and was working on her master's degree. She caught my eye for sure and I asked her out. Four months later, I asked her to marry me and she accepted.

We had some early miscarriages before our son, Chris, was born. Four years later, we had a second son, Jeffrey, who inherited my red hair and fair complexion. But four days after his birth, he died from a devastating form of meningitis. The grief I felt was kept private, and I wasn't much help to Ann at that time even though I knew she was hurting. My intent was to go on without any real emotional processing. I was afraid to expose my deeper inner feelings. Ann and I hadn't talked much about Jeffrey's passing until a year later when we started the process of adoption. That's how we became the proud parents of Steve, who rounded out our family.

Ann was the perfect Air Force wife. She has given me great support. She understands me, and who I am, and accepts me even with my many faults. She is very solid in her faith and in her caring manner. Her strong faith in God has been a powerful witness, inspiration and strength to me. She held the family together when I would be away for two, three months on temporary duty. The longest I was away from home was fifteen months in Taiwan.

Though I was stationed in Taiwan, this was the period of 1968 to 1970, during the Vietnam war. We had an ongoing mission of flying cargo in-country, meaning Vietnam. I spent two-hundred and seventy days in-country; this counted as a Vietnam tour. I didn't have it as bad as the guys who actually were stationed in Vietnam, especially the ground troops. I wasn't as intimately involved in the fighting. We could see small-arms fire coming up at us at night, but that's nothing like anti-aircraft guns or SAMS being fired at you.

Still, there was an intensity about our mission, because we carried out a lot of body bags. With my active rationalization and denial system, I blocked out the person inside the bag. I'd see a name tag on the bag, but often would not read it so as not to personalize the reality of facing a dead American boy. That might be too overwhelming. Again, my irrational reaction of loss of life was present. I would rationalize the death as a "normal" consequence of war.

Years later, I grieved for all those young men and their families who gave so much in response to their country's call. During the time I was flying the KIAs, I often said a prayer that God would sustain the families so impacted. There wasn't an overt grief process among the crew. You didn't hear, "This damn war, look what it's doing to so many of our men as well as the Vietnamese population." There had to be a lot of internalizing. You had a job to do and you did it.

Looking back, I was aware of the protests taking place back home, and the unpopularity of our presence in Vietnam. A part of me said we were doing the right thing, partly because I was over there doing it. Probably wishful thinking. I did have a hard time understanding how we were going to win this thing, but hopeful that the situation would be settled peacefully. I didn't think we would ultimately be overrun. I also was aware of people going to Canada to avoid the draft, but I've always accepted the rights of conscientious objectors.

Adding up the human toll in Vietnam and seeing it up close in terms of bloodshed, and having a chance to reflect on it, I don't think our military presence in Vietnam was worth the price of what we accomplished. I do believe in a strong military arm as an instrument of national power, but it needs to be utilized with great wisdom and foresight. Former Secretary of Defense Robert McNamara admitted, after the fact, that, in effect, the USA was playing a game in terms of justifying our continued military presence in Vietnam.

I'm seeing similarities with the current military situation in Iraq, with our stepping into another country via "shock and awe" and declaring, "This is the way you need to be." I'm concerned about the arrogance of such a move and how it can be counterproductive in its polarizing effect against the United States. A good rule of thumb is if you're going to get into a power struggle with someone, make sure you can win it, or you can limit it, or you can admit that where you're coming from has subsequently been proven wrong. Then get out. It truly is a strength to be able to say, "I made a mistake."

I've gone from being a hawk to becoming more of a dove in my thinking. I'm still a work in progress, but I am able now to look at a situation from a more universal perspective. I want us to be an honorable nation, but I have trouble with some of President Bush's policies and priorities. We are truly a great nation, with so many advantages and options as to how we manage ourselves. If we do own a sense of worthiness and a healthy national self-esteem, maybe we can more humbly face, and influence, those vital issues facing us today, without so much of the ego-oriented, hip-shot, "shock and awe" perspective. We might not only help ourselves and our confronting the terrorist threat, but we can do a better job of helping all the other citizens of the global community.

Durring my time in Vietnam, I did a lot of personal soul-searching, not in regard to the political question of the war itself, but more in regard to the person I was in God's eyes. It was later in my life and during my years as a counselor that I came to know Jesus Christ more intimately, and I could understand that Christianity can be defined as more of a relationship than merely a religion.

I rose to lieutenant colonel in the Air Force. I always received superior ratings. And I had obtained a bachelor's degree and a master's. But I was surprised when I made colonel. That little boy fear and negative self-concept still was a part of me. I'd notice other people's abilities and compare them to my own. There were other guys I thought deserved to be colonels who didn't make it. But I've grown to understand that I earned it.

I was on active duty in the military for twenty years. I was really ready to get out after doing so much traveling and being away from my family so often. I was thirty-nine at the time. I was always interested in psychology, as mentioned earlier, and thought maybe I could get into a helping profession. I felt my best avenue into such a career would be a master's degree in social work. We retired in Texas, where I attended The Graduate School of Social Work at the University of Texas at Arlington.

Then I spent the next twenty-six years as a psychologist/family counselor, working with adults, adolescents, children and elderly people at various clinics. I was part of a private practice for four years. I also worked as a group counselor in the psychiatric unit of a local hospital. I discovered a lot about myself. Besides my training, I had personal insights about my patients' pathology, from what I had experienced in my own past. Such insights as avoiding otherwise healthy self-disclosure and not confronting the real issues.

I could relate to loneliness, fears, anxiety and even the death of a child, which I had experienced. But I always tried to focus on the person I was counseling and not on me. One of the biggest satisfactions I received was (tears fill his eyes)....whew!....their discovering that they could feel good about themselves, and that they deserve to feel that way. Everybody is unique and gifted and should have a valid sense of their worthiness. When people can do that, they are in a much stronger position to cope with life's struggles.

Studying my high-school graduation picture, I remember feeling very good about being a graduate. Maybe my smile reflected that. I had achieved something. But behind that smile, I was pretty anxious and scared. What do I do now? I didn't have a clear road ahead of me, and even if I did, there would be self-doubt. However, thanks to the grace of God and a very loving and supportive wife, my life has turned out well. I've changed a lot from that discouraged little boy.

Belle of the ball
Merry Davenport

★21★

Queen Merry

By popular vote, Merry Davenport Montaudon was Menlo-Atherton's Senior Ball queen in 1956. But wearing a tiara didn't enhance her popularity or make her feel prettier. She didn't spend her life on some throne either, having to deal with her husband's job loss and their son's difficult return from Iraq.

We had lots of queens at Menlo-Atherton—three classmates my senior year. Joyce Keller was Football Queen, Mikel Ann Edelen was Homecoming Queen, and I was Senior Ball Queen. In my situation, every queen candidate was nominated. When you arrived at the Senior Ball, that's when everyone voted.

I didn't even know I was up for it, so I was very surprised when I found out I had won. That's because all of the Senior Ball princesses were popular: Martha Wright, Gerrie Keely, Mikel Ann and Beverly Wells. I didn't consider myself to be popular. I wasn't the cheerleader type.

There was one group we all looked up to in our class, but I wasn't in that group. I didn't think I was particularly pretty, not any prettier than the rest of these people. I felt kind of average. But I knew everybody. My boy friend, Sonny McNitt, had a group that was different from my group, and I knew all of them. I don't know if the other candidates knew everybody like I did.

It was wonderful that all these people voted for me. It was very exciting—and shocking. It was an honor, but it didn't make me feel really good. It boosted my ego, but I had a good-enough ego. I don't think I had a swelled head. I couldn't even find my shoes that night when I went up to the throne. I had been dancing and we took off our shoes. That's why you don't see my bare feet in the queen's picture in the yearbook; I was on yearbook staff.

But I wouldn't be Queen Merry the rest of my life; just Merry. I was named Merry, not Mary, after my paternal grandmother's maiden name. Her last name was Merry. It's a burden having that name; it's misspelled a lot and you're always supposed to be cheerful. I'm not always cheerful. But I'm not a downer. I'm sort of in the middle. I don't smile automatically as much as other people. I do have a good sense of humor, and I enjoy others who do, too.

At M-A, I was the good queen. I dated Sonny McNitt from late in our junior year through our senior year. He was a great guy, always happy. It was a delightful relationship. Basically, relationships back then seemed innocent. Not too many pregnancies like you get now. I was terrified of the sex part of anything. My family would have been crushed. Because of that, I didn't do it. I don't think that's true today.

There were people I actually was scared of at M-A until I got to be a senior. I wouldn't have run for an office; that would have scared me to death. The yearbook staff was a very exciting time for me. I got interested in writing and went on to major in English in college.

I look back on the Fifties as "Happy Days," a very innocent time. I enjoyed my childhood. My family was wonderful. I was the oldest of four children. My dad built homes in Menlo Park and Atherton. We lived in Atherton, near the Lindenwood gates. In the third grade, I rode my bike all the way across the railroad tracks and across El Camino Real to Fremont School. I can't imagine kids doing that today. Nothing ever happened to me on my bike. It was a safer time.

I had polio the summer before eighth grade at Encinal School. That colored my life a lot. I became a lot more serious about things. My parents became a little more protective of me. But I enjoyed Menlo-Atherton. All of it. Politically, though, I just didn't pay attention to what was going on in the country. That's terrible. Nowadays, I don't think that's true of high school kids. I think of myself as being an air head in high school, even though I graduated with a B average.

I had lots of friends at M-A: Susan Samuels, Jackie Cook, Joanne Broeren, Alice Taylor. Chris Cochrane, Susie Holt and Lynn Nicholas. We still get together. Susan Samuels Drake is a catalyst. She keeps up with people. We usually wind up by a beach, and we giggle like we did in high school. We just have a ball, like a big slumber party, talking about all kinds of stuff. It's therapeutic for me; we don't have to go get counseling. We're getting together again right after our class's fiftieth reunion, when I'll see Sonny for the first time, practically, since we left high school.

I loved boys. I loved dating. But I decided to attend all-girls Stevens College in Missouri. I picked Stevens because it was farther away than Mills and Scripps, two California schools which had accepted me. I needed to be away from my family. I was very protected growing up. There were things I could do and things I couldn't do. Then I regretted my decision about Stevens because it was a school with too many girls. The best thing that happened to me my freshman year was meeting my future husband, Al Montaudon. He attended the University of Missouri. I transferred to Missouri for my sophomore year.

Choosing Stevens was a good decision in another way, and that was getting to know the Midwest, which is very different from California. Midwest people are very friendly, very open. Their lifestyle is very different. They talk slower. They'd tell me to slow down when I spoke to them. California is very nice, beautiful, manicured. Being in the Midwest was very broadening. Al's from the Midwest, from Missouri. We dated my last three years of college and got married in 1961, a year after we graduated together.

Al was a business major. After our wedding, we moved to the Bahamas, where he ran the Nassau branch of a company that made loans to servicemen. We had a ball those two years, especially skin-diving. Then we moved to Savannah, Georgia, which we didn't enjoy because everyone was into their families. We couldn't break in. Next stop was Augusta, Georgia, where we saw the Masters Golf Tournament, which was wonderful. Then Al decided he wanted to go to California. We lived for a while in my parents' basement in Los Altos Hills.

We waited five years before having children, then had four boys. I love boys of all sizes, but it's an adventure every day with little boys. I felt that way even when I was a little girl. Boys are just more enjoyable to be around. They're funny, and rough, and they're a lot more fun than playing jacks with the girls.

I really enjoyed being a mother. Life was good. Al was one of four vice-presidents in a large corporation. We bought into the lifestyle with a new home in Los Altos and a second home on Anderson Island in Washington state. The kids each got a new car when they graduated from high school. We took them to Hawaii and on many fun vacations. Then Al got canned and everything changed.

We sold our house in Los Altos and moved into the house on Anderson Island. We were there eight years. Al didn't have a job for five of those years. It's a very demoralizing thing for a man. Al is the stoic type, doesn't talk about things. He'll just say, "Everything's fine." Drove me insane. But he always wanted to start a restaurant, and so he opened Montaudon's on the island. And he loved it, working fourteen-hour days, doing the cooking himself. He wasn't available to us for Thanksgiving or Christmas. Financially, we lost our shirts. People lived on this island for a reason: They didn't want to go out for dinner much. We should have done more investigating.

Then we had a bit of a problem: Al wanted me to be the restaurant hostess and I didn't want to be. Fortunately, his sister moved up to the island and became the hostess. I went to work, instead, for the county library system, something I really loved doing, though it meant working evenings. I didn't always make it home on the last ferry. I've worked in libraries ever since, mostly at schools. Reading is important to me as an English major. Being around books and helping kids to read is very fulfilling.

We had friends who went through the same thing, the husband losing his job. Some couples didn't make it and divorced. We've fought throughout our marriage; Al loves to fight and is good at it. Besides, we were in Washington state, which was depressing enough, so dark and dreary and rainy. We had a lot of rough times, but we never thought we were going to split up. That whole experience was good for our kids, who were used to money and having everything being hunky-dory. Then they realized dad's not going to be there for them (financially) all the time. We didn't go on vacation for a long time. One son had to get funding to finish college. But the boys never complained.

Al got out of the first restaurant and then managed a second one at a country club. Finally, we had to do something because our bank statement was getting very low. Al decided to take whatever was out there. He started looking at low-level jobs. My sister lives in Tucson, Arizona. We had visited there, liked it, and Al looked for work in the Tucson area. He found a job with this company that has done nothing but go up ever since. Al just got a big promotion for someone his age, almost seventy. We've been in Tucson seven years and life is good again, except for one area of our family.

One of our sons went to Iraq, and that experience did him in. There's stuff wrong with him now psychologically. He joined the Army wanting to work in intelligence. He met his wife in the Army. They both went to Iraq, but are back now. He's thirty-seven, she's thirty-six, and she wants babies. Now. He doesn't want any kids because he feels it's a sucky world and he doesn't want to bring kids into a world where they're going to have to go off to war and maybe get killed. I talk to him all the time. I tell him, "It's not just your decision. There's two of you to consider." He has had lots of counseling. His wife made him go because he awakened in the middle of the night screaming. He is sort of lost now, withdrawn, and we don't seem to know how to help him.

I don't think America should be in Iraq. I've been against it from the beginning. My son went over with the impression that he had to go, and maybe he can do some good. His attitude is that we need to get all the terrorists because they're going to get us. Well, you can't get all the terrorists.

I don't see an outcome to this war that's going to be very good. What we're doing is creating more people who hate us, creating more people who are going to become terrorists. This is political, and I'm much more political now than I was as a high school queen. I certainly hope that the democracy we're trying to install in Iraq holds, but I'm not sure what our agenda is over there. There's so much hate in that part of the world, hate based on generations of hate. You can't convince these people that they have to get along. Will we ever get to the point where their getting along is the case?

We did the same thing in Vietnam. We decided to go in there and fix it. Looking at the results, we didn't do anything. And what did it get us? I'm more dove-ish today. Looking at World War II, our fighting men were heroes. My dad couldn't go in the service at the time because his eyes were bad. But our military back then were the good guys. I don't feel that way today because of our government. It's all about retribution. We have friends from the Vietnam conflict who were damaged, too. They saw really awful stuff. You feel sorry for people like that.

Oh, here it is, my high school graduation picture. What was I thinking? I wanted to go to college and graduate. I didn't know what I wanted to major in, but I knew I would figure it out. And I looked forward to getting married and having kids. I didn't have any career aspirations. Compared to kids today, I wasn't very—what's the word?—ambitious.

But that girl in the photo would approve of what I did, of becoming a mother, of working in the library, and working with kids. Some people who went to M-A did more exciting things. Stevie Nicks was the lead singer on Fleetwood Mac. When I told my kids that I was being interviewed for this book, they said, "It must have been a boring high school. Can't they come up with someone more exciting than you?"

* 22 *

The Midas Touch

Jerry Berger was a college dropout who became a multi-millionaire in the building parts business, furnishing exclusive hotels in Nevada and New Jersey. He owns six apartment complexes, nine condominiums and two car washes. He does well in the stock market and holds his own as a high-stakes gambler.

I could open almost any kind of business and make it work. My accountant always told me I have the golden touch. I could find a strip mall and make a pet shop a success. I could make money opening a restaurant. I don't feel I'd ever have a problem making money. It's confidence, I guess.

I didn't go to college very long. I just use common sense. It's about making friends. It's about personality. Give me a million dollars, you can trust me. I'm relatively honest. I have the ability to organize and get things done. I feel I know how I want it done, and I can get it done that way. If I turn it over to somebody else, it may get done only eighty per cent of the way I want it done. So if I do it my way, it will be done the right way.

I was an entrepreneur even as a kid. I had a newspaper route in grammar school. I paid a guy to deliver the paper on Fridays, paid him half-price. That's because at a local supermarket, a guy named Sam needed help selling fish. And Catholics ate a lot of fish on Fridays.

I had that supermarket job six months until people found out I was too young. But in front of that market, you could sell four different San Francisco newspapers on Saturday. I could make as much money in one

Dropout to millionaire

Jerry Berger

day selling papers as I could in a whole month of delivering papers. But I always did the collecting on my paper route; that way, I got the tips.

After my family moved to Menlo Park before my sophomore year in high school, I worked in Marcel's Bakery. Plus I mowed the lawns of nine or ten customers. I got an Menlo-Atherton classmate, George Tygret, and one other guy to cut the lawns while I worked at Marcel's; I'd give them half of what we made cutting grass. I also worked at Purity Market in Palo Alto. I had a brand-new Ford when I went to college, although my dad and I each paid half.

I was thinking even then on how to make money. I didn't know how, really, except to get a bunch of customers and get somebody else to do the work, and then make double by working another job at the same time. I got that mover-and-shaker personality from my mother. She was very vivacious, a singer on the radio in her younger days before getting into the cosmetics field. Everybody liked her. Maybe that's why I've wound up as president of almost everything I get involved with. They keep electing me and re-electing me.

I went to San Jose City College for two semesters. I hated it and quit. My dad was an architect. He designed markets, and I worked for one of them, QFI. I moved up quickly to head clerk in charge of frozen foods, ordering frozen foods for all six QFI stores. It was a pretty neat job. I had tickets to 49ers games, Roller Derby, baseball games at Seals Stadium.

Then my father was hired to work on this lift-slab project in Reno; that's constructing a building slab by slab and then filling in between. He felt he could be a big fish in a small bowl in Reno instead of a small fish in a big bowl in San Francisco. My parents moved to Reno right after I got married. My younger sister, Judy, was at the University of Nevada. My wife, Barbara, and I visited them. There was snow on the ground. I thought that was wonderful. The next time I came up, there were guys in shorts standing in the Truckee River, catching trout downtown. Where do you see that in Menlo Park?

I asked my dad what kind of job could I get in Reno. He knew of a small roofing company, Spesco, that was just starting out and looking for a salesman. Barbara got pregnant on our honeymoon, but Spesco held a job open for me until the baby was born and we could move to Reno.

I sold roofing, siding and insulation. I found it easy work. My company said "go fishing" because they couldn't handle the volume of business I was bringing in. They were selling twenty five to thirty thousand dollars worth of roofing a month before I got there. A year after I joined them, they were selling two hundred thousand dollars worth a month. That's why they made me a junior partner.

I worked at Spesco seven years with only weekends off, sometimes, and only one or two days of vacation a year. We were open six days a week. I suggested we sell more hardware because of the markup. The senior partner said, "I'm a roofing man." That's when I decided to leave. But when I tried to collect as a junior partner, they wouldn't even give me vacation pay.

And so I started Berger Building Supply by borrowing twenty five thousand dollars from the bank and by buying supplies from Spesco at ten percent over cost. The senior partner made me pay, even though I had made a ton of money for him. After I left the company, he told everyone I would be broke in two years. The funny thing: He went broke two years later.

I did starve to death the first seven years of my own business, making one thousand dollars a month. And that was after working my butt off. Then I got in with the right people: the giant high-rise hotels. I became the biggest distributor of redi-frames door frames in the world. In Reno, I did all the Circus Circuses, the El Dorados, the Peppermill, the Atlantis. In Las Vegas, we did the Excalibur, which amounted to four-thousand rooms, plus the Rio Hotels, the Stardust, Treasure Island, Sam's Town and a lot of smaller hotels.

We also found business in Atlantic City. We did the Boardwalk Regency One, the Boardwalk Regency Two and the Playboy Club. Door frames became a big deal. And so did hardware. At Spesco, many general contractors liked me. Now on my own, I felt they would buy their medicine cabinets and door locks from me. And they did. I opened a warehouse in Las Vegas so that all the stuff could be delivered there for the hotels we furnished.

I made a lot of money, thirty percent profit on each job. When the job runs four to five million dollars in labor, you get a pretty good hunk. Same thing with materials. But after twelve years of doing it our way, we started getting competition. I pulled in my horns. I scaled back, because I didn't want to bid jobs for three or four percent. The installation company was union and there was no cushion for error at three or four percent markup.

Then a guy came to me about a business deal: building car washes. I flew my own plane to Salt Lake City to check them out. I was impressed, because for the first time in my life, I could have a business where people don't charge anything and then don't pay you. With car washes, they've got to pay you before they get in there. So I built car washes. If I was younger and just starting out, I'd have built ten to fifteen. I decided on three, but the one in Sparks was so far away from me that I sold it and paid off the other two. The two car washes I have left are very profitable. My junior partner, who owns twenty percent, does all the maintenance. Every night, he comes to my house with the money we've made that day. We pulled in one hundred thousand dollars more on the two car washes in 2005 than we made the year before.

I don't fly any more. I'm overweight and probably couldn't fit in the cockpit. I do have a sixty-three-foot yacht that was one-point-six-million dollars off the floor. We keep it in a boat house just north of Victoria, British Columbia. I drive it myself. I bought five condominiums in Maui that I paid for in cash. I'm building a condo in Mexico, right on the water. I also bought a high-rise condo in downtown Reno that overlooks the Truckee River. There's really not much of anything that I need or want.

Though it has been fifty years, I still remember a lot about Menlo-Atherton High. The journalism teacher, Mr. (Douglas) Murray, made me sports editor of the school newspaper. I still can see the layout of the school and our "senior prank." That was the day we locked a horse in the administration building during the teachers' morning break. Gene Smith had these tempered big straps with padlocks that were impossible to cut. We strapped them around the glass doors at each end of the building after coaxing some freshman who lived a few blocks away to bring his horse to school. We threatened him if he didn't. Fred Gayer was another ringleader. I was only a helper, but we cut the telephone lines so the teachers couldn't call out. Then three of us threw a body block on Mr. (Jimmy) Coffis, the dean of boys, to prevent him from keeping the doors open. That took some doing because he had been a star halfback at Stanford in the 1930s.

The only teachers who weren't locked up were the coaches in the gymnasium across campus. I think it was Mr. (Howard) Costello, the varsity football and baseball coach, who came over later because he couldn't get a phone call through to the administration. He called the fire department, which let the teachers out. We were happy because we had them locked up for two hours and forty-five minutes, a "senior prank" record. I don't remember the teachers getting mad; they took it pretty well. And I don't know of anyone who got caught. I went home and changed clothes so I wouldn't be recognized. I knew Mr. Coffis hadn't gotten a good look at me.

I also remember guys dropping cherry bombs down the toilets. Cherry bombs stay lit under water. When they went off, every toilet blew because they all had the same pipes. The girls would get all wet. Someone got caught, and it cost his family a thousand dollars, because the pipes were cracked.

The wrestling coach, Sam Lugonja, didn't like me very much. He bought a brand new Oldsmobile with spinner hubcaps. Somebody stole them and he was told Jerry Berger did it. Lugonja purposely bumped into me several times in the locker room. Mr. Costello saw what was happening and chewed him out. Well, there was another Jerry Berger in school, one year behind me, and I think he stole the hubcaps. But Mr. Coffis told me to have my dad at school the next day. There were a bunch of people in the room. My dad got very upset and grabbed somebody by the shirt. But I really didn't take those hubcaps.

I didn't take school too awful seriously. I did what I had to do to pass my classes. I was part of a hot rod club, The Shocks. Donald Day was in it; he always had a nice car. We had parties where I played the accordion. That song, "Smoke, Smoke, Smoke That Cigarette," we played it all the time. We had blue jackets and a big patch with a red shock absorber on it. I had a lowered, tan 1949 Mercury, even though I wasn't mechanically inclined. We had enough guys in the club to do those kinds of things.

I filled in for Jerry Juhl a few times as a disc jockey, playing music at noontime. The Fifties were a great time. High school was fun. I went to all the dances. You talk about Donald Day being the jitterbug champ; I agree, but I gave him a run for his money a few times. One of my neighbors was Dorothy Crofts, who was a year behind me at M-A. She was Mormon, and the Mormons had dances every weekend up and down the Peninsula. So every weekend, I went to a dance. We were welcome as long as we minded our manners.

I kind of liked the girls at Notre Dame, a Catholic girls high school in Belmont. Catholic girls like to sow their wild oats on Saturday night, then go to church on Sunday and pray for crop failure. George Tygret and I decided a great way to meet girls would be to have a teenage club. At Nativity Church in Menlo Park, there was this big hall. We made friends with the priest, who agreed to let us hold dances there once a week on a weekday night. I was the club president. George and I passed out messages all over the Peninsula. The turnout was three to one, girls to boys. We had an old jukebox. Some football players from the San Francisco 49ers even came by.

After high school, George and I opened up another social club at St. Pius Church in Redwood City. I was the club president. We had a dance, "Autumn Leaves," at Hillview School in Menlo Park. I needed a decoration committee chairman, but no one would volunteer. I saw a girl there for the first time. I said, "You look like a good decoration chairman." She said, "How would you know? You don't even know me." Everybody laughed at me. Her name was Barbara Vinciquerra. She was Italian, and her last name meant "win the war." I married her a year and a half later in 1960.

The Salk polio vaccine was discovered in the 1950s, a major discovery, but it came too late to help me. I had both bulbar and spinal polio as a kid. I missed the fifth grade after being isolated nine weeks. I was fed intravenously because I couldn't swallow. They put hot packs on me twice a day. It was horrible. I'm still missing a muscle in the side of my neck, which made it hard to play football in high school. So I quit after my sophomore year. The polio made me 4-F from the military. Today, if I see a needle, it shakes me up. That's why I won't take Novocain whenever dentists work on my teeth.

Even though I hate needles, I've had two knee replacements, mostly from playing racquet ball three, four days a week, two hours a day, in Reno. All that activity wore out my cartilage. Plus the rotator cuff is gone in one shoulder. And I'm a diabetic. With my knees, I'm reluctant to do anything exercise-wise. I also have a little water around the heart; I take two water pills a day. A friend uses a personal trainer, but they come over too early in the morning. I hate getting up early. So I'm just waiting.

Barbara and I have lived in only one house in Reno. I don't drive fancy cars, although I could easily. I have a twelve-year-old Cadillac, the oldest car in the family. I'm a multi-millionaire, but I'm too fat for a Maserati. I'm just one of the regular neighbors in our neighborhood. I have two daughters, and I've given each thirty percent of my business.

I've accomplished a lot. Twice a day, I get on the Internet to check the stock market. I'm pretty heavy into stocks. I told Barbara we should move into that condo downtown, maybe buy some furniture, live in it a month or two, then see where we want to live. But we'll keep our home and the building supply for my employees. One person has worked for me nineteen years, another twenty-six years. I'm not going to sell the business out from under them.

I do like to gamble, and the casinos fight over me. I'm in the top ten percent of high rollers at the Atlantis. I'll go by the car washes and Berger Building Supply in the morning to check up on things. About 1 p.m., I meet friends at the Atlantis. We have lunch until 2 p.m. Then I go to the high-limit area and play poker machines and other objects until almost 6 p.m. Then I go home. I do this Monday through Friday. I usually lose, but not all that much on the average. Had my best day ever a few weeks ago, won forty-two thousand dollars. I went to the Peppermill and won three thousand, only to go back there and lose the three thousand.

That's my high school graduation picture? I remember him, skinny guy. What did I want to be? I didn't do too well in mechanical drawing; I couldn't draw a straight line. So being an architect like my dad was out. I knew journalism wasn't too good because I'm a lousy speller. I'm trying to remember if I had any ideas back then about what I wanted to be.

That same uncertain kid would think I've accomplished a lot. The only thing is, I've gotten fat, old and ugly. But that happens to a lot of people, two out of three. I didn't become a garbage man and stay that way all my life.

I'm sure a lot of people are more intelligent than I am, but I'd have to think I got somewhere.

Making a splash

Carol Tait

★ 23 ★

The Swimmer

Carol Tait Harkins Macpherson Remen—she goes by Carol Macpherson—was the Class of 1956's finest athlete, a national swim champion when college team sports and athletic scholarships weren't available to California girls. She missed the Olympics by the slightest margin, but teaches swimming today.

George Haines was my Santa Clara Swim Club coach. George also was an Olympic coach. He's a legend, the greatest of all swim coaches. I've been told many times that I was his first star. He gave me this important bit of advice when I was a young girl, advice that I've carried with me ever since.

George always said, "No matter how tired you are, and no matter how you feel, you never stop in the middle of a race." One time, he had me swim the 100-yard butterfly, which wasn't even my event. I'm a freestyle swimmer. I still am to this day. I hadn't ever trained in the 100 fly, but George needed me to swim it this particular day because it involved a team trophy.

I believe in the team concept, so I entered the 100 fly. I thought I was going to die. I was in an end lane, at a time when swimming pool gutters were really tiny and all the backwash would come into the end lane. So every time I tried to breathe, I'd inhale all this water. But I was thinking, "If I stop, George will kill me." So I finished the race.

I've used George's philosophy my entire life. I'm a go-do-it-and-finish-it kind of person. My average work day even now extends from 5 a.m. to 11:30 p.m. I coach the masters swim program, which is year-round and takes up three mornings, plus two nights and Saturday. In the summers, I also have my Carol Macpherson Swim School four days a week.

And if I find the time, I'm training myself for masters competition. During the winter, I do maintenance training, swimming 2,500 yards a session three days a week. That takes an hour and fifteen minutes. On Tuesdays and Thursdays, I do weights for an hour, weights specific to my swimming. After a workout, I feel refreshed, just like I've always felt after a workout.

My ninety-four-year-old mother always asks, "When are you going to sit down?" Sunday is my day of rest. But that's when I do the yard work, mowing the lawn, trimming the roses. On Sundays, I also do housework and the laundry. I'll sit down sometimes and watch TV for four hours. I don't read a lot, because I'm on the computer. But I always stay busy. That's who I am.

If I have the chance now to train seriously, I can come within five percent of my best times as a teen-ager. I've made swimming my vocation as well as my avocation because it's a good quality of life. You use your whole body. It doesn't stop you from having a heart attack or other medical problems, but your quality of life is so much better. My specialty is distance swimming. I had good stamina as a teen-ager. I still do as a senior citizen.

I started swimming at seven years of age in Palo Alto at the Rinconada pool—the same place where I now coach swimming. I was born in San Francisco, where my parents grew up and met as high school sweethearts. My mother thought I should take swimming lessons. I have a sister, Carleen, who's three years younger and also was successful nationally as a swimmer. But she wasn't as dedicated as I was, so she quit. She was more into art and horses.

We didn't inherent our swimming genes from our parents. My mom would swim with her head up. My dad didn't swim; he was like a rock in the water. He was an auctioneer by trade. His business was called "Tait Auction." My mom worked with him and they auctioned antiques from all over Europe and from local estates in Burlingame, Hillsborough and Atherton.

Haines' swim teams trained at the Santa Clara High School pool—six lanes wide, twenty-five yards long. George had started the swim club in 1951. I swam there until 1956, competing in my first nationals in Portland, Oregon. I was fourteen and placed fifth in three events. The next nationals were in Fort Lauderdale, Florida; a short-course nationals of 25 yards. I won my first national title there in the 500 freestyle. I was fifteen. Then I made the Pan-American Games team and placed third in the 400 free in Mexico City, competing against twenty-one other countries.

Though I entered Menlo-Atherton as a freshman, M-A kids didn't see a lot of me until my senior year. That's because I worked out once a day for George after school, five days a week, all year long. We also trained on Saturday morning. So I didn't make many friends in high school. I was never there. I went to some of the dances. But after school, when kids would hang out, I was down at Santa Clara, training. A lot of my social friends were down there with me. Swimmers every one.

I wasn't on M-A's campus all that much except for classes. I became more visible my senior year after I got this gray Cadillac, a late-1940s Fleetwood, from my parents. That was so my mom wouldn't have to drive me to practice any more. I had five or six M-A girls I drove around with, having fun, although I'm having a hard time remembering their names.

I've been to one or two class reunions. People come up to me, but I don't remember them. They ask me if I'm still swimming. I've had a good time at the reunions, because I love to dance. And I've enjoyed these same kids as adults. It's just that I don't know them.

That same summer I graduated from Menlo-Atherton, I went to the 1956 Olympic Swimming Trials in Detroit. I was intense about making the Olympics, which were held that year in Melbourne, Australia. Maybe I was too intense. I swam a fairly good 400-meter freestyle, but I could have done better. The girl who won, Dougie Gray, beat me by two-tenths of a second.

Though I finished second, I didn't make the team. That's because in those days, they took only the first-place swimmers—except in the 100 free, where they needed four swimmers for the 400-meter relay. That was my bad luck. It's not like that any more; second- and third-place finishers at the Olympic Trials make the American team. I also felt cheated when I found out later on that high school sports now were available to girls. In the 1950s, I didn't think much about it; they just weren't available. So you didn't feel cheated.

Still, I was devastated that I didn't make the Olympics. Swimming had been my whole focus for six years. My first reaction after losing in the Trials was to break into tears. George knew I was upset, so he didn't even talk to me. I went over to the other pool, got in, and swam for twenty minutes to a half-hour until I got it out of my system. That settled me down.

After that, I retired. There was nothing for girl swimmers, no college scholarships. So I quit swimming at eighteen. Swimmers back then didn't swim when they were older, not like they do today. But I didn't want to swim some more and go downhill. I saw an Olympic swimmer do that. Dougie Gray didn't do much swimming after winning those Trials. I wanted to leave on top.

But the next year, George needed someone to swim relays. He asked if I would come back and train. I did and swam a lot of relays for him. That was the first year the Santa Clara Swim Club won the national team title. It was great to be a part of that. Then I retired for good.

I didn't experience any serious withdrawal from swimming. After my disappointment in the swim trials, I had to decide what to do next. I went to the College of San Mateo, a local junior college, for a year. But college wasn't something I was interested in. I was only an average student, but I've done well as a teacher. A teacher of swimming.

In college, I started going out with Virgil Harkins, who was one class behind me at Menlo-Atherton. He belonged to this car club, and I think I met him that way through some other people. We got married when I was almost nineteen. Because my parents always had a good relationship, I felt you got married and had kids. And I wanted to have them early, so that when I got older, I wanted to be really active.

Virg and I had three children together. I loved being with my kids. I love kids. I teach water babies now. They're just the greatest. My three kids were all water babies. Debbie started swimming at three and a half, Bryon at six months, and Carl at a month old.

After marrying Virg, I started teaching swimming at Addison Jane's Swim School on Willow Road in Menlo Park. That enabled me to get free swim lessons for my kids. I discovered teaching was something I was good at. I still feel the same way. I will continue to teach swimming until....whenever. As long as I feel good, I'll teach at the swim school and in the masters' program. And I'll keep swimming as long as I have the time to do it.

Virg had a great sense of humor. He worked for his dad's sign-painting business in Menlo Park, then started his own sign-painting company. But he was doing a lot of running around. After seven years of marriage, we divorced. It turned out I was ready for marriage and Virg wasn't. Whenever we'd meet people after our divorce, he would tell them, "It was my fault for the divorce. I wasn't mature enough." Virg passed away in 2004 from cancer.

I married again not that long after divorcing Virg. I met Joel Macpherson at a local party. He was a carpet layer. We stayed married twelve years, even though he was in and out of jobs. My kids were in high school, we had just bought a house, and it was getting to the point where I was supporting Joel. It was getting worse and worse, so I left him.

By then, I had gotten into masters swimming. Anne Warner Cribbs, who graduated from M-A after I did and won a swimming relay gold medal at the 1960 Olympics in Rome, Italy, called me in 1972 with the masters idea. She said, "Let's get some swimmers together and train." So we trained for six weeks and entered the first masters nationals at the College of San Mateo.

"Six weeks," I told myself, "I'm in shape." I entered the 1,650, 800 and 400 freestyle events. Halfway through the 1,650, I thought, "This is not the right thing to be doing," I died so bad, but I finished. George would have found out if I hadn't.

What a shock. I wasn't in good shape at all. I had taught swimming since I was twenty-one, and thought I was in pretty good shape because I was in the water with the kids, training them. Well, this was a starting point anyway. But we needed someone who would coach us year-round. Only we couldn't find a coach.

That's when Tom Osborne, the aquatics director at the Palo Alto Recreation Department, said to me, "Why don't you and Cindy Baxter do it? You know all the strokes." So I said OK, and started with this early bird program at Rinconada three days a week, where people did their laps. Those workouts at 500 yards aren't really much by today's standards.

From there, we progressed to an intermediate workout, then to an advanced workout. After a three-month trial, we started with a team of fifteen swimmers. In 1973, we took our team to the nationals in Santa Monica. And we did really well, clocking some good times.

The next year, the nationals were held in Santa Clara. I started finding my old Santa Clara teammates. I told them they had to get back in the water. There were three masters teams in the area—the San Mateo Marlins, De Anza and Rinconada, which has a twenty-five-yard, fourteen-lane pool.

Masters swimming groups start at age twenty and are broken down into five-year increments all the way up to one hundred. Don't laugh. The oldest swimmer I know of is one hundred and four. He might be the only swimmer in his age category. But my mom is swimming pretty fast for a ninety-four-year-old, and she's relatively new to the sport.

What I discovered about myself as a masters swimmer is that I'm still competitive. It's all part of swimming fast, feeling good. I like teaching, but I also like training. And, being the competitor, winning.

I've found you can improve your swimming times into your forties, but not after. But I feel as good as my body feels. In 1994, the whole feeling I had when I was a younger swimmer came back to me. That year, I decided to really train. Weights didn't come into popularity until the 1980s. So for six months that year, I swam five to six days a week and lifted weights three days a week. I got down to 136 pounds, which is as close as I've been to my high-school weight of 125 pounds since I left M-A.

I felt really good in 1994 even though I was in my fifties. I felt as good as I did in the 1950s, when I really was in shape. In '94, I swam the 1,000, 500 and the 200 free. I did the best time I've ever done in the 100 free, which was not my favorite race. I won all five of my events, all within five per cent of my all-time best times. Although you can't improve your best times in your fifties, you can get close.

It's finding the time to train that's the problem. I have other things going on, like a business to run. I have ninety swimmers in the year-round masters program. With my swim school, I run six sessions during the summer with six-hundred kids. I'm on the computer setting up scheduling. So I do my 2,500 yards swimming at 7 a.m. after coaching at 5:45.

While swimming and teaching, I married a third time, four years after my second divorce. I stayed busy. His name was John Remen. He worked for Lockheed for a while, then he was a consultant for Lockheed and for NASA. He had five kids who were all grown when I met him.

I like being married. I like a relationship. Single isn't where I like to be. I was married to John about ten years. We just stopped getting along. It turned out that he wasn't a happy person. He was fighting with his kids, having problems. I'm really a positive person. I like being up. When I started getting negative vibes in the house, John and I ended up getting a divorce.

I didn't keep John's last name because I'm well known in swimming as Carol Macpherson. All three of my husbands have passed away. And I've dealt with death in another personal way. My youngest child, Carl, was killed at eighteen. He was on a bicycle, holding onto his friend's mo-ped, when he let go, kind of veered off, and a car hit him head-on. He went over the car and was knocked unconscious.

I went to the hospital. They tested Carl for three days, but he was brain dead. I donated all of his organs. Unfortunately, there was nobody at the time to take his heart, and he was in great shape physically.

Losing Carl was really hard. All my kids were close to me, but Carl was the baby, really kind and sweet. Never did much wrong. I had a hard time going to funerals for a while. I still have trouble talking about Carl.

The way I look at life, people come into the world for a purpose, to teach or learn. And when your purpose is done, you go on. I'm very spiritual, so I believe in reincarnation. I don't believe that you just die and you're gone. You come back. That belief helps restore your faith.

And I still think there's a right man out there for me. I've had two relationships since my last divorce, but they weren't anyone I would marry. I'm a really strong person. When I'm coaching on the deck, guys look at me in a different way. I'm very outward. Some men could be a little intimidated by that. Even when I teach the kids, I coach in a way to give them confidence. But I have a soft side which shows itself when I'm married and with kids.

In 1995, I was inducted into the Menlo-Atherton Hall of Fame, the first person from my graduating class to receive such an honor. It's a neat thing to be considered the best athlete in my class. It's progress for women, too, making them understand they can do things like that. Back when I was swimming as a teenager, you almost had to retire at a young age. I would have kept on swimming if there had been college scholarships for women, because I really enjoyed swimming and the competition. But I don't have too many regrets in my life. I've done well. My parents are proud of me.

I wasn't timid at all in swimming. The confidence was there. But I didn't have confidence on a social level at that age. I wasn't that sure of myself. Even today, in a big social group, I'm kind of quiet. But I am more outward now than I was in high school, much more social.

I look at my graduation picture and I think "Terrible hairdo." But I see a happy person. That's always been me. I don't see the competitiveness in that picture, but it's here inside me. My life has been a great improvement since then. That girl in the picture would think I've progressed quite well.

There's one more thing I want to do with my life. I want to build an indoor swim school. This would mean teaching year-round for me. But you can't teach little kids when it's cold. If they aren't performing well in the water, it may not be because they're scared. They could be cold.

An indoor pool is where I'm headed in life. I've got my business plans done. I've got my financials done, my blueprints done. It will be a six-lane, twenty-five-yard-long pool inside a building with glass sides and a ceiling that opens up.

I have a piece of property in mind. If I can buy it, that would be great because it gives me a better chance of getting loans. If I have to lease property, I'm going to have a hard time getting money. I have a bank in Redwood City willing to work with me as long as I can raise the money.

The "Carol Macpherson Aquatic Center" is something I want to leave behind. It's part of me, part of my teaching, why I was meant to be on this earth. This aquatic center would be my legacy, what I want to give to the world, and to the children. I want them to have the same love of swimming for life that I have.

It would be a great moment for me one day to stand in front of an aquatic center with my name on it. That would mean success, but it would also give me the wonderful feeling of knowing I accomplished what I set out to do. As George Haines told me years ago, "Never give up. Never stop."

The rich kid

Stewart Morton

✶24✶

Mr. San Francisco

Stewart Morton contends he wasn't the richest kid in the Class of 1956. But no classmate was more privileged. He's still enjoying the good life, though occasionally re-inventing himself. He is the consummate urbanite, caught up in San Francisco's social swirl. It is all, he feels, terrific.

San Francisco is where I've lived since the early 1960s. It is very special, like nowhere else. That's because we care about lifestyle. If you ask me what San Francisco has over other cities, it's the sophistication, but not the largeness. The size is really important. We are only forty-nine square miles, with seven-hundred and fifty thousand people. It is a very tolerable, do-able city. We use the word "Manhattanization" as a negative. We work against becoming that type of city.

My next favorite city in America? I don't have one. But, all right, it has to be New York. I'm there several times a year to enjoy the restaurants, museums, theater and opera. I support the San Francisco Opera, but the Met is far superior. Our weather is far superior, and the pace here, as I said, is tolerable. We do work hard to continue to make San Francisco wonderful.

In 1971, I was one of the founders of the San Francisco Architectural Heritage, and I remained on its board of directors for more than twenty-five years. I served on the mayor-appointed Landmarks Board under mayors George Moscone, Dianne Feinstein and Frank Jordan. Willie Brown was to appoint me, too, however he forgot. I saw him at a party many months later. He said to me, "Oh, shit, I forgot." I told him that it was probably wise, because he would have fired me from the board by now, for I wasn't in his pocket, I know what is best for the city, and I'm quite outspoken about preservation. Brown stalked away from me, and he didn't speak to me for a year or so.

In the early years of the Architectural Heritage, we fought for the retention of the City of Paris department store, which we lost after six years of confrontation. However, the Architectural Heritage gained much support. Financially, we were among the leading preservation organizations in the country. And we're still active in helping to maintain architectural integrity in San Francisco.

These days, I spend most of my volunteer time involved with the activities of the Port of San Francisco and its development. I have spent much time on various technical and advisory committees, and continue to do so. I was one of the main players in the Loma Prieta earthquake of 1989. Our committee held weekly meetings for about six months, cleverly making sure our adversaries were present (Mayor Art Agnos and Chinatown, North Beach and Fisherman's Wharf merchants). With continued information supplied, we slowly convinced them of the value of demolition, and the value of the rebuilt and redesigned Embarcadero Freeway. Today's resultant product justifies our efforts.

In the 1970s, I would have run for the position of San Francisco supervisor. However, I decided to marry Natasha instead. I met Natasha, a blonde Australian, in Bali, where I was visiting for a month while a house I was designing in Jakarta was being worked on. I had just completed a twenty-thousand-square-foot home in Manila's Forbes Park. With my scuba gear and a lot of time, I visited the great places of Southeast Asia.

That's where I found Natasha. She was visiting Bali with her husband's attorney and his wife. But not with her husband, who remained in Sydney. We fell madly in love instantly, which was very easy to do in Bali. After one week, Natasha flew home to Sydney and started divorce proceedings. We were married in San Francisco's Grace Cathedral two years later with a Bohemian reception. It was all really terrific.

For ten years, we lived in Sydney, London and San Francisco, doing all the good things. We were in the newspaper columns a lot with very high visibility. Natasha was a Grace Kelly lookalike. When she entered a room, the room stood still, just like the time I first met her in Bali. She affected people easily. In Sydney, we lived in the Eastern Suburbs in Point Piper, which was very much like Belvedere in Marin County. In London, we used an apartment behind the Atheneum. In San Francisco, we used my home on Russian Hill which overlooked the bay from the Golden Gate Bridge to Treasure Island. It was a grand life.

Natasha had three boys from her previous marriage. Their ages at the time of our marriage were four, six and eight. Becoming the father of three boys at thirty-nine was terrific. We had great times together. We shared the boys with their father, but we were able to have them in San Francisco each year, either at Christmas or during their school holidays.

Natasha and I divorced ten years later. I found out that I was still growing intellectually, and Natasha was not. The lady I now see, we have similar IQ's, which is so important. However, I would not have missed the Natasha years for anything. Living the international life was incredible.

I think I was the last one in the Class of 1956 to be married. I won a bottle of champagne at one of our reunions for being the only class-mate still single. The previous reunion, Olin Hughes and I were the only single ones.

Growing up in Woodside, I had the best parents in Richard Edward Morton and Helen Stewart Morton. My mother's maiden name became my first name. My parents and I were the best buddies. They gave me the choice of attending private Menlo School or public Menlo-Atherton High School. I needed a coed school, thus M-A was my choice. Our Woodside home, which was the location of two M-A graduation par-ties—one planned, one impromptu—was the home of Lurline Matson Roth before she moved into the exquisite Filoli on Canada Road.

Our house, on the "Why Worry Farm" property, had twenty-six rooms and was constructed of the same sandstone from a Stanford quarry. It is mentioned in "Here Today," the architectural heritage book published by the San Francisco Junior League, which became the first acknowledged inventory of significant architecture. The original struc-ture was built in the late Nineteenth Century, and was added on, then added on some more, to gain its current size. Captain Matson of the Matson Lines added the most, then gave the home to Mr. and Mrs. Roth as a wedding present. John Arrillaga bought it in the 1990s, refurbished it over several years, and just sold it for twenty-four million dollars. Mother and father bought it in the 1940s for thirty-seven thousand, five-hundred. California real estate is truly wonderful.

My family was totally "Ozzie and Harriet," with two sons and a great relationship among us. However, my brother was ten years older than me, so he and I were never close, not like David and Ricky Nelson. He went to Stanford. I'm the only one from my family still alive. But I doubt if any of my friends at M-A had the same relationship with their parents that I did. I was blessed, and I'm certainly glad they allowed me to attend M-A. I loved the school. I remember lots of great times during those four years, including driving around in my 1949 red Ford convertible with lots of friends. Got my first ticket in that car, driving over the double line of El Camino Real after leaving Marquard's, our drive-in spot that we hit after dates, games and dances.

After the red Ford, I had a 1955 Buick convertible, white with red interior, which I kept through college. I was always extroverted, always knew everybody, always was interested in everybody. Sheila Gray was Social Commissioner at M-A. Rhoda Maxfield was Spirit Commissioner. I helped them both. I remember assisting Sheila with the Winter Wonderland dance. We built a tall snowman out of wire. Then, because of no budget, we stuffed it with all the toilet paper from the school johns.

Remember the dirty boogie? I loved dancing, still do. I think we still gyrate like Elvis Presley when we dance. It was naughty then, but who cared? I thought the class ahead of us was a little more advanced and the one behind us a little more playful. We were quite serious in comparison. We seemed to do what was expected of us. Definitely, the Eisenhower era. We didn't seem to have any causes. We just got along beautifully. Boy, hasn't that changed.

After graduating from M-A, I spent the summer touring Europe, then flew directly to the University of Colorado. Twenty of us from M-A attended Boulder. I spent five years and three summer sessions before

I graduated with a bachelor's degree in Sociology. Boulder really changed my life. I had been accepted at Oregon and Arizona, but Boulder seemed a bit more sophisticated at the time. I was social chairman of my fraternity for four years and vice-president for one year; I missed the presidency by one vote to a very good-looking jock. Boulder's enrollment was only ten thousand then, and I seemed to know nine-thousand, nine-hundred and ninety-nine of them. One summer, I was the house boy at Delta Gamma. My last year, I was relief hasher at the six best sororities. I would just pop in and have some fun. Terrific idea. Boulder certainly lived up to its reputation as a party school.

Upon graduation, I moved to Pebble Beach and stayed in a guest house on one of the big properties. The Casa Munras hired me as a hotel management trainee. What else can one do with a B.A. in Sociology? I found myself driving up to San Francisco two, three times a week to parties. Not a bad pace working six days a week. After thirteen months and two Bing Crosby golf tournaments, I moved closer to home in Atherton, securing a job at the Stanford Shopping Center's Emporium store as manager of the toy department. That kind of job usually is given to a guy who has just taken the bar exam and is waiting for the results. I loved the job, but did not like the Emporium. Ed Carter of Carter, Hawley, Hale—the Emporium owners—offered me a job in their executive training program. I declined.

I went instead to the president of the City of Paris store in San Francisco's Union Square—I mean, directly to the president—and asked for a job. I indicated that I was at the right age, so that when he decided to retire, it would be appropriate for me to be his replacement. He hired me on the spot. He told the personnel director to put me in sales. I was in men's furnishings. Though bored, I became the top sales person of the fifteen people who worked in that department. When I was forced to join the Local 1100 Retail Clerks—the store was a union shop—I was promoted to training director. So during the Sixties, I moved from selling men's socks to training director to assistant personnel director to manager of the Marin County store at Northgate, where I also was president of the Merchants Association, to personnel director of the one-thousand employees, which meant dealing with nineteen unions. I was twenty-six.

I was living on Telegraph Hill at the time, a good place to be in the Sixties. In 1970, I was fired from the City of Paris, which was slowly reducing its executives—I was the fourth of ten to go—before the store finally closed in 1972. So what does one do when fired at the age of thirty-two? I bought a home on Russian Hill, taking a six-month escrow. Then I bought the first of nine Mercedes that I've owned. With a European delivery, I spent the next six months touring Europe in my Benz. Had a terrific time.

Since that time, I have been self-employed, buying and selling real estate, and creating a design firm for residential interiors. I also got my California real estate brokers license. I bought property at Pajaro Dunes from Hare, Brewer & Kelley, and then built houses. My own beach house at the Dunes has been rented often by Merry Davenport, an M-A classmate. I found that out at one of our reunions. I won many design awards at the Dunes. I was treasurer of the Pajaro Dunes Homeowners Association for many years. I got to know future United State senator Dianne Feinstein quite well; she and her husband owned one of the houses there.

I bought and sold more than thirty properties during the 1970s and 1980s. Living abroad, though, limited the rhythm that real estate requires, and it came to a halt. I envisioned the same success in Sydney, but jealous financial executives found a way to stop the Morton success in buying and selling. By a very weird and illegal maneuver, I lost my Australian empire, about ten-million dollars in profits.

After the very carefree life with the lovely Natasha, I returned to San Francisco full time, just in time to participate in the real estate bubble-bursting of 1991. Because of my divorce from Natasha, I lost my Russian Hill home of twenty years, my Pajaro Dunes beach house of twenty-six years, and therefore the ability to use the properties as the "Bank of Morton" for loans necessary to continue real estate speculation. I had given Natasha eighty-five percent of my net worth. I now had no money.

With my Newfoundland dog, Molly, my Benz station wagon, and a whole lot of friends, my life continued on, but with nowhere to live. You can only stay a short time with friends. You can only stay a short time with a New York lady by earning one-million-five per year, actually spread out over two years. She had an apartment in Greenwich Village, a house in Southampton, and a house in Palm Springs. So we did all those scenes for a while. Incredibly enough, that lady and Natasha had the same birthday, June 14.

But, again, with nowhere to live and a lot of furniture and accessories, I figured out it was very smart to start marketing real estate by "staging" unfurnished properties. The market was very difficult, particularly with interest rates in double digits. It was not easy to convince sellers to allow someone and his Newfoundland to move in with furnishings and accessories. However, when the first staged property sold in one day for more than one-million, it was easy to convince the second seller of the advantage of staging. And then the third seller, the fourth, the fifth, etc. I lived in the first twenty-five properties I staged. I had enough money to rent a loft in the Hayes Valley, behind City Hall and the Opera House. Terrific location.

I have staged more than one-thousand properties now. According to my accountant, I have an inventory of more than two-million dollars in an eight-thousand-square-foot warehouse on Townsend Street. My stagings are primarily in San Francisco. But for Sotheby's, I will do Stinson Beach, Healdsburg, Sonoma, Napa and Half Moon Bay.

Oh, my. You're showing me my Menlo-Atherton graduation picture. I'm thinking, "Wasn't he young." What was I thinking back then? We weren't thinking back then. We just went with the flow.

I am certainly not the same person, but I am exactly what the kid in the photograph wanted to be. That kid would be proud of me. He'd like my aggressiveness, my success with manipulating people, and my happiness with life. I have had a great life.

And I am still having a great life, and shall do so until the age of one-hundred and twenty-five, as there is so much yet to do and enjoy, Oh, yes.

A man's man

Bill Lawson

★ 25 ★

The Carpenter

Bill "Whitey" Lawson, the son of Menlo Park's mayor in the 1950s, prefers the country lifestyle, the way he remembers the Menlo Park of his childhood. Like his father, he found his true calling in construction. But he then had to re-build his own life before discovering his "new" Menlo Park.

Carpenter work is grunt work. If you're just driving nails all day, and you're just framing walls, that's all you do. But if you get to start a project as a foreman or supervisor, and you go through the whole thing, you've created something. A monument. Well, I have monuments all over the Bay Area: the south terminal of the San Francisco International Airport, 655 Montgomery Street, the Fairmont Hotel in San Jose, and a twenty-eight-story high-rise.

Those were the biggest jobs I did in a forty-five-year career. But whatever I built, I created something for someone to move into. To me that's a satisfying, self-pleasing thing. How many people can say that? Those were my projects, and I lived and died with every project. It was not an eight-hour-day job. It was a twenty-four-hour day job. I'd wake up in the middle of the night, thinking of things, putting them in order.

I really felt I owned those projects. I felt responsible. They had to be done, and done right, and on budget. So I became very possessive on a project. I took it personally when something didn't turn out right. But when it was over, and you handed the keys to somebody, it wasn't your baby any more. It was like losing a child, seeing something grow from nothing in a year and a half.

And after I walked away, I never went back. It was hard to let go, but it wasn't mine any more. There was another project to do, and people would change things after you left. It was the same project I built, but it wouldn't look the same. But I can still say it's mine. See that? I did that. Look, I accomplished something. Here it is. It wasn't like writing a paper in school, which was useless to me. But here is something that everybody can see.

When I was named to the Menlo-Atherton High School Sports Hall of Fame along with teammates from the undefeated 1955 water polo team, the committee sent out a letter that said to be prepared to make some comments. I thought about what I had learned from that sports experience that helped me in life. I came up with four things. I spelled them out at the banquet.

No. 1, you work hard. My parents came to my M-A basketball games. After one game, they congratulated coach Bob Ayers. He told them, "I don't know what I'm going to do with your son." My parents thought something was wrong. Then he said, "Your son has the least ability of anybody on this team, but he has the most desire, and I can't find a better combination."

No. 2, you have to have teamwork. Nobody rows this boat alone. I carried that idea through my construction career. Sometimes you worked twelve hours a day, sometimes twenty hours a day. I would tell my workers, "If I need you at four in the morning, I need you at four in the morning. You're mine until I'm through with you, then I send you home to your wife."

No. 3, you need to learn to lose. I don't like losing, but I try to turn it into a positive. What did we do wrong? What do we need to do right the next time?

No. 4, you learned to be a good winner. You didn't taunt, flaunt, arm wave, scream and yell. You shook the other guy's hand and you walked off. It was a nice way to treat a loser.

Sports at M-A taught me those four things—forever. In sports or work, you pick up your jock and you get it done. I never took a sick day. They weren't allowed. You still had to pay your bills. The rent still goes on. So I worked in the rain and the mud. I sprained my ankle playing adult city-league basketball. The ankle was at a right angle. At first, I thought it was broken. The next morning, I shoved it in a boot, laced it up tight, and went to work. It hurt, but I made it through the day. When I took the boot off that night, the ankle got bigger. I shoved it in ice water, then shoved it back in the boot the next morning, and went back to work again.

I've ripped off a fingernail on the job. I've broken the same finger twice, and I really don't know how I broke it either time. But I still have all my fingers, and they all work. I remember being sixty feet in the air when this panel I had just been standing on kicked out and fell to the earth below. My life flashed in front of my eyes. You just had to be careful.

On sunny days, when I was a carpenter, the men worked all day long without a t-shirt to see who could get the best tan. It was fun, until you got skin cancer. It takes twenty to thirty years before it shows up. Skin cancers have been removed from all over my body. One part of my lip is lower than the other part because of a cancer that was cut out. I've got scars around my eyes, back, arms and head, and a very deep scar on my left chest where cancer was removed. Thank God they have all been benign. Why so much cancer? I'm blond. Nordic. Why do you think my nicknames are White Owl and Whitey? But even with the skin cancers, I would do it all over again in a heartbeat.

When things were going well, just like clockwork, those were the good times. When you had to fight with people, those weren't good times. I retired in 2003. It was the right time. Construction had changed.

When I was a carpenter, we used to race among our crew. We'd ask ourselves, "How much framing do we have to do today?" Well, if we had to get ten walls done, we'd say, "Let's get twelve walls done." Then you were racing. And that way, the days went by, the weeks went by. It was fun.

I started to think of retiring because it wasn't fun any more. With carpenters today, it has become drudgery on the job. I don't think they race as much. As a supervisor, I didn't see them having the same fun I thought

I had as a carpenter. There has been a change in attitude. It has become, "Pay me. All I care about is the money. I don't care about the job."

I said to someone, "You look like you could be a foreman." He said, "Pay me and I'll be a foreman." And I said, "Show me you're a foreman and I'll pay you." It's that attitude I'm talking about. I never asked for a raise or promotion, and I got them. I wasn't brought up that way, to ask for something. You worked your way up the ladder by producing. Nobody ever had to tell me I wasn't carrying my weight because I knew myself. When I was working with my tools, I had to do more work than the next guy, because the guy that does the most work, that's the guy they kept.

So I had to produce. Today, it's, "Time to go yet? Time to go yet?" You can't look at your watch and produce. When I was a carpenter, if there was time to get another wall up, and it meant staying past 4:30, we did it.

I liked being a leader, in sports and at work. In basketball, you had to make decisions; you couldn't analyze because they had to be split-second decisions. It was a reactive game, and I'm not one who sits still. Work is the same way. You look at little pictures, but sometimes you had to step back and see the big picture. After a while, you saw things that were wrong just by feel.

One time, this building was going up, but I saw that it was off in measurement by five feet. It was a gut feeling on my part. What happened was the surveyors were off in their own measurements. Getting older and more experienced, it was easy for me to see problems that were up ahead. I could envision what carpenters would be doing two weeks ahead, three weeks ahead.

Being the son of a builder, I should be able to tell these things. My dad owned Sunlite Homes. He never put the name of his construction company on the side of his trucks. He never promoted himself. He felt if you did a good job, people would know it. I turned out to be the same way. My dad was very honored when Menlo Park named Lawson Plaza after him in Burgess Park; they even erected a permanent bust of him and his familiar hat turned askance.

Dad was on the Menlo Park City Council for nineteen, twenty years, serving as mayor from the 1950s into the 1960s. He never considered being mayor a big deal. It was something he wanted to do and liked to do. There was no pay in it; he was just interested in the growth of the town. He also wanted to bring BART rapid transit all the way down the Peninsula and loop it around the Bay Area. Amtrak would have provided the tracks for nothing. The vote was nineteen to one against him. Now there's a real need for what he proposed, but it'll never get done because it's too expensive. Dad was a visionary.

There was no pressure on me being the mayor's son. That never bothered me. I was just another guy. Am I going to get in more trouble because my dad's the mayor? You didn't want to get in trouble in the first place.

My dad, also named Bill, was born in San Francisco in 1900. He remembers the 1906 earthquake. The house his parents owned didn't burn down in the fire, which destroyed the city more than did the earthquake. Their family had to go live in Golden Gate Park. When they came back, they cooked outside. You weren't allowed to cook inside because there was concern about gas.

My mom's name was Helen. Her father, Paul Scharrenberg, was a ship boy who became shipwrecked. He then swam ashore and founded the Sailor's Union of the Pacific. Senator Joseph McCarthy called him a communist. My grandfather went through a trial, then it all went away.

My parents met on a blind date. When my mother's father asked my dad if he knew what the electoral college was, and he did, that got the blessing of my grandfather. My dad was a graduate of Cal. He married my mom in their thirties. My older sister, Paula, and I were born during their late 1930s. We moved to Menlo Park in 1947, and lived on the outskirts of town. There was one store, a grocery, across the street from the presbyterian church. My classmate Jerry Terhune's father ran the meat market inside the store. There also was the Sunshine Market down on College Avenue. That was it. People mostly shopped in Palo Alto, which had a bigger downtown.

In San Francisco, it was too crowded to run on the playground at school. But in Menlo, the playground at Fremont School was like a big playing field. You could run, climb trees. Menlo back then had a few houses and lots of open fields. We lived on Bay Laurel Drive. The fellow behind us grew hay—harvested it, stacked it and sold it. There were orchards all around us.

As kids, we didn't have the restrictions you have now, or the problems either. Our folks weren't looking over our shoulders every thirty seconds. If we went to Nealon Park, we had to be home by 5 o'clock. Nobody came by and checked on us. There was no Little League, no soccer or dance classes, no structure in our lives like you see today. We were just independent. We made up our own games, like kick the can or five-on-five baseball at Nealon Park. If you got hit by a baseball, nobody came by to fix you. You either sat and cried or you got up and played.

Dianne Pritchard lived next store to us. We'd have this bicycle race around the block. I'd go one way, she'd go the other, and she always beat me. We had such freedom. I was on my own. That was the neat thing of growing up.

My mother, if she liked you, you were wonderful. If she didn't like you, you were toast. My friends were on stage all the time. They didn't know it because my mother never said a thing to me about it until much later. I'm like her that way. Can't you see my mother sitting on my shoulder?

My dad was very quiet. He never got into the discipline thing unless you really did something wrong. He never hit you. He was so smart that he could make you feel like a dummy. He had a very logical mind. I have a lot of common sense; I know I can survive. I think I got that from him.

I got spanked only once. I made the mistake of hitting my sister in the stomach with my fist, probably while we were washing dishes. We always did the dishes after dinner while my parents sat in the living room. Well, after hitting Paula, I saw my father coming. I tried to duck under the dining room table. He threw it aside, grabbed me and smacked me good. Then he told me, "Don't you ever let me see you hit a woman. Never. Gentlemen do not hit women. Period." Even today, I open doors for women and pull out their chairs.

By the time I got to high school, I was calling my father "Bill" and my mother "Helen." They never had a problem with that. It was a respect thing. But my mom used to say I had concrete brains. My dad disagreed; he said that I just stood firmly on my convictions. So did my father. He made sure we had family dinner every Friday night at 7 o'clock. If I had a date, it wouldn't start until 8 o'clock. That's the way life was.

I played lightweight basketball for three years at Menlo-Atherton. We had 110-pound, 120-pound and 130-pound basketball teams, which were determined by exponents: height, weight and age. The 110s and 120s played in the fall. I was all-league in the 130s and team captain. I started all three years. Then I tore a knee cartilage as a senior and couldn't play varsity that season.

I grew six to eight inches between my sophomore and junior years, to where I now was six-feet tall. I went out for water polo because my autumns were free. I was competitive, but at one hundred and fifty pounds, I was too small for football. But you could get rough in water polo, and I made second-team all-league as a senior.

Where I grew the most in high school, though, was those two months my mother was in a hospital having a tumor on her spine removed. Paula was away at the University of Colorado, but my father expected the house to be maintained the same. So I did the shopping and planned the menus, cooked dinner, and did the dishes every night. I even changed the sheets and did the laundry. I learned to take care of myself and others.

I wore khaki pants at M-A. Somebody made fun of me one day because my cuff wasn't folded just right. I remember thinking if the way I folded my cuff makes me a better man, then that person is wrong. That's when I realized what I am is more important than the clothes I wore, or the people I hang out with, or the car I drive. What registered with me is that I've got to be me.

I never was a good student. My parents always wondered how my sister and I went to the same high school. She always had homework and I never did, and we got the same grades. It also upset my mother when friends started calling me "Whitey" because of my hair. There was a popular cigar then called "White Owl." Somebody, possibly my friend, Chuck Weesner, named me that. Then it became "Whitewall" or "Whitey." My mother told my friends, "Don't call him Whitey. I named him Bill. His name is Bill." Then she learned that those who called me Whitey were my friends. Those who called me Bill were somebody trying to sell me something. It's that way today.

I had my first serious relationship at M-A. with Sharon Hutchinson. She was blond, pretty, popular. We went together our junior and senior years, and probably two years more. I did a lot of things wrong in the way I treated her. I was probably an asshole. Friday night was boys night out, Saturday was date night. But I was protective of her, and it was a good relationship. We talked about growing up, getting married, and what we were going to do.

On Saturday nights, you usually found us at Marquard's, the popular local drive-in restaurant where all our friends would hang out. We called it 'Quards. That was our "Happy Days" place. But did you know I remodeled Marquard's while working for my dad during high school? We rebuilt the kitchen and remodeled the insides. My dad told me that Mr. Marquard said I was a very good worker. Yes, there really was a Marquard. I think his first name was Frank. Nobody ever saw him because he had that office in the back. He was an old man even then. He had gray hair and was cheap, cheap, cheap. My father told me that. Think of it: You're making money on French fries and milkshakes. It's nickels and dimes, not dollars. So Mr. Marquard was very frugal.

After high school, Sharon and I attended a junior college. She wasn't a student, and I wasn't much better. I did all right in JC; she didn't because she was working. Then I got sick and had to drop out of the College of San Mateo. I was diagnosed with pleurisy, which meant the pleural lining inside the lung secreted fluid. Basically, I was drowning from the inside. I found myself getting more tired, and I just wanted to sleep. After an intramural basketball game at CSM, I couldn't breathe. My parents took me to the doctor.

I spent the next three months in the same bedroom. I'm not a reader so I'd watch television. Sharon was away at Santa Barbara City College.

Thank God for Bill Schaffer. He was a year older and going to CSM. He'd come over twice a week and we'd play chess or War, a card game. For the most part, though, I entertained myself, which reinforced that feeling of independence in my mind.

I stayed out of school a full year, then started over at CSM the next year. Sharon came home and went to CSM, but dropped out to go to work and do some modeling. Two years later, I graduated from CSM and transferred to the University of Arizona. That's when Sharon got sick. She was a tall girl, and not at all fat, but while losing weight for modeling, she became bulimic. We didn't see each other until I got back from Arizona. She was healthy by then, but we never dated exclusively again.

I paid for my own college education. I worked through high school at the same Menlo Park gas station. One summer, I had three different jobs. It was easy for me to save money. I've never been a clothes horse. I don't have fancy cars. I don't spend money just to keep up with the Joneses.

Then I decided I didn't want to go to school any more. It's hard for me to read and write, and why was I wasting my time working in the summer for something I wasn't interested in? I called my folks and told them I wanted to quit school at Arizona and go to work. They agreed, so I came home.

By that time, the Fifties had moved into the Sixties, and you knew things would change. The music our folks listened to wasn't the music we listened to or the music our kids are listening to. The things that happened in the Fifties—the Korean War, McCarthyism, the Republican and Democratic conventions that were on television twenty-four hours a day—had seen their day. Those conventions were a huge thing, though. There's more news on TV today, but people don't pay as much attention to the news as we did back then.

Our age was very innocent, but we had a great time. You won, you lost, you played games. You weren't expected to run the world at age fourteen. When my parents had guests, you said hello and then went to your room. You weren't the center of attention. That's all changed now.

Ours was a very mellow, fun generation. Today it's an uptight, under stress generation. What's wrong with you people? It's too much of a magic pill to solve all your problems. There is no magic pill. The magic pill is you, and you can pick yourself out of any mess you want to if you want to do it. If not, you can wallow in self-pity. Oh, poor me. Everything's changed.

To the people we hung around with, the Sixties weren't much different from the Fifties. We weren't affected. We ran around and drank. We didn't do drugs. We didn't have flowers in our hair or cohabitate before marriage. In 1964, I married Susan Brott, an honor student at the University of Wisconsin who had come to California with some college girl friends to teach school.

The first nine, ten years of our marriage were fun. We didn't have kids and did a lot of things. We trained dogs for competition. We trained them together. I hunted, though not as much as I do today. A bunch of us went to the Cal-Stanford Big Game for eight, nine, ten years. We went to New Year's Eve parties together. We went skiing and I would make my famous omelets.

Then Susan and I adopted Matt. It was a fun time while he was a kid. I got into coaching his teams. Then he grew up and I wasn't doing that stuff any more. Susan and I made twenty-four years together. The first twelve, fifteen years were fine, then the remaining years weren't too much fun. I supposedly wasn't fulfilling her needs. I was the same person she married, but she wasn't the same person I married. It became very obvious the marriage wasn't working.

Susan was convinced I was an alcoholic. All during my supervisor's years, I kept a bottle of bourbon in my office drawer. If you got wet, you had a shot before you went home. On paydays, the crew would sit around and have a beer or two on the work site before we went home. Or I'd call the foreman in after work and talk about the next day's work over a beer. And the next day, things went smoother.

Did I drink a lot? I drank. But I never missed a day's work because of drinking or any other reason. Susan complained about my drinking when we went to see a marriage counselor. The therapist asked me if I could stop drinking if I had to. I said sure and didn't touch a drop for three months. Then when we saw the therapist again, Susan complained about my drinking. I got up and walked out. When I got a divorce, I heard that no-man-is-an-island bullshit. Hey, I could take care of myself.

My sister, Paula, died from breast cancer when she was thirty-eight. She became a school teacher after college, met Jim, got married, had three kids, then had a mastectomy. She lived in Hacienda Heights, near Los Angeles. She had a Fourth of July party, then walked me to the airport gate and gave me a kiss and a hug. That's the last time I saw her. I think she knew.

It was through the construction company I worked for, DPR, that I met Bernadette. I had been single fourteen years. We got married January 26, 2002. It has been a good marriage. We're old enough to know that I can't change her and she can't change me, though I don't drink as much any more. The most important thing is her family. If they call, we go, unless it's hunting season. Everyone in her family goes to grandma's house on Christmas Day. But I don't do well with forty-five to fifty people, so I go hunting. I tell them I'm in God's church, not in any church that man built. I hunt ducks, and afterwards I have a shot for baby Jesus.

After I retired from the building trade, we left the Bay Area and moved to the Auburn-Lincoln area in the Sierra foothills. On a clear day, we can see the Sacramento skyline and even Mt. Diablo in Contra Costa County. I don't do well in cities. That's not me. Where we live now is very similar to the Menlo Park I remembered when my family moved there. It's outside, it's quiet, it's a long way from town. We have freedom to do whatever we want. We can make all the noise we want and nobody can hear us. Bill and Cathy Schaffer live close by. We do things together. Bill and I hunt, and we train dogs.

I came here to get away. We're on a dead-end street. I don't have to listen to somebody's radio or boom box. I hear a donkey that goes off, a horse, or some chickens. It's what the country should be like. I was probably born in the wrong century. I should have been born a hundred or two hundred years ago. I could have been a cowboy going over the next hillside, the next draw, free-lancing across the country. I would have loved to just explore.

I'm still the carpenter. I love to putter. But now I don't have to do it to anybody's time table. I remodeled the kitchen, rebuilt the cabinets in the bathroom, extended the porch. I'm building an overhang right now. The pay is not very good: Budweiser or Jack Daniels.

When will my projects be done? Never. I'll live here until I can't physically take care of it any more. Then I'll live in some rest home somewhere. Right now, I take satisfaction in sitting on my lawn mower, cutting the grass on the hill. Afterward, while having a cocktail, I look at how I cut the corners and I say, "What a good job. Look at how the sun goes down over that pretty lawn."

We have lots of company with all the critters around here. I went down to get the newspaper and there were five wild turkeys at the bottom of the driveway. We have deer, quail, dove, rattlesnakes. Two years ago, I killed six rattlesnakes. I keep a gun on the four-track and a gun on the lawn mower.

You want me to look at my M-A graduation picture? What I see in his face is that life was good. I don't have to go to high school anymore. I'm not tied down to rules. I've got good friends. The world is great. I don't know what I'm going to do, but what's over the next hill? I'm going somewhere.

If that same kid was looking at me now, he'd say, "Awesome." I'm happy with my life, tickled pink, wouldn't change a thing. If I could have said back then what I wanted to be when I retired, I'd be right here. I got a good life, a good wife. I can do what I want. How many people can say that?

★26★

The Salutatorian

Rhoda Maxfield Stanley was a graduation night speaker at Menlo-Atherton High School before leaving Stanford with two degrees and a husband. She later faced two serious issues, breast cancer and her own adoption, and came through each much stronger emotionally, largely through her deep faith.

I was the new girl. When I entered Menlo-Atherton in my junior year, it was my fourth high school. Unforeseen family moves had made this a pretty traumatic time for me. At each school, it seemed that everybody had their friends, and I never knew if I would have the right stuff to be accepted.

I thought I was probably pleasing enough in appearance, but a certain kind of looks seemed to be very important in high school. I feared that maybe I didn't have the right kind of looks or maybe just not the right kind of interests. Maybe I was too prim. Maybe I wasn't considered a lot of fun by some people. When student body elections came around, I thought running for office might help me fit in. I ended up as School Spirit Commissioner. This was an executive office and a good thing for me because I really wasn't little or cute enough to be a cheerleader.

I remember first thinking of dieting in high school, when it was Marquard's drive-in and lots of hot fudge sundaes and French fries. I smoked my first cigarette at Marquard's with Barbara De Angeles and Nancy McDowell. I had become friends with them through riding the bus to M-A. And they still are my very good friends. We get together at least four times a year.

Evolution of a lady
Rhoda Maxfield

But when I smoked, I didn't inhale, long before Bill Clinton. It was weight-related. I was struggling with weight, and if I had inhaled I would have had another thing to think about besides my weight. So I didn't go there.

Marquard's was a drinking time, too. On Friday nights, there would be some booze secreted away in the cars. It was a fun time to be rebellious. There was talk about who was having sex. There were couples who dated a long time, and I imagine it would have been the same thing as my birth parents, with all that testosterone. Those were not my values. I had my adopted parents to think about. So for me it was not the right thing to do.

I hear Marquard's now is a vacant lot surrounded by a cyclone fence. That's prophetic. That's what it was then, too. I think a lot of what went on there was just vacant high school play or mindlessness. You just went there to unwind completely. It was a totally frivolous and unproductive time, though Menlo-Atherton turned out to be a very positive time for me.

My dad worked for Borden's, the dairy company. Remember Elsie the Borden's cow? I was born in Chicago, started high school at Main Township in Park Ridge, Illinois, and then attended West High in Madison, Wisconsin, my sophomore year. That summer we moved to Los Angeles after my father's company transferred him there. I went to University High before my dad was transferred again, which is how I got to M-A. My mother battled with the school district to get me into M-A, because we lived close to Sequoia High in Redwood City.

I lived on the edge of Atherton with Barbara and Nancy. We were not on the big deal side of Atherton. Steve Cobe and Greig Gowdy from our high school class lived across the street. I took part in plays directed by Mr. (Stanley) Dorfer, the drama teacher. These were plays designed for high school kids, family type plays about appropriate values.

I didn't have any serious romances at M-A. I dated a guy a year ahead of me, Richard Meredith, who was in drama. And there was Stew Morton, who was more of a pal and a very good dancer. I went to the Senior Ball with Chuck Holland, but he was a great flame of Susan Erstrom, who set it up. She was a mover and shaker. She was going to the ball with somebody else, but Chuck wanted to be with her, so we double-dated.

I was very driven in school. I worked my tail off, though I wasn't very good in mathematics. My math ended with Geometry. I was picked to be the class salutatorian, but I don't recall myself being No. 2 academically. I might have been fifth or sixth in the class, I really don't know. Being chosen salutatorian might have been a matter of speaking poise. It wasn't hard for me to speak. It was like a little gift I could present to my parents. So my feelings were, "Oh, good, they'll like this." And they did. Ever since I was a little kid, I'd do something like write an essay or win a prize to please them. So it was kind of a surprise game between me and my parents.

My graduation night speech was "Aim High," the standard graduation speech of that time. My dad didn't want me to go back east to college. My guess was he didn't want me to meet someone there and stay back there. He wanted to be part of my life, for I was my parents' only child. I was happy to get into Stanford, an important place to go, and I enjoyed it very much. I wanted to go into theater at Stanford. I still wasn't cute and little, but I had long legs, so I got into the chorus line in "Gaeties Review." That's when I knew the theater wasn't for me. My family, for whom it was a sacrifice to get me through Stanford, wanted me to take something I could use later on. So I majored in Speech Pathology and Audiology, and received my Bachelor's degree and a Master's in Audiology at Stanford.

The Stanford experience is a confidence-builder, and I grew in self-assurance there. One of my M-A classmates, Andy Schwarz, was there. I thought it would be nice to date him. Andy was giving Barbara Rhoades, another M-A classmate at Stanford, a ride home. I was going to ride along, then this guy, Jim Stanley, steps up and says, "I'll walk Rhoda home." And I'm thinking, "But I want to go with Andy." So Jim walked me home. It wasn't romantic right away. He was a class officer at Stanford and on the rally committee. He was interested in pre-med and was really driven. I studied a lot with Jim, which meant that both of us graduated with honors.

We dated off and on, but I was dating other people and so was he, though not as much. The ratio of men to women at Stanford was six to one, so you didn't have to do much to get a lot of action. Jim also had a car. I didn't and he let me use his as much as I wanted. My girl friends and I would borrow it to have dinner in Palo Alto. I think Jim got tired of being used by me. I didn't hear anything from him that summer after he went home to Arizona and even after he returned to school that fall. I knew I had overstepped my bounds. So as a peace offering, I invited him to a dance. It worked. We started seeing each other again.

Jim was much more serious about school. He was more substantial, goal-oriented, a man of outstanding character. One day he said to me, "There are two things important to me in my life, my family and my career, and I consider my family an equally important job. I want you to be the mother of that family." That was not the kind of thing people talk about in their sophomore year of college, and I didn't think like that at all. But I was impressed he thought that way, and eventually I took his fraternity pin. On the back was engraved "Love to Rhoda." He took the chance that I would accept it.

That was the beginning, though it wasn't the smoothest courtship. We were engaged three different times, mainly because of his drive. He was very intense. His senior year, he got really involved with research, working all night and sleeping all day. So I broke off the engagement. He went to medical school at Yale. By October, he was calling daily. He came home at Christmas and asked me to marry him again. I said, "Yes, but I'm not taking a ring. I'll just see you at the altar."

I did see him at the altar after his freshman year of medical school in 1961. Someone played a prank at our wedding, emptying all the birth control pills from my traveling bag. So we went off on our honeymoon with no birth control pills. And the pharmacist in the town we were honeymooning in wouldn't sell us any. Tearfully, I called my doctor back home to speak with the pharmacist, who finally gave us the pills. How things have changed!

Jim and I have had a wonderful marriage, with three children and six grandchildren. My father thought I could do anything, and do nothing wrong. I was daddy's girl. I had this sense that I couldn't disappoint my dad. With Jim, it was the same thing. Oh, he knows I can do many wrong things, but he's been very affirming, like my dad, always focusing on the positive.

You can't find a better grandfather than Jim. He was a good father, too. But there were many years when his work-alcoholism kept him away from the family night and day. He started a huge psychiatry practice with a partner here in Newport Beach in 1972. I'd walk him to the car in the morning and he'd hand me the McDonald's wrappers from the night before. I grew hostile and started drinking martinis and wine at home. Finally, when I became worried that I was drinking too much, I took our liquor cabinet and put it in Jim's car trunk, so I wouldn't have a drink until he got home late at night.

And even though he was dead tired, he'd say, "Let's sit down, have a drink, and tell me how you are. What went on today?" Still, I was pretty unhappy. I was making plans to leave him. That's when people reached out to me, giving me a faith and a peace, a way of processing what I was feeling. Things also got better once the kids left and I started doing Jim's bookkeeping. Doing this made me see what he had to deal with, the emergency intervention sessions that he would do. He never turned anyone down. I learned that I had been shortsighted, that I could have been more gracious. There was something about Jim that kept us together. There was something about God, too. About this time, He intervened in our lives. As a result, we put down spiritual roots that continue to nourish the five of us today.

What I've learned is how sweet it is when you hang in there. It's so neat to have that partnership. My heart goes out to couples who have some of his, some of hers. It sounds like a lot of fun, the "Brady Bunch," but it's not the same as having the natural father and the natural mother, who are both committed to the kids.

A month after my sixtieth birthday, I was diagnosed with breast cancer. I couldn't have had more loving care and support from Jim and our three children. Doctors found a lump. Jim said, "We'll just get through this." He began researching it. I saw five different oncologists. About the third oncologist, when I was hearing more about my "options," I had to struggle to keep from breaking into tears. I realized people thought this was a big deal. In years past, I always felt I could control my life. You know, get up earlier, stay up later, work harder.

After making a spiritual commitment to Christ, I did understand that I control nothing. But, oh, that control illusion creeps back. It was running up against an aggressive cancer that brought me to the end of myself; in other words, the end of striving. What takes my breath away is knowing that the end of striving is when we really meet God. I know it sounds strange, but I see that illness as one of the best parts of my life.

I don't meet that many Rhodas. My parents named me Rhoda after an aunt. My parents had tried a long time to have a child. But it wasn't until an unwed pregnant teenager from Wisconsin came to Chicago, so her parents wouldn't know about the child she was about to have, that I was adopted. I was that Wisconsin teenager's child.

I finally know about my birth parents. I wasn't interested when I was younger, because I was very committed to my parents, who had a solid life and who adored me. So I felt this great responsibility, like if something happened to me, what would become of their lives. I felt this burden of wanting to be there for them and to do well for them. So I didn't look for my birth parents.

I knew my mother had in her possession a letter written to my aunt from my birth mother. My cousin found the letter after my aunt died, but I didn't take it then because I didn't want to hurt my mother, especially after my dad had just died. When my mother died, Jim found this strongbox. He forced the lock and inside was the letter. I read it, kept it for two years, then someone suggested I contact a private investigator. A Wisconsin address was on the envelope. In two weeks, the P.I. found my birth mother living in Florida.

Jim is an easy-going guy. He told me he would support me in whatever I wanted to do. So I called my birth mother and told her I was her child. She said, "Oh, my goodness, what do you want to know? Do you want health records?" I said, "I just wanted to let you know that the baby is fine, and that I've had a good life." And she said, "Oh, aren't you sweet."

This was five years ago. Jim and I flew to Florida to meet her. She was very petite. She told me her husband, my birth father, had died at forty-one of heart disease. They had two more children after me, both girls, and that my birth mother's parents never found out about me. She said if they had, her father would have killed her.

One day, I got a call from my birth sister, who found a note after her mother had gotten Alzheimer's. My sister took from the note that her mother had another child, and that the child was me. She wanted to know if this was true. I told her yes. She was delighted. Jim and I returned to Florida and had dinner with my sisters and their husbands. It turned out great. We would have had pleasant relations with them if they lived closer, but we still exchanged Christmas and birthday cards and e-mails.

My birth mother died in October 2005. Seeing her was like a closure. I didn't get a rejection, although it wouldn't have mattered. My husband is supportive. My children are supportive. I have a network of supportive friends. I know who I am at this age, so I didn't need to visit with my birth mother to complete anything for me emotionally. But you know what's funny? I do look a lot like my adopted parents.

What was I thinking about when they took my M-A graduation picture? I was happily anticipating the future. I was looking forward to going to the university and maybe finding somebody there I would fall in love with. That was pretty classic for girls coming out of high school back then. I saw myself as a wife and mother.

If she were looking at me now, that girl would feel very fortunate and blessed to know that she is happy and basically satisfied, though maybe a bit of a whiner. I have a self-critical bent, usually about over-programming. I'm waiting to see what happens next, which could be any minute now.

★27★

The Homeless One

Jerry Baker didn't fulfill his dream of becoming a major-league baseball player. He became, instead, a big-leaguer in the advertising field as an award-winning creative artist. He then abandoned this life of status to become a housesitter, which freed him to concentrate on his own mortality.

The life of a pet/housesitter isn't a lonely life. Quite the contrary. It gives me a lot of freedom and choice. I'm a pretty private person by nature, and I really do love my freedom. I have no home. I have a post office box. I have a small storage unit. I have a cell phone. I have an e-mail address. I have a simple and wonderful lifestyle.

Freedom is more important to me than climbing the ladder in the executive corporate world. I got to where I could not stand the endless meetings, the focus groups, etcetera. I did it for enough years to become very successful in the advertising agency business. Then I didn't want it any more. I found that coming up with advertising concepts for television commercials and magazine ads were, in a way, like some mini-Hollywood showtime life—very make-believe and not really that important.

Now I'm in such a personal business. People trust me to come into their homes and take care of their animals. My business card reads: "Critter Sitter Plus: Pet & House Sitting w/care. Jerry Baker. Top Dog." It's a wonderful life. I've stayed in little quaint shacks in Fairfax and multi-million-dollar homes in Tiburon. The owners are so nice. They almost always tell me to help myself to any food in their homes, to use their stereos and TVs, and to even use their computers for my e-mail. And they pay me to do this while I take care of their pets.

Pet-sitter for hire

Jerry Baker

I just feel fortunate to have gotten out of the advertising business when I did, at fifty-one, still a young man. What if I had worked until now, at sixty-seven, then have doctors discover all these health problems I'm having? I'd have never fallen into this lifestyle of pet/housesitting. I've kept a photo album of the dogs and cats I've enjoyed. I've met some of the nicest people and ended up in some beautiful neighborhoods I wouldn't have ever known about otherwise. I also live in the San Francisco Bay Area, one of the best locations in the United States. And no rent. And no mortgage.

Like I said, it's a wonderful life. Oh, sure, there have been disappointments. I was a good father in many ways, but in other respects, I was a horrible father. I was more concerned with drinking and partying instead of wondering how my daughter was doing in school, and how my marriage was doing. Our daughter, Nicole, got into drugs as a teenager. She has had a hard time ever since. My wife, Jackie, and I got a divorce in the early 1980s. There are regrets, absolutely. Regrets that can haunt you.

But we must move on. If we didn't have the low spots, we couldn't really appreciate the good things. And one good thing is I have a great relationship with my ex-wife. She remarried a good guy, they live in Sonora, and I've even house-sat for them! I feel happy for Jackie. She's a good lady.

Meanwhile, Nicole has been through two marriages, had a child by each marriage, and has been in drug rehabilitation more than once. I just keep my fingers crossed. It's tough, really tough, going through high school these days with all the drugs. That's what happened to Nicole. She got involved with the wrong crowd and would walk in the front door of school and walk right out the back. She never graduated from Redwood High School in Marin County. So high school for Nicole is not a fond memory either for her or her parents.

We didn't worry about drugs when I was a teenager. I didn't have my first drink of alcohol until the very end of my senior year in high school. And I really didn't start drinking until my junior year at San Jose State, when I got into the fraternity lifestyle. The music of Louie Prima and Keely Smith blasted out across the yard. Or The Kingston Trio was singing about the MTA. Good beer-drinking music.

My drinking then got out of hand in the advertising business. One company I worked for had a bar right in the conference room. Then there were all the softball league parties at the local bar, with dancing and drinking until closing time. It's no wonder I got divorced.

I finally realized I needed help and joined Alcoholics Anonymous. I didn't drink for a year. Then I went on a photography cruise around the Hawaiian Islands. I met a fantastic lady from Indiana and started to drink and party again. After I returned home to Marin, I didn't go back to AA meetings.

Well, now it's 1993, and I'm sitting at home alone, watching TV, drinking a beer. Three people from the AA program showed up. I turned off the lights and tried to make them think I wasn't home, when they could see the TV reflection on the ceiling. I didn't answer the door, so they called the police. I finally opened the door. A short time later, the paramedics showed up. I ended up in the old Ross Hospital for a few hours before I was admitted to Serenity Knolls, a rehab center where I spent the next twenty-eight days.

That got me sobered up. Alcohol for me is so addictive. It relieves the classic inhibitions. It gave me a false sense of confidence socially. Plus I liked the taste of it. I drank everything—martinis, scotch, beer, wine. You name it. At Serenity Knolls, I learned to live without alcohol. I finally admitted I was an alcoholic after twenty years of heavy drinking and denial.

It's 2005, which makes it twelve years since my last drink. I don't have any desire to drink. I go to AA meetings several times a week. Wherever I'm staying, I can find an AA meeting in that area.

When I don't have pet-sitting jobs booked, I like to go up to Lake Tahoe or Reno and play blackjack. I'm a semi-professional gambler; that's how I help support my lifestyle. I've entered many blackjack and dice tournaments, and I've won my share. I can win a few hundred dollars a week. The hotel room is pretty much free, because the hotels and casinos want you to come up, thinking you're going to lose. But if you're sharp and play conservatively, you're getting the room practically free. I generally win or come out even.

Eighty to ninety percent of the time, I'm booked up as a pet/housesitter. When I want some time off, I don't always go gambling. Sometimes, I'll take my camera and go off on a photography cruise along the Mendocino coast or in the Sierra Nevada mountains. During my advertising career, I took several cruises while doing my photography—through the fjords of Norway, up to Alaska, down to Mexico and through the Panama Canal. Plus the Caribbean, Hawaii and—the best one of all—flying to Tahiti and photographing those fantastic islands for fourteen wonderful days. Pet-sitting, gambling, photography—it continues to be a good life.

And I plan to continue housesitting, taking care of these wonderful pets, as long as I'm healthy. Three years ago, they took out part of my colon. I had diverticulitis and it got pretty serious, affecting my bladder. I was on a colostomy bag for a year. Thank God they were able to get me off that and reconnect my colon. Then in 2004, I had some prostate cancer problems. I had external radiation treatments for twenty-eight days straight. Then they put sixty-eight radiation "seeds" into my prostate. My PSA count this last time was zero-point-four. That's way down from point-sixteen.

But my biggest medical concern is the melanoma cancer on the top of my head. I asked the doctors if they could do radiation. They said surgery would be better. When I asked them how extensive would be the surgery, they told me they would have to take off a good chunk of my head.

"It will probably kill you if you don't do it," one doctor said.

"Hey, we're all dying," I told him. "I'm sixty-seven years old. If I can get another four, five years, that's enough."

The length of life, I added, isn't as important to me as the quality of those years I have left. And I didn't want to go around with half my head missing. Also there's no guarantee they would get all of the cancer. It's OK, though. I believe I can accept dying. If that's the near future....I've had a good life, a lot better than so many others.

Marriage to Jackie was good when it was good. Going to the Art Center College of Design after graduating from San Jose State was one of the best decisions I ever made. Playing semi-professional baseball was great. I've won awards for my creative advertising and for my photography. All the traveling I've done through advertising, all the friends I made in the profession....I always feel things happen for a reason, whether it's a job situation or relationships with people. Good or bad, it's mostly out of our control anyway.

Playing baseball is the same thing. That's all I ever wanted to do as an only child growing up in Waukegan, Illinois. My father worked for Johnson Outboard Motors, but he was a player-manager on a semi-pro baseball team. I was his batboy. My dad also was a bird-dog scout for the Cleveland Indians.

He was a second baseman in the Brooklyn Dodgers organization for three years, then quit when he married my mother. Johnson Outbard transferred him in 1951 to California, to Redwood City, right below San Francisco. He was their sales representative for northern California. We rented for a year before my parents bought a home in Menlo Park, where I was lucky enough to attend Menlo-Atherton High School.

Like my father, I was a second baseman. I played on the M-A freshman-sophomore baseball team my first year. I also lettered in wrestling and lightweight basketball, starting on a team that won the league championship. After that, I concentrated on baseball. As a sophomore, I walked into the office of Howie Costello, the baseball coach, and asked him if I could try out for the varsity. That's how I became the first player at Menlo-Atherton to play three years of varsity baseball.

Except in art, I was an average student. Baseball and art were my life. Dan Umberger, an art teacher, saw that I had talent and encouraged me to push it. Socially, I went to school dances and enjoyed them, but I always felt self-conscious. I didn't feel smooth in a crowd. Later, alcohol would solve this problem for a while.

I wasn't big in size, but I wasn't shy about facing a good fastball or curveball pitcher. I was shy otherwise. I was fortunate to date some special girls in high school. I took Carmelita Arroyo to a drive-in movie and

I don't think I even kissed her. I took Linda Price to Bean Hollow Beach, north of Half Moon Bay, for a picnic. We built a fire and just talked. When we got back, Linda said, "That's the first time nobody tried to kiss me."

Unfortunately, I was a gentleman. I didn't have my first sexual experience until I was a college freshman. Even then it was with a special girl who was a year behind me at Menlo-Atherton. I also dated Emily Merk and Gerrie Keely, but no one for any great length of time. Friends are so important. That's how I look at it. Recently I got together with my old high school buddies: Jim Degnan, Otello Ascani and Adrian Ledda. Still great guys.

My senior year at M-A, I set eight school baseball records. My batting average that season, .453, is one of the highest in school history. I was elected team captain and was voted all-league along with my double-play partner, shortstop Bobby Wendell. M-A classmate Bill Brodie and I played in the league all-star game at Stanford's Sunken Diamond. This game matched the senior all-stars from the North Peninsula Athletic League against our South PAL team. Bill pitched and I played the whole game, hitting a double to drive in our first run as we beat the favored North.

Don Dorfmeier, who coached football and track and field at M-A, then talked me into trying out for the Palo Alto Oaks, a semi-pro baseball team that had a bunch of former professional and collegiate players. Don personally introduced me to Monte Pfyl, the manager. I moved right into the lineup at third base, and I tore up opposing pitchers. It was a great summer.

I hadn't really thought about college, but classmates Alan "Muggs" Robinson, M-A's catcher, and Dan Tapson were going to San Jose State. So I joined them. Ed Sobczak, San Jose State's new baseball coach, had seen me play when he was at Willow Glen High School. In my last game for M-A, I hit one over the 370-foot fence at Flood Park against his Willow Glen team. I just missed a second home run my next time up, hitting it off the top of the fence for a double. So going to San Jose State seemed like a natural thing to do.

I played freshman baseball for the Spartans. Even though I was a second baseman, I volunteered to pitch a few games as we had only one regular pitcher. Against Menlo College, I struck out the first five batters. Then I walked the next six before being taken out. But I hadn't given up a hit.

My sophomore year, I moved up to the varsity. I played the first couple of games and didn't do that well. After that, I couldn't get back into the lineup, and I ended up playing mostly junior varsity. The following summer, I played for a Santa Clara semi-pro team called Southern Nesbitt. That probably was my greatest baseball experience. Everyone on the team had played in the majors or minors; I was the only one still in college. I ended up sixth in the league in hitting with a .344 average, and I was picked for the all-star game. We won the championship, beating out Sobczak's Falstaff team. Scouts from the Boston Red Sox and Philadelphia Phillies talked to me about my future plans. Imagine how thrilled my parents were watching from the stands.

But my junior season at San Jose State, Sobczak still was acting strange. I just couldn't seem to do anything right by him. In one doubleheader, I got four hits. Then I played just once over the next ten games. When I talked to him about it, I couldn't get a straight answer. He was kind of a strange duck anyway. When he'd get mad and yell at the umpire, he addressed him as "Mr. Umpire." Weird.

My junior year, I joined a fraternity, Phi Sigma Kappa, with my buddy, Muggs Robinson. In our pledge class was Tommy Smothers, the comedian. He had that deadpan humor even then. We'd go see Tommy and his brother, Dick, at the Purple Onion in San Francisco. We'd get in free. The Kingston Trio and the Limelighters played across the street at the Hungry I. Those were great times.

But getting into the fraternity scene, I was drinking, and my grades began to slip. My senior year, an art professor told me I had to make a choice, baseball or art. I told Sobczak of my decision to quit. He played me in the next game, my last game. I got a couple of hits and that was it.

I graduated from San Jose State in four years with a Bachelor of Arts degree in Commercial Art. I got a job at the Channel 11 television station in San Jose, working in their art department and acting as floor director during their record hop show. I did this for over a year, then spent six months on active duty at the Ford Ord Army base in Monterey. I was now dating Jackie Garlinger, who was born in Oakland and grew up a country girl in King City.

During that time, I found out about the Art Center College of Design in Los Angeles. I enrolled the next semester and specialized in advertising art. I loved it, studying under real working professionals. After graduating with honors in two years with a BPA Degree in Advertising Design, I headed up to San Francisco, job-hunting, and was hired by Hal Riney, an advertising legend in San Francisco with Batten, Barton, Durstine & Osborn. I had a damn good job, but my ambition was to get involved with television art directing. I was informed that I'd have to go to New York City to gain such experience.

Jackie and I then decided to get married in 1968. Otello Ascani was my best man. Jim Degnan was an usher. Jackie and I packed up her 1958 Chevrolet and drove across country with no jobs awaiting either of us. Some Art Center buddies were in New York City, so we crashed with them for a short while.

I had one name to look up, Jack Mariucci, at Doyle, Dane, Bernbach Advertising. He was my second interview and my timing was perfect. They were looking to hire. I became an art director on the Clairol, Monsanto, Seagrams and Burlington Woolen Mills accounts. Jackie had gotten a job as an executive secretary. We settled into apartment living on East 88th Street.

New York was fun and we loved the excitement. I had a great job with the hottest advertising agency in the 1960s. Advertising budgets were huge and creative people were kings. On one of my TV commercials for Naturally Blonde Clairol, we took three Clairol models to Scandinavia to mix into the street scene of Stockholm, Sweden, with all the natural Swedish blondes. The concept and the theme were, "If you can't tell who the Clairol girls are, we're not going to tell you." That one TV spot sold a lot of products for Clairol.

Jackie and I were in New York almost four years, knowing one day we would return to California. Nicole turned two when that day came. I gave my notice at DDB and we headed back across the country with, once again, no jobs promised. It was Christmas of 1969.

The first person I checked in with back in San Francisco was Hal Riney. He had no openings, but gave me a list of names, including Cunningham & Walsh. Again, my timing was perfect. C&W had just landed the Royal Viking Cruise Line account and was looking to hire. I came in as senior art director on RVL, Fireman's Fund Insurance and Pendleton Woolen Mills: Three solid accounts with creative possibilities. The ships for RVL has just been built in Finland. The very first chance I got, I hired New York photographer Elliott Erwitt. We flew off to the Norwegian fjords for ten days to get the pictures we needed for RVL's brochures and advertising. Tough duty.

It was two great years at Cunningham & Walsh. Then Grey Advertising of New York opened a San Francisco office. Warren Peterson, who worked as a copywriter with me at Cunningham & Walsh, went over to Grey to head up the creative department. He asked me to come along as executive art director with the additional title of vice-president. Grey had gotten the Bank of America account. They also had Kikkoman Soy Sauce and Knudsen Dairy. Then they got Challenge Butter, the St. Francis Hotel and San Miguel Beer. We won numerous awards, and it was a fun place to work, with many super people.

But my personal life had changed. Jackie and I separated. A lot of it had to do with me, wanting to drink and party. After two years, we got back together and bought a home in San Anselmo in Marin County. We took a cruise to Mexico, through the Panama Canal to the Caribbean. But even that didn't work. After four years, Jackie was so frustrated, she had an affair with a man she worked with. I wasn't an angel; I had a couple of brief affairs myself.

We separated again, which was terrible timing as Nicole had started high school. Our splitting up was very tough on her. Then came the drugs. Jackie and I didn't know how to handle her situation. We were in denial for a while. Our attitude was that she couldn't be using drugs.

It was a lack of responsibility on my part, settling down and being a better father. I lived in the Larkspur Apartments, within walking distance of the ferry. I commuted daily to San Francisco by boat. And I was really enjoying the single life.

When Jackie and I divorced, I bought her out of our house and moved in with Nicole. Jackie then married Paul Davis, and they bought a home near Sonora in the gold country. Nicole also moved up to Sonora. There she met her first husband, Mike, a real jerk who physically beat her. Thank God she got out of that situation, but they did have a beautiful daughter, Kayla, my first grandchild. After her divorce, Nicole and Kayla lived with me for a few months. Nicole always has had a guy in her life, and she got married again, and pregnant again. She had a wonderful, sharp little boy named Jadon.

That marriage ended in a little more than two years. Then Nicole got back into drugs and was arrested for breaking probation. She was sent to a rehabilitation center. Kayla is with Jackie. Jadon is with his father, Todd, and his girl friend, plus his two children from a previous marriage. I feel both of my grandchildren are in good, safe environments.

Nicole now lives in Santa Rosa with a new boy friend. She's trying to rebuild her relationship with her children. She is thirty-six.

In November of 1989, I took another big risk. I had complained about the advertising business long enough. I walked into Warren Peterson's office and told him I was leaving. The business was no longer fun. Budgets tightened up. Computers changed the way business was done. After sixteen years at Grey, I was losing my artistic desire, feeling I was doing the same things over and over again. The business wasn't the same any more. So I resigned. Friends told me I was crazy. Some of these same friends remain in the business, and they feel very frustrated with how the agency business has changed. It was very nice to leave on my own terms and on my own time table.

I wasn't really sure what to do next. I could do a little photography. I had a nice chunk of profit-sharing built up as a nest egg. I did some real estate photography for a small agency, and I photographed a Calistoga bed and breakfast. The biggest account I had was the Napa Valley

Wine Train. Although my photography was good, it wasn't going to knock your socks off.

By 1996, unfortunately, I had made some bad investments, like so many other people in the stock market. So I made another decision, to really simplify my life. I sold the San Anselmo home and gave away most of my furniture and clothes. I got my own PO box and a storage unit. I planned to do some traveling and just let things develop. Talk about simplifying!

Two of my best friends, Joe and Lauren Scott in Calistoga, then invited me to stay at their beautiful home while they vacationed. I took care of their two dogs and cat for almost two weeks. Click! The light went on upstairs between my ears. This was a pretty good deal. They even wanted to pay me. One thing led to another and I started picking up clients. I charged twenty dollars a day. Slowly, I moved it up to thirty dollars. Some people have paid me fifty, and others have sent me an extra hundred-dollar bonus. When you're single with no rent or mortgage, no household expenses, and a base income from social security, one person can live quite comfortably.

Checking out my M-A graduation picture, there are no credits next to my name. Who is this flake! Everybody else has some activities listed. They were in the band or varsity track or some club activity. I had earned several block letters for sports. I had won some art contests. I was on the Student Council. But there's nothing listed, like I was the invisible man.

That same kid with the glasses, though, I think he'd be pretty happy right now. He kind of let life develop, and he didn't push things too hard. But if he was looking at himself now, he'd say, "That guy did all right. It's been quite a ride."

Jerry Baker. The homeless one. By choice.

28

The Prisoner of Words

Dave Newhouse didn't stand out at Menlo-Atherton as a student, athlete or campus leader. Self-confidence was his biggest obstacle. At a crossroads, he joined the Air Force and discovered journalism. But not until he became a senior citizen was he able to conquer his identity problem. Well, almost.

The majority of my life has been spent writing about the games people play. I wrote about teams and I wrote about athletes. I probed them, analyzed them, projected their legacies. It was a huge responsibility and I strove mightily, though not always successfully, to present my viewpoints with insight, balance and fairness.

Athletes I've written about, specifically those I've treated with disfavor, would relish a return shot, preferably at dawn with me blindfolded. They found my analyses utterly biased and devoid of intelligent thought.

Well, they all can relax. I'm about to take that shot for them. I'll probe myself harder than they ever could. I'll expose myself in a way they know nothing about. And I'll aim right between my eyes, so I won't miss.

Writing about myself will be the hardest thing I've ever composed on a typewriter, lap-top computer or on lined or unlined stationery.

I've hidden these feelings from others, including family, until now, feelings I've held inside my entire life. Because I've asked M-A classmates to be candid about their own lives, I must ask the same of myself.

For starters, I've treated life as a masquerade, putting on a smile for others while beset with doubt, lack of confidence, and deeply ingrained

Insecurity's vise grip

Dave Newhouse

insecurity. The intertwined roots of this insecurity: I have the hardest time giving myself credit, and I can't stop putting myself down.

A self-administered pat on the back should be welcomed. For I've achieved a certain level of importance in the print and electronic mediums, including writing awards, book contracts, and my own radio show. But for some strange reason, these accomplishments have failed to elevate me within me.

From early childhood, I showed an awkwardness in the classroom and on the playground. Academic tutoring occurred for me as early as the first grade, to see if I had enough smarts to enter the second grade. I made it, barely. I wasn't a pretty picture either when playing games. In baseball, my first love, I couldn't hit the ball well or consistently. And I ran the bases with the gait of a tortoise rather than a hare. Summed up, I was a banjo-hitting fatty.

Around classmates, I was naive, lagging behind, for instance, in sexual knowledge. I was cowardly, scared of defending myself, and there was a lot of me to defend. But by being nice—this meant smiling through my mask of deception and being the silly boy in the sandbox—I found that classmates accepted me. And I needed acceptance as much as I needed fresh air to breathe.

Though no one knew, I was the great pretender.

Perhaps if my home life had been easier, there wouldn't have been such pretense. My Polish immigrant parents weren't the most loving couple. My mother was unhappy, largely because my father was an alcoholic. It was an awful scene whenever he came home drunk from his second-hand clothing store, which would be once a week like clockwork. He would be abusive verbally to his wife in front of us kids. It was also embarrassing when my friends came over, perhaps to watch boxing on television. If the fighters were African-American, my father, if tipsy, would unloose a barrage of racial epithets as I crawled inside my own skin. Alcohol could make my father into a monster.

One night, he stood outside my bedroom window, bombed, yelling at me to let him in. My mother had locked him out. I wasn't about to leave my bed, not with my mother ready to pounce. Naturally, the temperature reading inside our home was coldest in the master bedroom. Dad had a Jekyll-Hyde personality: He was a good, decent, kindhearted man when sober. That's why the marriage lasted, although divorce then was rare. However, in a pique of revenge, my mom bought a mink coat. She dressed like the nines anyway—a very attractive, peroxided blonde Lana Turner type. Well, Lana wasn't a natural blonde either.

There were three children, with me in the middle. My older sister, Phyllis, had it the roughest. In her mother's eyes, she wasn't thin enough or pretty enough. Finally, as a teenager, Phyllis rebelled. She left home, first for college, and then as an escapee.

Meanwhile, little brother Bobby could do no wrong. He was the baby and his baby talk persisted until the seventh grade. This was perfectly fine with his parents, for he was the favored child. All three of us, though, watched sadly as our father's drinking drove away many of his and mom's friends.

Regrettably, I was denied the male role model I needed desperately. And coming from a home that lacked a loving environment, I entered into an early state of confusion, and formlessness, that stayed with me for many years.

My early awkwardness persisted into high school. My first year at Menlo-Atherton, I was cut from a lightweight basketball team and the freshman-sophomore baseball team. Watching my elementary school classmates excel immediately in athletics at M-A was demoralizing. Compounding matters, I had braces on my teeth, a serious case of pimples, large cheeks that brought me the nickname "Moonface." I also was born with a chest cavity, and M-A kids called me "Soup Bowl." The popular guys at M-A didn't have these issues.

I didn't travel in the same social circle as the rich kids at M-A. That wasn't a big deal, though, because the rich kids and the not-so rich kids were friends. There wasn't a caste system at M-A, but the rich kids had the fanciest cars. Andy Schwarz's parents bought him a brand-new 1954 canary yellow Ford convertible for his sixteenth birthday. One night while circling Marquard's Drive-In in my ratty 1937 Pontiac coupe, I accidentally dented Andy's right rear fender. I vowed to pay for the repairs. I don't think I ever did, not fully, but the fender was fixed and Andy and I remained sociable.

Unlike Andy and the other class intellectuals, I wasn't considered college material because of my so-so grades. I envisioned myself as a big-time sportscaster, but I didn't apply myself in that direction. Plodding along, I turned out for track and field as a sophomore. I had size so I tried the shot put. But I was clumsy and didn't compete in a single meet that season.

I wasn't much better at romance. The same day I received my driver's license, I escorted Carolyn Gerbo to a summertime party. Carolyn played a special role in my life, for she was the first girl I ever kissed, at a flashlight dance in the eighth grade. That kiss left no effect on her. Nor did my driving skills the Saturday I turned sixteen.

I practiced for my driver's test in my parents' automatic Buick. They went dancing most Saturdays at The Casino, a San Carlos night spot, and always in the Buick. This meant I had to pick up Carolyn in the '37 Pontiac, which had a stick shift. Well, I hadn't driven a stick shift. It takes no imagination to guess what happened. The Pontiac lurched and stopped, lurched and stopped, as I couldn't figure out how to coordinate the clutch and brakes with the gear shift. That was my first and last date with Carolyn Gerbo, and there would be no kissy face this time.

Even so, my junior year at M-A evolved into the best year of my young life. I improved in the shot, qualified for the league finals, and set the school record. That wasn't a monumental achievement as M-A was only four years old. But at the spring awards banquet, which I talked my father into attending, I received the "most improved" trophy in varsity track—the only significant athletic award of my life. My father was so proud of that trophy, he had it engraved with everything but my birth certificate.

That same year, I had my first serious relationship, with Barbara Beise. Her father was an All-America football player at the University of Minnesota in the 1930s. He met his future wife at the East-West Shrine Football Game in San Francisco when she, a University of California at Berkeley coed, served as a hostess. They lived in Minnesota and Texas before the father's insurance business, which replaced his coaching career, transported their family of four to Menlo Park.

Barbara was intelligent, sarcastic, with a strong sexuality. She let me explore her body, which was extraordinary. And she explored mine, which was less extraordinary. Our heavy petting didn't lead to sex—not in the 1950s. Her burly dad would have hospitalized me if we had gone that far. "My father says not to play with fire, I might get burned," Barbara told me repeatedly in the heat of the moment. But I can't ever thank her enough for teaching me how a man should feel next to a woman.

I was a weekend usher at the Guild Theater, which showed foreign films exclusively. I would seat Shirley Temple Black and her husband, who often complained, justifiably, about the poor air conditioning. At the Guild, I saw my first nude movie, Sweden's "One Summer of Happiness." The nudity lasted but a few seconds—an unclad lass running on the beach toward the waves. I became a huge fan of Alex Guinness, who was in such memorable British comedies as "Kind Hearts and Coronets," "The Ladykillers" and "Captain's Paradise." I've remained a devotee of foreign cinema, subtitled or otherwise.

I sat my very last movie-goer at the Guild about the time Barbara and I broke up as seniors. I wasn't thick-skinned enough for her barbed tongue, so I ended it. She later told me she was about to do the same thing. Neither of us won or lost, though. She always will be a special person in my life.

But with my weekends free, I got into trouble. Dan Tapson and I stole Pendleton shirts and Levis, and sold them to schoolmates out of the trunk of Mrs. Tapson's car. And I began drinking heavier stuff than cherry Cokes. Country Club malt liquor only cost one dollar and six cents a six-pack. M-A kids preferred "CC" because it was a cheap high. Another preference: Rainier Ale, a ridiculously high one dollar and twenty cents a six-pack, which was known as "Green Death" to us underage drinkers. I'd throw up either way.

One night, Henry Edwards, Dickie Plowman and I bought some cheap wine at a Safeway. We went to the M-A basketball game at Palo

Alto High acting as if we had a "heat on." Henry was caught and kicked out of school; he had previous transgressions of which I wasn't aware. Dickie and I were spared, but I later went to court. I was a lost soul. Graduation couldn't come soon enough. My final track season regressed. I lost my shot-put record, didn't even make the league finals. To this day, I regret not lifting weights at M-A to improve my shot-putting. Just like my sportscasting: No ambition, no drive.

Out of the three-hundred and fifty-two kids who graduated from M-A in 1956, I ranked two-hundredth and eleventh academically. Thus my college possibilities boiled down to junior college. Classmate Gary Dodson talked me into accompanying him to Santa Rosa Junior College, two hours from home. Getting away appealed to me, so I found a room at a Santa Rosa boarding house. But the heavier sixteen-pound college shot basically ended my track career. I still had my sights set on broadcasting until Speech 1-B. A ten-minute self-written speech was the assigned final. I didn't time my speech beforehand and it ended after only six minutes. Thus my semester grade was a D-. Dumbkopf!

How could the next great sportscaster get a D-? I was flummoxed. Instead of retaking the class to improve my grade, I switched majors to physical education, having convinced myself I wanted to coach. I no more wanted to coach than drive a cab. As a P.E. major, I had to take chemistry, which was like reading hieroglyphics. At the first chem midterm, everything went blank, including my blue book. Also that semester, I began dating pretty Marilyn Mason, who became more important than school. My life now in a mess, I left school.

In the 1950s, if you weren't in college and you could walk upright, you were military draft material. Larry Ludgus was a year behind me at M-A. We visited a recruiting office in San Mateo. As I talked to the Army recruiter in the front, Larry chatted up the Air Force recruiter in the back. It was a six-year military obligation either way, but Larry informed me that after four years in the Air Force, there would be no active reserve duty. Yes, but it's still four years! All my friends would be out of college and likely married by then, and I would have three years of college left, majoring in who knows what. But four years, Larry reminded me, could take me to far away places I had only dreamed about. So the two of us took off into the wild blue yonder.

Unfortunately for Larry, he was stuck all four years in Colorado Springs, Colorado, while I spent three years in France, stationed just ninety miles from Paris, only the world's greatest city. Sorry, Larry. My assignment was the Laon Air Force Base gymnasium, running athletic programs. Getting away to France's sugar beet country really matured me, enabling me to finally think for myself, and to make important decisions.

Growing up in a Jewish home. I was confirmed, or Bar Mitzvahed, at thirteen. But I wasn't exactly the religious type. An Air Force chaplain asked me about attending Jewish services. I didn't want to be Jewish just because my parents were Jewish any more than I wanted to be a Democrat or drive a Buick for the very same reason. I needed time to decide. The chaplain understood my dilemma and he left me alone. You can't imagine how important he made me feel.

But I still had no concept of life after the military. Jack Wendell Jones showed me the way. He edited the Laon Sentinel, the weekly base newspaper, and needed someone to write sports. Because I worked in the gym, he hounded me to do it. I said no twice, then came to my senses. My best grades were writing assignments. Essays, three-act plays, I'd get A's or B's with ease. A sportswriter instead of a sportscaster? Well, it's still sports. The third time Jack asked, I accepted.

My last two years in the military, I was the Sentinel's sports editor, working for free, writing at night in the barracks in between gym responsibilities. I had my own sports column, "Riding With The Rangers." There was plenty to ride, or write, about as the Laon Rangers had the premier Air Force sports program in France, and sometimes in all of Europe. I had frequent seven-day work weeks because of weekend athletic events. But I felt more inspired than overloaded as I now saw a future for myself. And partly because of sports, I traveled to Paris, Copenhagen, Brussels, Madrid, London, Morocco and Garmisch, Germany. But the best trip of all, if you'll hold this thought for a moment, was the 1960 Summer Olympics in Rome.

I had one brief military romance with Vera "The Countess" Grupen. She was very pretty, a German girl working in Paris as a children's governess. We planned to meet in Berlin, her hometown, in the summer of 1961. That's when the Berlin Wall went up, and our romance went down.

I was discharged from the Air Force right afterwards. As I foresaw four years earlier, most of my old buddies were no longer bachelors. Some had started families. I lived at home that first year, attending Foothill Junior College, trying to raise my grades. Old girl friends had married, too, or were about to, such as Linda Turner. But I rekindled a relationship with Marilyn Mason, the tall redhead I met at Santa Rosa JC. She was teaching, but didn't mind dating a student. After one year at Foothill, receiving the best grades of my life to that point, I transferred to San Jose State. I worked for several local newspapers while finishing up my degree. Then I was hired by the Oakland Tribune just before getting my college degree in 1964.

That same year, I married Patsy Lewis. Now here's the Rome, Italy, story. I met Patsy through Fred Hock, a stranger I happened to sit next to in the sold-out Olympic track stadium. Fred was stationed in the Army in Germany. We practically were neighbors in California, we learned that day. Fred was from nearby San Mateo, where I was born. He was at Menlo School, a private high school, while I was at Menlo-Atherton. We both graduated in 1956.

After we came home from Europe, Fred introduced me to some University of Wisconsin alumnae who had come out to California to teach. Fred dated one of them, Bev Vaughn, who later became his wife. Bev's roommate one summer was Patsy, a University of Nevada graduate from the tiny mining town of Ely, Nevada, who taught with Bev in Cupertino.

Visiting the Wisconsin ladies, I spotted Patsy by the pool. We started talking, but didn't date immediately. Then I realized this attractive, bright, caring, fun-loving, balanced, brown-eyed girl was the one for me. She accepted my marriage proposal the following winter and we married in August, 1964.

Patsy even helped me land my first post-college job. Oakland Tribune sports editor George Ross' first newspaper job after graduating from Nevada happened to be the Ely Daily Times. During my job interview, he interviewed Patsy more than me as they talked about good ol' Ely and the U. of Nevada.

My first sports beat at the Tribune was women's track. I was so eager, I covered women's track like it was the No. 1 beat on the paper, even though it didn't exist before or after me. The University of California, Berkeley, basketball, football and crew beats opened up during an interesting time, the explosive 1960s. Most of America's revolutions originate in the Bay Area and at Cal—the Haight-Ashbury drug culture, Marin County communal living, the free-speech scene in Berkeley. Also the black athletes' protest, which happened at Cal. I'd cover press conferences all day long on campus, then rush home and watch them, and me, on the CBS news with Walter Cronkite.

In 1970, my brother Bobby died of cancer. He was thirty. He had battled lymphona throughout his twenties. He left behind a wife, an adopted son, and broken hearts all around. My parents were devastated. Dad moved two steps slower and died ten years later. My mom had a nervous breakdown after Bobby's original diagnosis. She lost a sister and their mother to the Nazis during World War II. So depression was the bane of her adult years. She's still alive at ninety-five, living in a care home, bed-ridden and slightly delusional, although looking healthy. My sister, Phyllis, was married for a short time in her twenties. She then took over my dad's used-clothing store after his death and transformed it into a fashionable women's boutique in Palo Alto.

When the 1970s arrived, I was ready for something different, and calmer, than campus protests. So I left the amateurs for the professionals, covering the San Francisco 49ers, Oakland Raiders and Golden State Warriors. It was a hallmark time. The Raiders won their first Super Bowl, the Warriors won their only NBA title out west, and the Oakland A's won three straight World Series. Plus the Bay Area had cornered the market on zany owners in Charles O. Finley, Al Davis and Franklin Mieuli.

As that decade ended, Gannett Corporation bought the Tribune from Combined Communications, which had bought the paper from the

Knowland family. Our publisher, William Knowland, had been the Senate majority leader. Then came my big career break. Ralph Wiley and I were promoted to lead sports columnists. I'm recognized mostly for my feature writing, but columns brought out my opinionated side. It wasn't always the most delicate balance as the human aspect of sports tugged the hardest at me. I tried to mix humanism with opinion, motivated by what the great sports journalist Red Smith preached: "Make them feel people always." I hated dry, boring sportswriting about contracts, labor negotiations, strikes. These issues have to be tackled, but the best sportswriting is done with soul, one thing I do know I have.

I'm not a great sportswriter—there I go again—yet I've had my share of local, state and national honors for column-writing and features. A Hall of Fame writer, Joe Falls from Detroit, told me no sportswriter in the country turned a phrase better than I did. Hearing that, I began to deal better with my identity hang-up.

My biggest hang-up? Somebody will praise what I've written, yet it's hard for me to accept praise. Instead, I'll say something sarcastic, make a joke at my own expense. Over and over and over. It just never ends. I should feel good about myself, because I've come a long way from that rather average, rudder-less teenager in Menlo Park. But I still can't seem to make myself say "thank you" whenever praise comes.

At the root of this self-flogging, I'm sure, is rejection. The same kid who was cut from his high school sports teams, and whose grades weren't good enough, and who hated his pimply appearance, later faced rejection in the form of pink slips as an adult. I had a fling at sports broadcasting thirty years after my D- as a radio sports talk show host on KNBR in San Francisco. For five and a half years, I was a sports columnist by day and a talk show host by night. I barely saw my family, which now included teenage sons Chad and Casey. I burned both ends of the candle, and even managed to write a book on the Heisman Trophy's fiftieth anniversary. Wearing three hats over a twenty-two-month period made my busy life even busier.

That maddening pace ended when the radio station fired me. In my defense, numerous KNBR talk-show hosts have been canned after me, including the screamers, the vile, and the dog-barkers. All clowns, which I refused to be, even for a buck. Though I have more sports knowledge than a whole bunch of goofs who followed me at KNBR, I haven't yet gotten over being rejected, nearly twenty years later. One hard truth I've learned about careers: It only takes one person to lift you up and one person to drag you down.

Then I was demoted as a full-time sports columnist. My sports editor said I lacked "oeuvre." I still have no idea what he meant. But as he was demoting me, I felt a new person emerging inside, someone I hadn't recognized before. Listening to my demotion, I had a serious talk with myself. I said, "Screw him, I'm going to make this a better situation. I'll write books." I've had a seven books published, six on sports. Three of those books followed that demotion. When that same sports editor left the paper, he informed me that no one had been more helpful to him than I had been. He even gave me a small raise, without my asking. But I avoided his going-away party.

One thing about me, I am highly principled. I will stand up for my beliefs. In 2006, I turned in my Baseball Writers Association of America card, which meant I was ineligible to vote for the baseball Hall of Fame. I had given up a cherished honor, all because I couldn't be sure if I was electing cheaters. To me, a cheater is a cheater no matter when he started or stopped using steroids. To honor Barry Bonds as the all-time home run leader, if that comes to pass, would make me nauseous. Hank Aaron set the record honestly. Bonds' arrogance in attempting to overtake Aaron is disgraceful, for he's only dishonoring the most cherished record in sports. Though I've sacrificed the opportunity, I'd never vote Bonds into Cooperstown. Same thing with Mark McGuire and Sammy Sosa.

As the finish line draws near, I've found my nirvana in newspapering. I felt I had the best sportswriting job in the Bay Area, writing features, question-and-answer interviews, enterprise pieces, and occasional columns. I felt some redemption in 2005 when I, the demoted columnist, won the top sports column-writing award in the San Francisco-East Bay Press Club competition, even though I had only a handful of columns to enter. Disillusioned or otherwise, my writing continues to make strides.

In early 2007, my career took on another direction, at age sixty-eight. After forty-eight years of writing sports, beginning at Laon AFB, I moved out of the Tribune sports section. I came up with a revolutionary concept, something no one else is doing, writing three columns a week on strictly positive subjects. Management bought it after agreeing that there isn't enough good news in the newspaper. Writing about mostly unknown local heroes, my batteries are re-charged. I feel like I want to write forever.

Life, I've learned, is all about re-inventing one's self.

My personal life is better than ever. Patsy and I have been married forty-two years. She teaches art and is perceived as a saint by the elderly and mentally disadvantaged whose lives she brightens. Our two sons, Chad and Casey, are good guys in their mid-thirties, still single and promising not to move back home. We love them dearly, though we worry about them daily. Once you become parents, Patsy and I have discovered, you parent forever.

Now the time has come to study my own M-A graduation picture. My hair looks like bleached wheat, with good reason. Karen Lindsay dyed my hair and the hair of my good buddy, Muggs Robinson, one day after school. Only my crew cut came out orange. I'm just glad our yearbook was in black and white.

Studying that same person now, I have no idea what he was thinking back then. He basically lacked a grand vision. The future unnerved him no end. But if that same undefined kid looked at his senior-citizen counterpart with the receding gray hair and the many wrinkles, he would have to say, "Not too bad for the two-hundredth-and-eleventh graduating member of his class."

And I'd gladly accept that compliment without belittling myself.

"Your class stood out"

Douglas Murray

∗ **29** ∗

The Faculty View

Doug Murray taught English and journalism at Menlo-Atherton High during the "American Graffiti" hot-rod era of the 1950s. He then served as M-A's principal during the late-1960's campus race riots. Reflecting on those dissimilar decades, he recalled the Class of 1956 with a particular fondness.

I retired from education in 1981 and moved to Santa Rosa. So I don't have the same association with Menlo-Atherton any more. But from what I read and hear, it's still doing well academically and otherwise. They have new buildings there. It's good to read of the success of the kids, and therefore the success of the teachers.

I was there with the bricks, when Menlo-Atherton opened in 1951. But I moved around the Sequoia Union School District quite a bit. I was at M-A from 1951 to 1958. I returned in 1968 after getting the news that I was the new M-A principal.

I remember that day vividly, saying to my wife, Barbara, "I got it." And we just stood at looked at each other. There were no smiles, no laughter. It was dead serious. I was going back to a different M-A from what I experienced in the 1950s. In the late 1960s, it was a militant time, like what UC Berkeley was going through.

I knew I wanted to be a principal, but I also knew it wouldn't be a picnic. And it wasn't. There was a big riot between blacks and whites my second Monday on the job. Fifty to sixty kids were hurt, not seriously, but seriously enough that some had to be sent to the hospital.

The campus atmosphere was kind of jumpy, not only because of the revolution on Berkeley's campus and campuses across the country, but because of the conflagration of black and white that reached all the way back to New York City. We found out from the FBI a year later that some non-students had been paid by forces in New York City to come on our campus and start the riot.

These were young black men in their late teens and early twenties who went after kids with sticks during the brunch break after our first two classes of the day. Things then stayed jumpy for a year afterwards.

I remember going to a parents meeting. It was as if a skunk had come into the room. I was persona non grata. I met with black parents in their homes in east Menlo Park, even on the day Martin Luther King was killed. I was thinking as I worked on papers in my office late at night that somebody could take a shot at me through the window.

The answer, and I knew what the basic part of the answer had to be, was a change from what we had previously at the school. That change was education as a profession. The administration didn't want parents involved in the school. I knew in my heart of hearts that we had to have parents involved.

I worked toward that end, and I met—it's emotional for me talking about it because I lived it and I can see it in my mind even now—with the people in Atherton. That's where the money and the power was at. And I met with poor black people in east Menlo Park. I had any number of meetings with people from both sides. And the hand was extended to both to get involved.

To have success, you must have involvement. This feeling supported the attitude I took into these meetings. And it was accepted. Both sides came together. The end result was UMA: United Menlo-Atherton. A polyglot of teachers, kids and parents, with the parents a strong third in that group. A real strong third. We brainstormed on what we needed to do, and that was to get parents black and white to walk the halls to show that they were working together: Solidarity. Whether you're black or white, you want quality education for your kids.

UMA put on fund-raisers and other shows. The bottom line was the community was behind the school. It was a marvelous thing, people working together. We turned the corner that first semester, but there still was some unrest, including some whoop-de-do the next year.

Some black students had called a meeting in the multi-use room at M-A. The room was full of students. I remember coming in and a black kid said, "We want your resignation." I laughed out loud and said, "I'm not a bit surprised, and you ain't going to get it." Those kids quieted down.

So while I was principal in a pastoral area, it was an explosive time in the 1960s. There hardly were any blacks when I started at Menlo-Atherton in the early 1950s. By the 1960s, twenty-five percent of our students were black. And we ended up with a bunch of black and white kids who were fantastic.

If you asked me if kids were easier to teach in the 1950s than the 1960s, I'd say, fundamentally, no. It's what faces kids individually in their communities that matters, whether they went to high school in the 1950s, 1960s or 1970s. There were more marriages in the 1950s. There's more living together now, and more single-parent homes. Therefore, more dysfunctional situations for kids to cope with while trying to learn.

On the teaching side, in order to make the field more attractive, paying teachers more money is only part of the picture. There has to be more of a community effort. That's the answer. But you also have an opiate like television. That isn't the greatest thing in the world for kids growing up. TV makes for a nice baby-sitter, which means kids aren't stretching their thinking muscles like they should. It wasn't like this in the 1950s, or the 1940s. And TV affects every household, rich and poor.

The 1940s is when I started teaching, in Turlock, California. Back then, California was number one in education in the country. That's because Californians respected education. Their hearts were there. Today, their words are there. Proposition 13, the Jarvis-Gann Initiative, was approved by California voters in 1978, thereby slashing state school budgets. Proposition 13 was the door that closed on California education. You get what you pay for.

However, the California state legislature was a laughing stock even before Proposition 13 passed, micro-managing education. They were saying that you got to do this, and you got to do that, but they weren't putting their money where their mouth was. Proposition 13 changed the whole ball of wax. All the power went to the legislature instead of to the local people, which is where education belonged.

Today, California is near the bottom of education in this country, and it goes back to getting what you pay for. The country is putting its money into overseas expeditions. Etcetera, etcetera. Educators are not respected. But I respect all teachers who go into classrooms and bring students up to where they should be. It's a helluva job. And with English being taught as a second language now in the classroom, it's very difficult. We need to have an ombudsman atmosphere in order to provide help for parents. I'm involved with the Kiwanis Club up here. We buy books so that every youngster has a book to take home. In many instances, these are the first books those homes have seen.

These are good kids. The potential is there. But they need to read at home, and that effort isn't going on. There needs to be a community involved. It's been said that it takes a village. That's true. What's needed, though, isn't just words, but formulating a program and putting it into action. Part of it is volunteer help, but these volunteers have to be able to speak Spanish. Schools have to be an encompassing thing, not something that's just set to the side.

Looking back on my life in education, I'd probably have to say I was meant to teach. As a kid in Ypsilanti, Michigan, I was active in the Boy Scouts. I achieved the highest scouting rank of Eagle, and I even ran the troop as assistant scoutmaster. With my work in summer camps, all this pointed toward a career as a teacher.

Teaching was regarded as a middle-class profession at that time, in the 1930s. People didn't look down on it. Teachers were respected and education was supported. I attended a high school in Ypsilanti that had just been built with an indoor swimming pool. With that kind of support from the community, you could see where education stood. It was top-notch.

Therefore, it was perceived as a sense of accomplishment to become a teacher. And it was something I felt I could do and be successful at.

First, I had to get more serious about my own education. After high school, I started college at Eastern Michigan in my hometown of Ypsilanti, which is thirty miles west of Detroit. But I was having too much fun, and after two quarters, I knew I had to get out of town. So I transferred to Central State, now known as Central Michigan, in Mt. Pleasant. That was my savior. I was very active there, going to school, working part-time as a desk clerk, and running matinee dances at the college. It was a marvelous experience.

With one semester to go before I graduated, we heard the news about Pearl Harbor. I enlisted in the Army as a radio operator and went to Camp Crowder in Missouri for basic training. Then I was stationed in Texas, New England and Florida before I got to Fort Ord in California.

A Michigan friend of mine heard there was a USO in Salinas. So off we went. I looked across the floor and here was this doll dancing with someone else. I said to my friend, "When they come around here, I'm cutting in." I did, and she became my wife.

But marriage would come a lot later. I knew Barbara only five weeks before I was sent off to Australia for more training. Then my company landed in New Guinea. This was General Douglas MacArthur and his genius at work. He made all these island stops, cutting off the Japanese to the point where they had no equipment, no food and so forth.

I was gone almost three years. Barbara and I still have in a box some seven-hundred and fifty letters, half of them hers, half of them mine, that we wrote to each other during the war. Soldiers I knew received "Dear John" letters from the states. They were devastated and spent a lot of time by themselves. Mail call for all of us was the most important thing, more important than the chow hall.

The end of the war was nearing, and I wondered when I got back home if things still would be the same. What will be the first thing I do when I see Barbara? Kiss her? She was going to San Jose State College, and I was coming down from Washington state, where I was ushered out of the service.

I called her. From the tone of her voice, she sounded different from what I remembered three years earlier. She sounded like some highfalutin' sorority girl. I didn't know she had a cold. We arranged to meet in San Jose on a street near the college. It was foggy, 7 or 8 o'clock at night. I was walking down the street, and here was this lady walking up the street. There was no hesitancy when we got together. We both will never forget that moment.

I went back to Michigan for two weeks to wind up my affairs. Then I finished up school at San Jose State. Barbara and I were married Aug. 17, 1946. I received an emergency teacher's credential. That way, while teaching, I could finish up my credential.

I enjoyed teaching every day of my career. I received a master's degree from Stanford and thought about getting a Ph.D. But I didn't want to become a superintendent. I wanted to be at the school level.

My first teaching job was in central California, in Turlock, teaching English and journalism, and putting out the yearbook as well as a bi-weekly newspaper. So my days were full. I was always interested in journalism. The Ypsilanti Press was right next to our house, so I had the smell of printer's ink very early on. I worked on the yearbook in high school, and I worked on the local paper in college.

I was at Turlock three years and knew it wasn't the place for me; they had a ceiling money wise. I was getting roughly three thousand dollars a year. I needed to moonlight in the summer as a peach inspector for the California Peach Advisory Board. I shopped around and got an annual raise of five-hundred dollars from the Sequoia district. That was a lot of money back then. And unlike Turlock, Sequoia paid you year-round.

At Sequoia, I taught Sociology and Geography out in the car barns, which required a heater. In the winter, it was nice and warm from the table top up, but cold as hell from the table top down. Teachers had a choice in the Sequoia district of where we wanted to teach. With my going to M-A, the opportunity was there to get back into journalism. I really enjoyed the kind of kid that came into that class. I also taught English at M-A and became a part-time counselor.

Barbara and I had three children right away, which meant I had to have part-time jobs. Like most teachers back then, there was only one income coming in, and it was from the husband. While teaching at M-A, I had a job on Thursday nights and Saturdays selling clothes at dandy Van De Sande clothiers in Menlo Park.

M-A was a good fit for me. The faculty bonded really well. We were starting a new school and there was a lot of work making M-A into M-A. Seven years later, after I had become assistant dean of boys, the district wanted me to go to Sequoia High as head counselor. I hated to give up what I was doing.

I spent the next two years at Sequoia, which is just up the road in Redwood City, where I lived. Then I went a little more up the road to San Carlos High as dean of boys and vice-principal. I was there seven years.

I remained active in the Menlo Park community, and in the local Kiwanis Club, doing things for local schools. I'm sure that had something to do with my being named principal at Menlo-Atherton. After ten years as M-A's principal, I was transferred to Carlmont High. My job there was to turn things around. But that was a sad day for me, leaving M-A a second time. And M-A, after all we had gone through together in the late-1960s, was sad to see me leave, I'm happy to say. They even had a "Doug Murray Night" in my honor.

Those four years at Carlmont represented my last four years in education, and it wasn't a happy time. That experience told me it was time to get out. I was sixty-one then. Now it's January 2005, and I'm eighty-four. But I play tennis twice a week, weather-permitting. Barbara plays, too. And I'm still involved in journalism, writing about our tennis club—we have more than three-hundred members—in our retirement community newsletter.

Even though it has been nearly fifty years, I do remember your graduating class from 1956. Honest to God. It's an intangible kind of thing why one class has a certain personality and another class a different personality. You were a stellar class, a class that was a lively group in sports and academics, a history that was very proud.

Your class stood out. Some classes are more withdrawn, not as outreaching. Your group was overt, working together. Truthfully, yours was a great class. It was special.

And Menlo-Atherton High School is a fantastic place. I love it.

Karley Marty

✯ **30** ✯

The Class of 2006

Karley Marty graduated from Menlo-Atherton with all A's except for one B grade. During her last day on campus before heading off to Duke, she relived her high-school experience and discussed what M-A is like. Much different, it turns out, than 1956, although her values do mirror those of M-A coeds in '56.

The biggest difference I see looking at your Menlo-Atherton yearbook in 1956 and my M-A yearbook in 2006 is that everything looked more uniform when you were here. All the boys look to be dressed a lot alike. The girls are all wearing their pearls, and their hair is kinda done the same. In my senior class, there's more diversity in clothing.

We don't have bobby sox like the girls in your class. We don't wear sweater skirts. A lot of kids just come to school every day in jeans, sweat shirts and flip-flops. It's considered dressing up if you put on a skirt, although I think it's nice, personally, if you dress up a little more. It's really casual now. There is a dress code at M-A in that the school says you can't wear clothing too revealing, but it's not enforced too strongly.

Cheerleaders aren't as popular as when you went to M-A. The girls who have replaced the cheerleaders, and who are the popular girls now, are on the dance team. The dance team has pretty much taken over for cheerleaders at football and basketball games, and at assemblies. We do have cheerleaders, but they're a smaller group. The dance team is a big thing on campus to make. They travel to tournaments, and they're really good, fun to watch.

As far as the big man on campus from your day, well, we had a big man on campus competition this year. That's kind of new, and it was done tongue in cheek. All the guys who thought they were super cool were paraded across the stage. Jocks are still looked up to here, but it's different than 1956 because there are so many other things you can be at M-A. People find their own niche; it's not like they're driving after that one title. There's really not that competition to be No. 1 at school. There are a lot of cliques, but it's not like the cliques are competing with each other. They stay separate.

There isn't one main hangout like you had, because social life isn't an M-A thing. There are a few restaurants where my friends and I hang out. We may go to the beach, which is close by. With cell phones, things happen at the last second. You can call up friends at 7:30 p.m., make plans, and show up at the same place a half-hour later. Do your own thing.

It sounds like football games were the place to be in the Fifties. Some kids go to games now, but it's not a big thing because our teams haven't been very good, and we can't have night games. The neighbors won't let us put lights on the football field because of the noise coming from there on Friday nights. Basketball games are different. M-A started a Sixth Man Club cheering section. Students pack the gym when we play our rivals: Woodside, Sequoia and Carlmont. They pack it for the guys, but they'll be at girls games, too. Basketball games represent the biggest school spirit that I saw at M-A.

You had a school fight song? Really? How did it go again?

("Here comes the Menlo Bears, here comes the Menlo Bears, beneath the maroon and gold on high. We are the Menlo Bears, we are the Menlo Bears, we shout our praises to the sky. We know our victory will soon be history, and all the foe will know our name. For Menlo-Atherton we hail to thee, Bears triumphant hail they name.")

I'd never even heard it. We don't have any kind of fight song at M-A. The Sixth Man Club makes up cheers at basketball games, but that's it.

There are lots of dances at M-A. The three big dances are homecoming, the winter formal, and the junior or senior proms. We have a beginning of the year dance, plus a Sadie Hawkins dance, and theme dances. Kids go to the big dances more than the Friday dances, which don't get the turnout your dances seemed to get from what you say. And we don't dance quite the same way you did. Slow dancing's still the same. You see people dancing cheek to cheek. We play rap and hip hop. It's not the boogie style from your day. The term we use now is "freaking." It's bump and grind, a lot of touching. Inappropriate? I guess. My parents think it's kinda gross. It's progression, I guess.

It's still a social status thing to have a boy friend or girl friend. Do boys open car doors for girls? If you remind them. But there's a lot more short-term stuff as far as relationships. You mentioned about your class that some high-school sweethearts married after graduation. That really doesn't happen any more. There are a lot of breakups right after graduation or right before you graduate. Most people are going off to college, and in different directions. There's a timetable, and the time has run out by graduation. I dated Ben Spar for the better part of our senior year. We broke up at the beginning of summer. He's going to the University of New Hampshire, I'm going to Duke. It's not practical to keep dating. We'll still be good friends.

Another thing that's different about your yearbook: No girls sports. Half my yearbook has as many girls sports as boy sports. Those short shorts in basketball in your day? I'm glad that style has changed, personally. I just like the longer shorts on guys, though the short shorts do seem more practical. Also, your yearbook is all black and white; mine is all color.

As for student-teacher relations, it's roughly the same as what you remember, with the teachers in control. There's a lot of respect for the teachers in the Advanced Placement classes. But if you walked into a lower-level class, there's not a whole lot of control there. We have a phenomenal teaching staff at M-A. They just don't care about teaching you a subject; they want to get to know you as people, This makes you want to do better in their classes. The teachers I had as a sophomore, I still keep in contact with.

Something else that's changed: We don't have a class valedictorian. There is a top ten-percent, and I'm in that group. Would I have been the class valedictorian? With AP schedules, some people might have had a higher grade point average than mine, a five-point on a four-point scale. My one B was in AP Biology my last semester. I already had been accepted by a college, and I got a little bit of senioritis, spending more time tanning than studying.

People know me at M-A as a basketball player. I was the team's Most Valuable Player as a sophomore and junior, and team captain my last two years. I started all four years on the varsity. I was injured most of my senior year, but I came back in time for our team to make the state tournament, which was incredible. I hope people saw me as a very focused person who was friends with a lot of different people. It's more important for me to be seen as an accepting person. I choose not to be a judgmental person.

It seems so strange looking at your yearbook because of the mostly white faces. Today, M-A is diversely segregated. Everyone gets along. It's harmless. But there isn't a whole lot of effort to inter-mix. Most of the middle schools in Menlo Park and Atherton are made up of white kids. Because they go to the better schools, once they get to M-A they get into the better classes, on the Advanced Track. So most of my classes were made up of mostly white kids, which looks like your yearbook. But when I walked around at lunch, you would see all kinds of kids. I think that's unique and really special. There would be a Polynesian wall or places where other diversities hung out by the bathroom. What I loved about sports, it all got mixed in (racially).

We have a really good leadership class at M-A that breaks down racial walls. But the kids you're used to are the kids you'll hang around with. Mixing is getting better, but it's getting better slowly. It's hard to go out of your comfort zone. The two biggest helps this way are the leadership classes and the sports teams. Besides kids from Menlo Park and Atherton, kids from East Palo Alto, Woodside, Portola Valley and Redwood City also come to M-A. It's a really good school. I believe fifty percent of our senior class is going to college, including junior college, and seven are going to Stanford. But there is a huge dropout problem at M-A. There were six-hundred kids in my freshman class, and only three-hundred and fifty graduated.

Living in Menlo Park or Atherton, both wealthy areas, there is a little bit of that stuck-up nature. But Suburban Park, where I grew up, is just the best area. We have street football games, pickup basketball games, lemonade stands in the summer. A lot of kids my age live in Suburban Park, which is very family oriented. Atherton, Portola Valley and west Menlo Park seem to have a little more of an elitist-type feel, though not really. People are really friendly.

But if you bragged about your wealth at M-A, you'd get brought back down to earth. When it comes to economic background or sexual orientation, this school is pretty good at accepting you and not trying to be too judgmental. There's a Gay-Straight Alliance at M-A, making that issue more of a non-issue. The majority of kids in this school are comfortable with someone's sexual orientation. People are pretty open when talking about it in classroom discussions, in leadership classes, or in a Gender Studies program that is part of the classroom curriculum.

Different from your day, there is gang activity at M-A. I've witnessed a few fights on campus. For the most part, gangs keep that stuff off campus, because if they bring it on campus, the police will get involved.

As for drugs and alcohol, it's much more of a problem today. If you want to get it, you will be able to, though most people will keep that off-campus, a Friday night thing. But there definitely are drug deals on campus. You can see exchanges. People occasionally bring alcohol to school in their cars or in a water bottle. People get creative. If you choose not to be involved with that kind of life, which is my case, you won't have someone pressuring you to do it. There's not that kind of peer pressure at M-A.

You can't go into the M-A parking lot at lunchtime like you were able to. A few years ago, people could eat inside their cars or sit on car trunks and eat with their friends. Now the parking lot is closed at lunch because of the drugs and alcohol in cars, and because some kids don't return to classes after lunch, or they'll return under the influence. That's why you're not allowed to leave campus for any reason unless your classes are done.

I haven't ever taken a drink. That's because I'm an athlete and also because I have a sister, Rachel, who's four years younger. I want to be a role model for her. I'm also involved with the Menlo Park Presbyterian Church, coaching basketball and being part of the church's Strive Group. But the party scene never appealed to me, though I got along with the Friday night kids. I've seen friends who felt the pressure to join that crowd in order to fit in at M-A. I've seen people I know well who've lost control, and it makes me worried for them. I'm still going to be friends with them Monday morning, because as I said, I'm not judgmental.

In talking about these issues, I'm representing mostly the kids like me at M-A. There's a whole other side I'm not able to shed light on. As for sex on campus, I haven't walked that path. I don't think sex is as big a deal at M-A as it was during your time, and I feel that's unfortunate. That's because kids nowadays take sex pretty casually. People spread rumors about it, and I've seen people hurt by that a lot. My faith is a big part of my life. I'm waiting (for sex) until I get married. I definitely felt in the minority at M-A with my decision, but I was respected for it. I wasn't made to feel uncomfortable.

I wasn't the only Marty to graduate from M-A in 2006. My twin brother, Chris, is attending William & Mary this fall in Williamsburg, Virginia. I'll be in Durham, North Carolina, three hours away by train. I love my family. My dad, Alan, is a NASA consultant and the founder of Noah Basketball, a computerized machine that helps players improve their shooting. My dad met my mom, Cindy, at Stanford Business School.

I didn't pick Duke to get away from home. I wanted to major in bio-medical engineering. Duke has one of the top programs in this field in the country. If Duke was down the street, I would have gone there. I'm getting into engineering because I like math and science. I know that makes me kind of nerdy, but hip replacements and artificial hearts come from the bio-medical field. My goal, though, is to get into business school and then into business.

I'm a very competitive person. Basketball didn't let me really develop friendships in high school because I was so committed to the sport. I'm looking for a balance in college, because when I look back on my life, I don't want it to be the achievements that stick out, but the relationships I made, and the people whose lives I've impacted.

Leaving high school, the world looks a little intimidating because of war and terrorism. There's a lot of stuff out there, but students my age are kind of numb to it, because there was so much of it while we were growing up. When you graduated from high school, there was no war. It was "Happy Days," right? My parents said it's important not to be too scared or overwhelmed by war and terrorism, that I still have to strive after the things I want to achieve in life. I really want to know what's going on in the world. I feel it's important to understand our history, where we've come from, and what everyone sacrificed for us to be where we are right now. I think some people forget about that. It worries me when people become too apathetic.

I am a patriot. My grandfather served in the military. I have a lot of respect and admiration for those people. My friends in Menlo Park have talked about going to Iraq. In my hometown, people are anti-war. I hear people say they'd go to Canada before they'd go to Iraq. But if the draft started up again, it would be boys and girls this time, wouldn't it?

I've grown up in a liberal area, though I'm a conservative with Republican ideals. It's hard to take too strong a stance on Iraq. Once we got over there, we just can't back out of it. Do you just put out the fires or do you get to the root of the problem? All these sacrifices have been made; it's really tragic how many people have died. It's hard to watch, but for freedom, some sacrifices have to be made.

Being on M-A's campus this final time before I head east, it makes me feel proud to be here. I'm proud of the way I went through M-A, proud of the decisions I made and the work I put into athletics and academics. I'm really comfortable with M-A, so it makes me a little nervous going off to new places. I also feel grateful because M-A prepared me for it.

I'm definitely ready for whatever life throws at me.

epilogue

Three members of Menlo-Atherton High School's Class of 1956 passed away after they were interviewed for this book: Wayne Chan, Jerry Juhl and Bill Brodie. They created legacies in different ways, especially among family and friends, who offered personal epitaphs on why they will be missed.

"Wayne truly enjoyed life," said Elizabeth "Pinky" Chan, his widow, "and he accepted everybody for what they are—rich, poor, black, white. He didn't care. He took you as a person. That's why he had so many different friends. This came out at his memorial service. Someone said, 'There are thirty people here who think Wayne was their best friend.' "

Wayne Chan was a dermatologist; he improved peoples' skin condition.

Juhl was a puppet-maker and a creative writer; he made people laugh.

"What was Jerry like? One big smile," Susan Juhl said of her late husband. "He was so generous. Everything about him was giving—giving of himself, giving of goods. He had this big heart. He was constantly giving.

" 'Fraggle Rock' was the thing he was proudest of; it ran on HBO from 1981 to 1985 and was cancelled while still on top. Jerry was all about bettering the condition of people. Make then laugh, but make them think."

Mike Skuse and Susan Erstrom Thomas were not only close friends of Brodie, but Menlo-Atherton schoolmates. Thomas graduated with Brodie in 1956 before he went on to a law career that was terminated by alcohol and prison. Skuse was his drinking buddy.

"Bill and I were roommates at one time," said Skuse. "We always had an honesty between each other. We could laugh at each other. And Bill never laughed in a malicious way. We did things in our lives we probably shouldn't have done. We also could look at it as 'That's who we are.' Bill was never phony about that.

"The Bill I knew was the kind of person where it didn't matter if you owned the San Francisco Giants or if you were a ticket-taker for the Giants, Bill would treat you the same. There was a goodness about him. He liked people. As long as you were honest with him, he was honest with you.

"People loved Bill. You couldn't walk into a bar—now he had problems in bars—where they weren't happy to see him. And he was always happy to see them. As they said at his memorial, he was the kind of person who would always be there for you. He would give you the shirt off his back."

This interview with Brodie's friends took place at the Dutch Goose, a Menlo Park burger-beer joint where Brodie would stop off to get a "pop."

"Bill had a center core that was always there," said Thomas. "In a strange way, he was very dependable. He was a good friend. Bill was Irish. That's how he looked at life. It would have been fun to take him to Ireland. He led a shitty life, but he was a happy and proud man until the day he died."

May these Old Bears rest in peace.

acknowledgments

Locating Menlo-Atherton High School classmates required a three-year search, and was accomplished without the author leaving California. This good fortune was made possible by out-of-state classmates who agreed graciously to be interviewed in the time frame around the Class of 1956's fiftieth reunion.

To the following "Old Bears," the author owes his deepest gratitude for allowing a long-ago classmate—a stranger, really, to most of them—to re-enter their lives and to hear their very personal stories:

Diane Sullivan Gayer Reynolds, Jerry Juhl, Carol Tait Harkins Macpherson Remen, Wayne Chan, Susan Samuels Drake, Bill Brodie, Lynne Kramer McCallum, Bishop John-David Schofield, Carolyn Gerbo Scherini, Bill Lawson, Gerrie Keely Miller, Joe Parodi, Josephine Booth Grieder, Jerry Terhune, Merry Davenport Montaudon, Gordon Plaisted, Linda Price Williams, Jerry Baker, Rhoda Maxfield Stanley, Bryon Farnsworth, Barbara Boucke Violich Rice, Andy Schwarz, George Carr, Marilyn Hareid McDowell Powell, Jerry Berger, Stewart Morton and Dan Tapson.

Thanks to Doug Murray, who provided valuable insight from a faculty point of view, and to Karley Marty from the Class of 2006, a special young lady who could have been in the Class of 1956 in the way she thinks and acts.

To Susan Erstrom Thomas and Donna Newport Ralph Fraser, who were interviewed and then changed their minds, there are no hard feelings. No conditions were set, no pressure was brought, it was all voluntary.

To Susan Juhl, Elizabeth "Pinky" Chan, Susan Erstrom Thomas, Mike Skuse and Lisa Brodie Dunham, for tying beautiful ribbons around lost lives.

acknowledgments

To Sean Connelley of the Oakland Tribune, whose artistic eye so brilliantly accented this book, including the smashing front and back covers. To Brad Greene for his brilliant text design.

To Kristine Clark, whose valuable insights assisted the author through the decision-making publishing process.

To Richard Grossinger of North Atlantic Books, who agreed to put his company's stamp on the author's work once again.

To all of you who made this book and filled its pages, the author says the next Oasis burger is on him.

the author

DAVE NEWHOUSE has been a journalist for forty-eight years, including forty-one years at the Oakland Tribune. He has won national, state and local awards for column and feature writing. He has authored seven books, including "The Jim Plunkett Story" and "Jim Otto: The Pain of Glory." He lives with wife Patsy, an adult art teacher, in Oakland, California.

the foreword writer

DARRYL BROCK is a heralded novelist, having written the baseball classic "If I Never Get Back," its acclaimed sequel, "Two in the Field," and "Havana Heat." He lives with his wife, actress-teacher Lura Dolas, and daughter Phoebe Zhilan in Berkeley, California.